Intensive Care

by the same author

EXTERMINATING ANGELS

INTENSIVE
- CARE -

a novel by

PETER DUNANT

ANDRE DEUTSCH

First published 1986 by
André Deutsch Limited
105 Great Russell Street London WC1

ISBN 0 233 97820 8

Phototypeset by AKM Associates (UK) Ltd
Ajmal House, Hayes Road, Southall, London
Printed in Great Britain by
Ebenezer Baylis and Son Ltd, Worcester

Chapter One

The room in the hospital had not been used for some time. In its emptiness it had taken on a surreal quality. First there was the bath. Large, angular and made of stainless steel. Then the machines, cold, grey missiles, their noses pointing downwards, like dentist drills targeted on the tub beneath. And the trapeze, a hoisting device strong enough to raise or lower the human body, should it prove necessary. Not now though. Now the room was deserted, save for a plastic cup discarded in the corner gathering dust. The air was stale. It had not been changed for some time. There were no windows, and the ventilation grills around the skirting board were sealed. The door was also closed, but not locked. Outside, another room, and another and another, all empty except the one that housed the console, swathed in heavy polythene. The door to the last room was locked. Behind it were further bolts, padlocks and chains. Out of bounds. The building waited.

Beyond this cluster of rooms there was a badly lit corridor, where a man sat reading a newspaper, squinting slightly in the gloom. He took a last drag at a cigarette and stubbed it out on the floor near a small cache of butt ends. He turned a page and glanced nervously at his watch. Ten forty-seven. He stared down the corridor, the silence buzzing in his ears.

Out in the real world the summer heat still lingered, despite a soft, steady drizzle which clung to the clothing of the few passers-by and obscured the windscreen of a car travelling north towards Archway roundabout in the London Borough of Islington. The driver switched on his wipers and rolled up the window. The sky above was still mottled with tell-tale streaks of fading light; high summer and the night was besieged by the day. The man frowned, acknowledging a certain weariness. He wished he had left the restaurant a little earlier, had drunk a little less. Still, he was not drunk. No sir. Just two or three glasses of wine and they would have been soaked up by the food. Later he would reassure himself with this fact.

A quarter of a mile away a girl on a bicycle was approaching the same roundabout from Junction Road in the west. She was unprotected from the rain, but seemed oblivious. Her head was awash with images of Tuscan landscapes: cypress trees against the skyline, luminous sunsets over olive groves, the rhythms of life on the land. She had left the cinema early, incensed by the film's romantic clichés, but the pictures stayed glued to the inside of her brain.

Ahead of her the car had already entered the roundabout. Then it suddenly stopped. Junction Road was barred to him by a No Left Turn and, momentarily disoriented, he had pulled over to consider his route. That's it, another circumference of the roundabout is called for. He glanced round. Nothing behind. If he moved swiftly he could do it. He signalled and pulled out. There would be times in the future when he would wonder if he only imagined the second glance in the wing mirror which failed to register the flickering beam of the cycle front lamp. She seemed to come from nowhere out of the darkness like a moth zooming towards the light and smashing itself against the shade. As the car recorded the thud of impact, his stomach lurched in sudden panic. The first thought hit him in terror. My God, I've hit someone. The second, fleeting but crystal clear, This could change everything.

He watched it all in the light of his headlamps. There was a flickering, slow motion quality to the action, like an early silent movie. As she careered in front of him, he caught a flash of face distorted in panic. She tried to regain control of the bike, but already it was too late, she and it were toppling to the ground, the machine crashing on top of her as she hit the road near the railings.

He was out of the car instantly, anticipating scenes of broken limbs and trickling blood. There was a body, lying half on, half off the kerb, but as he ran forward to help, it began to move. She slowly picked herself up from the pavement. She seemed to be unhurt, though a little dazed.

Thank God, he thought. 'Are you all right?'

'Of course I'm not all right.' It was then that he noticed her arm, and the way she was holding it awkwardly away from her body. 'You bastard. You fucking well nearly killed me.'

She bent to pick up the cycle. The handlebars locked and twisted out of her grasp, falling against her left hand. She gasped with pain, and the bike slid back onto the road. The man took hold of the frame and propped it against the railings.

'Is your arm broken?'

'I don't think so,' she replied, but without much conviction. In the car headlamps she was crouched in the road, using her good hand to retrieve the contents of the bag, which had spewed out in a wide arc around her. He picked up a tattered cheque book and handed it to her.

'We should get you to a hospital.'

'I'm all right,' she said through clenched teeth, not looking at him.

'Well, you don't look all right. Listen, just let me move the car somewhere safe, and we'll check the damage.'

Back in the driving seat he noticed, to his intense displeasure, that his hand was shaking. Twenty years without an accident, not even a scrape, and now this. Damned cyclists. They had no road sense. Still, there was no denying how lucky she'd been. How lucky they'd both been. He parked close to the kerb a few yards ahead, and walked back to her. She was examining the buckled front wheel by the light of a streetlamp. For the first time he got a good look at her. Small, maybe late twenties, a pointed little face under a bushy halo of black, curly hair. She glanced up at him accusingly.

'You know we should report this to the police?'

He noticed she was cradling her injured left forearm close to her body. It's probably the pain, he thought, that's making her aggressive.

'O.K.,' he said evenly. 'Where's the nearest station?'

She shrugged. 'I don't know. Anyway, Archway on a Friday night – they're probably all out beating up black kids. I'll skip it, if you're willing to pay for the damage. It was your fault, you know.'

In the distance behind her he was aware of a figure swaying towards them. Across the street a group of men were trickling out of a pub. Whatever the rights and wrongs, this wasn't the best place to conduct an argument. He knew the last thing he should do was to accept liability . . . but then why risk a breathalyzer and the loss of a no claims bonus? Better to turn the other cheek. It was a good night's sleep he was looking for, not a squabble over thirty quid.

'O.K. I'll give you twenty pounds for repairs. But I want to make it clear that I don't accept liability, and that should you wish to make a further claim you must get in touch with my insurance company.'

That sounds suitably formal, he thought. There was a pause. 'Thirty,' she said.

'What?'

'A new wheel costs £25. And the gears will need re-aligning.

A likely story. Still, at least that was an end to it. 'O.K. Done.' He took out his cheque book. 'Who do I make it payable to?'

'Josephine Ridley.'

He signed with a flourish, tore out the cheque and handed it to her, along with his work card. 'Do you want a banker's card?'

'No, I'll trust you,' she said, lingering over the card. 'What does the W stand for?'

'William.'

'Nice one. Well, thanks William.' She pocketed the cheque and the card, and picked up her bag with her good hand. 'Now, if you'll just drive me home, we'll call it quits.'

The temptation was considerable. And it was not entirely altruism that made him hesitate. But he had in effect accepted liability by giving her the cheque. If later her hand was to cause trouble . . . It was clear from the way she was nursing it that this was not a simple bruise. William liked to think of himself as a man who saw things through.

'I'm afraid it's not that simple. We really should get that hand checked out. I'll take you to Casualty.' She opened her mouth to speak. Sensing disagreement, he talked over her. 'And if we stand here bickering in the rain, neither of us is going to get home this side of midnight. You'll be perfectly safe with me, if that's what's worrying you.' He risked a slight smile. 'It's not in my nature to take advantage of women in pain.'

'I'm glad to hear it,' she said tartly. 'We wouldn't want to both end up in hospital.' She pulled herself up to her small full height and walked past him towards the car. At the passenger door she waited. Ah well, he thought, following her. One more Friday night.

The hospital began only a hundred yards away, but this closeness was deceptive. The Royal Highgate, founded in the last century, sprawled its way across the south slopes of Highgate Hill almost down to Archway. Expansion and the aggressive demands of the motor age had had the effect of major surgery, cutting the site in two so the smaller part was now marooned between highways like some displaced urban castle surrounded by a moat of cars. Ten minutes later William was still negotiating the labyrinth.

'I'm just telling you it's possible,' his passenger remarked sourly. 'I don't remember the exact names, but if fourteen casualty units have been closed down in the city, then it's a fair chance Highgate is one of them.'

Wonderful, he thought. Just what I wanted to hear. 'Damn it, you'd think they'd have the place better signposted.'

'Why don't you take the next left?'

They entered a sleepy, tree-lined street with a long, high wall on the right. Behind it lay the hospital, but no entrance. They turned right at the end, following the wall until it turned into railings, and an opening of sorts presented itself, invitingly marked Visitors. No Parking.

'This'll do,' she said. 'I think I know where we are now. If I'm right, Casualty is on the other side of the compound. We can get to it from here.'

'How do you know?'

'Because I've been here before.'

'Oh great,' he said, parking on the almost empty roadside. 'And we've been driving round like zombies for the last half hour. Why didn't you say so before?'

'Because I didn't recognize it until now, that's why.'

She led the way, up the slope into the expanse of a large, ill-lit compound, surrounded by hospital wings. It didn't feel like an official route. 'I hope you know where you're going,' he whispered, in automatic response to the invalid silence around them. Their steps echoed in the night. On either side the buildings loomed dark and shapeless, connected by low-slung iron corridor bridges with outlines so black they stood out even in the darkness. The architecture reminded William of a prison. It was unnerving to find such quiet near the centre of a city.

'Highgate Cemetery's just over there,' she remarked, unconsciously tuning in to his apprehension. 'Very handy. I wonder how the patients feel when they look out of the window.'

'What were you doing here?' he asked, more to hear the sound of his voice than to know the answer.

'I was taking part in a demo. That's how I remember the wall. I climbed over to get in. It was during the occupation of the kidney unit. You must remember it.'

Vaguely, William thought. There had been so many rows over the national health service. Wasn't it something to do with some space age machine for kidney stones? What was it called? 'The lithoblaster?' he asked aloud.

'Lithotripter,' she corrected him automatically. 'The patient sits in a big bath and gets bombarded with sound waves. It shatters the kidney stone into fragments so they can piss it out. All without surgery. Cost a million and never used. Going cheap to BUPA.'

It came out pat, like a speech she'd made many times before. Was it that simple? William didn't know enough to challenge her. Now he thought about it he did recall some pictures of angry faces and placards staring out at him from the front page of his *Times*. The demonstration had degenerated into a punch-up. So she had been part of that. Clearly she was the kind of girl who could look after herself. He began to wonder if his gallantry wasn't misplaced.

Too late now. They were approaching a more modern building, its forecourt bathed in light, like a landing stage in a sci-fi movie. Two ambulances stood there, one with its doors open and a stretchered patient being carried out. A few yards away a police car slouched in attendance. This was Casualty.

Inside, the building had not aged well. On the glass reception booth a sign, CASUALTY FURTHER DOWN CORRIDOR, was partially obscured by a Health Not Wealth sticker. In front of them the corridor stretched empty, its institutionalized green paint jaundiced by the glare of strip lighting. The instantly familiar death and Domestos smell crept into William's nostrils, transporting him back to childhood and memories of sprained ankles and tonsil operations. The surroundings had seemed more impressive then. Meanwhile the girl had more immediate aims than reminiscence. She forged ahead, obeying a large arrow marked Casualty. He followed.

At first glance the room they now entered looked like a shabby community centre that had recently been burgled. It was a large square area with a reception cubicle at one end, chairs round the outer rim and a makeshift playpen in the corner. Save for a coffee machine and a couple of posters on the wall, that was it – no tables, no magazines, just a great expanse of linoleum floor.

The woman at the desk looked as if she'd been there since adolescence, a number of years before. As she took down the details William stood to one side and calculated the wait. There were five or six people before them. All but one, a middle-aged man with a bandage on his hand, looked up as they came in, but fast lost interest again. There was a definite quality of fixtures and fittings to them. It did not inspire confidence. The whole scene left William feeling uncomfortable, like someone returning to a home they had once lived in and finding it changed beyond all recognition. From the desk he made out rumblings of trouble.

'I don't have to answer those questions. It's not compulsory.'

The receptionist looked up at her. 'The information is entirely confidential. It's simply for the records,' she replied, with the ease of a practised response.

'I still don't wish to fill it in.'

The receptionist sighed slightly, distancing herself from the problem. 'Very well . . . If you'll just take a seat. The nurse will call you when the doctor's ready to see you.'

'You couldn't give us a rough idea how long that might be?'

As soon as he opened his mouth William realized the audacity of the question. She gave him a look more in sorrow than in anger. 'There are two doctors on duty, a traffic accident just in, and all these people in front of you. You'll be seen as soon as possible. But, as I'm sure you know, we're operating on limited resources.'

On the far side of the room they settled themselves into the moulded plastic chairs. William thought with longing of his leather sofa, *The Big Sleep* on late night television, his traditional last whisky of the evening. Begrudgingly he pulled himself back into the present. 'How's the arm?'

'Not bad. Throbs a bit.' She was again cradling it to her chest. 'You can go home now, if you like. I'll be all right. You heard what she said. It'll be hours. You've done your duty.'

There would be many times in the days to come when he re-ran this moment. He imagined himself getting up, shaking her good hand, and saying, 'Well, if you're quite sure. I'll give you a ring to see how you are. Goodbye.' Just like that. Pleasant, but formal. And final. Normal life to be resumed as soon as possible. Instead, with a chivalry he could later only attribute to stubbornness, he said, 'No no, I'll wait. I don't want to leave without knowing you're all right. And anyway, you have no transport home.'

'You could always leave me a fiver for the taxi.'

Her tone could have been provocative. He rose to it. 'I said I'll stay. Why don't we let it go at that?'

She shrugged and looked away. William's attention wandered round the room. A few yards away sat a middle-aged woman in a faded patterned dress. She looked tired but hardly seriously ill. Maybe she'd come here to get off the streets. People must hang around in hospitals the way they do in public libraries. He'd never thought of that. The woman caught his eye and stared back. He broke first. Next to him, the girl was saying something.

'You're not used to being in NHS hospitals, are you?'

The remark was neutral, conversational almost. He was lulled into replying, 'I was just thinking it must have been years—'

'Things have changed, haven't they? How long have you been private?'

'It's automatic with my work.' He added defensively, 'But I haven't been ill for years.'

'Lucky for you.' She leaned back in her chair. 'This isn't bad actually. I've been in a lot worse.'

'Do you often fall off your bike?'

It was a calculated risk. A gentle gibe among acquaintances. She let it pass, her mind evidently on weightier things. 'No, but I've been to a couple of demos in the last year. You know, the Health Not Wealth campaign. God, there are some hospitals that look more like Victorian workhouses. But I suppose that's the point. The worse hospitals look, the more people go private. And the more people go private, the less people care how bad they look.'

Midnight on a Friday was not William's ideal time for political confrontation. He hazarded what he thought was a careful comment. 'But you still have a choice. No one is forced to pay for health care.'

'Yeah. Would you choose to have a brain haemorrhage in this place? Why do you think I refused to fill in their bloody questionnaire? You know what the leaked memo said. It's the biggest open secret in the country that the government is planning to get everyone earning over £7000 into private health insurance schemes. Which means that those left stay in a health service that gradually grinds to a halt, and no one - except them, of course - notices. State charity. Why should they expect more?'

She waited. He let her wait. 'What's wrong?' she asked. 'Don't you like discussing politics with a woman?'

'What makes you think this is a discussion? I thought it was a lecture. I was just wondering how many other unsuspecting motorists you've conned into knocking you down so you can harangue them in the bowels of an NHS hospital. You're a very effective one-woman pressure group.'

'Thanks.'

'I'm not entirely sure I meant it as a compliment.'

'I know,' she nodded pleasantly, 'but if you think about it—'

'Do you want some coffee?'

'Why, are you having trouble keeping awake?'

'No, but I thought you might be getting thirsty.'

She looked at him suspiciously but nodded. 'O.K. Thanks.' He got up. Her voice followed him, 'But I bet you the machine doesn't work.'

He walked determinedly towards the brightly-lit Have-a-Cuppa monster. The light was on, so the machine must work. He put in the right change and pushed the button. Nothing happened. He pushed again. Still nothing. He kicked it, just a small thump to let it know he meant business. At the desk the receptionist frowned.

'It doesn't work,' he said, attacking in defence.

'No, it doesn't.'

'Well, why isn't there an out of order sign?'

The woman shrugged. 'There was one earlier. It must have fallen off.'

'So what about my money?'

'You write your name and address here.' She held up a notebook. 'You'll get your refund in due course.'

Behind his back William could feel Josephine's enjoyment. 'And what if I died in the meantime?' he asked.

'Then you wouldn't need the money, would you?'

He admitted defeat. 'No, I suppose not.'

'If you want a cup of coffee, there's a machine on the lower ground floor by Physiotherapy. You could try that one.'

The information, offered voluntarily as it was, felt to William like something of a victory. 'Thank you. Is it far?'

'You'll make it there and back before your turn.'

'Game, set and match,' he murmured as he walked back to the girl. 'Well, Physiotherapy?'

She was grinning broadly. 'Why not?'

Physiotherapy was easy. Back along the corridor, down a flight of stairs and through a set of swing doors. Even finding the coffee machine did not prove a major undertaking. There it sat, next to a few forlorn chairs outside a treatment room. It was not, however, working. William was ready to give in but it was Josephine who suggested they go further, and who now led the way. After all, as she said, since they had time to kill, why not see some of the sights?

The corridor snaked onwards, taking them, William thought, further underground. It intersected with other passages, signposted Paediatrics, X-ray, Orthopaedics, before splitting into two. The left branch was marked EMERGENCY OPERATING THEATRE, the right simply NO ENTRY. She chose the right.

Of course, he thought. This is probably how she gets her information, snooping around hospital corridors gathering ammunition for her soap box. He didn't feel like accompanying her on a fact-finding mission for the Health Not Wealth campaign. 'Hey, can't you read the sign? There's nothing down there.'

'Oh come on,' she said good-naturedly over her shoulder. 'Don't you have any natural curiosity? It's obviously one of those corridors that leads through to another building. We might even find a working coffee machine. It's not as if we're in any kind of hurry.'

She walked on, not waiting for an answer. There was no doubt about it. She was clearly one of those people who, on principle, have to break rules. His instinct was to leave her to get on with it, but it wouldn't help either of them if she got lost. He sighed and set off after her.

The corridor led further underground. Through another set of heavy swing doors it became a broader, older passage with huge boiler pipes running the length of the walls, lagged in rolls of grimy cream padding.

'Oh great,' he muttered. 'All this and asbestos too.'

'God, it's just like the bowels of some vast ship.'

'Yes, the *Lusitania*,' he said, this time more audibly. 'Look, I'm not going any further. We're clearly not supposed to be here, and it's the last place on earth anyone would put a coffee machine.'

She stopped, seemed to hesitate for a moment, then glanced at her watch. 'Oh come on. Just a bit further. We must be near the end of it.'

They stood there, both refusing to give in. The silence around them was broken by the dull hum of the pipes echoing in the baked air. Then from some distance in front came the sound of footsteps. Both of them heard it clearly, amplified in the tunnelled acoustic. Damn, thought William, now we're going to be caught like a couple of schoolkids out of bounds. He didn't move. Neither did she. The steps got louder, clearer, more insistent. He felt a prickling at the back of his neck. Old childhood guilts revisited. He stood his ground until around the corner there approached a white-coated figure walking swiftly, head down, bag in hand.

William let out his breath. Stupid. A doctor on call. What had he expected, some mythical bogeyman? Her snooping had made him nervous. He waited for the doctor to notice them and order them back out of forbidden territory. But it didn't happen. In fact, when he did raise his head and spot them, twenty yards off, he seemed for that split second almost as confused as they were. Instead of stopping, he quickened his pace and passed without a sign of recognition, his head down almost onto his chest. In the pasty light William registered a broad, pale face made large by a receding hairline. Then he was gone. A few seconds later they heard the clap of the swing doors behind him. But something remained. Josephine had turned to watch him go. She made a face. 'Phew, what do you think all that was about? He looked like he'd seen a ghost. He was more uptight than we were.'

'He was probably on his way to a cardiac arrest or some such emergency. We're lucky he didn't bawl us out for being where we shouldn't.'

'Felt to me like he was trying to ignore us.' She shrugged. 'Weird. I wonder what's down there?'

'The morgue, I shouldn't wonder,' William said impatiently. 'Now, can we go back?'

She shot a look longingly into the distance. 'Listen, you wait here, O.K? I'll only be a few seconds. Just a quick look round the next corner, then I'll come straight back.'

It's pointless to argue, he thought. She'll go anyway. He nodded wearily, making sure she could read the disapproval in his eyes. She walked quickly away, light on her feet, her good arm swinging by her side, and disappeared round the corner. What am I doing here? he asked himself. By nature William would have described himself as a mild-tempered man. His profession of personnel manager required a graduated response to conflict, an ability to get on with both sides. Yet here he was suffering the unusual distinction of being annoyed at being annoyed. There was something wilful in her behaviour that made her tiring to be with, a kind of deliberate unpredictability. Now, if it had been Penny . . . Penny. Strange how these comparisons were always jumping out at him from nowhere, even though they were no longer together. Certainly if she had been in the car with him . . . Still, no use speculating, the split-up had been his decision.

He looked at his watch. Ten past twelve. How much longer? He took a few steps along the corridor to call her, and say he was going without her. There was no need. She was already heading towards him. He turned and started walking back. At the swing doors she caught up with him. He glanced at her. There was a certain gleam in her eyes that made him uncomfortable. He decided not to ask.

'Don't you want to know what I found?'

'No doubt you'll tell me anyway.'

If she heard the sarcasm she didn't react. 'That wing directly above us is the kidney unit. You know, the place that was occupied. It looks like Fort Knox now. I walked straight into a security guard. Scared the shit out of him. He gave me a real earful.'

'No more than you deserved. What did you say?'

'I told him the truth. That I was a casualty patient who had taken the wrong turning. That seemed to soothe him a bit, and I beat a hasty retreat. Boy, I had no idea the security was so shit-hot.'

An unpleasant thought struck him. 'You weren't by any chance looking for the unit?'

She shook her head. 'Of course not. I thought it was over the other side of the compound. I never saw it from underneath. I didn't even know there was an underground entrance.'

He let it pass. By now they were back in the reassuring grime-green landscape of Casualty, away from underground passages and threatening security guards. It seemed almost normal second time around. There were still three people before them, plus a few newcomers. They resumed their wait. He ignored her, taking out his diary and studying next week. After a few moments she touched his sleeve.

'Look, I know this will probably piss you off, but I'd really prefer to go home. My arm is feeling better, and quite frankly I think the sleep would do me more good than any bandages. I can always go to my GP tomorrow morning. Otherwise we're going to be here for hours.'

The suggestion was music to his ears, but he contrived to look doubtful. 'Are you sure?'

'Yes, I'm sure.'

'As long as you do see a doctor.'

'I will. I said I will. Now can we go?'

Outside she rubbed her eyes with her good hand.

'Tired?'

She nodded. 'You don't think . . .'

'What?'

'Nothing.'

He didn't feel like pursuing it. 'Do you want to wait here while I get the car? I could drive it round and meet you at the main entrance.'

She shook her head. 'No, I could do with the fresh air. Anyway, with your sense of direction there's no guarantee you'd ever find me again.' This time the dig was not malicious, merely familiar.

They set off across the dark compound. The place was deserted save for a solitary figure they overtook near the exit. How remarkable, he thought. Four hours ago I had never set eyes on this girl, and tomorrow, apart from maybe a phone call, she'll be a stranger again. Yet now here we are exchanging insults as though we've known each other for years.

Out on the road she stumbled slightly at the kerb, and he put out a hand to steady her. As she straightened up he noticed her staring at something over his shoulder. She said softly, 'How good's your eyesight?'

'I usually see cyclists coming up behind me, why?'

'Well, don't be too obvious about it, but as we cross the road take a look to your right. About thirty yards down the street on the other side of the road there's a man standing close by the wall. He's got a cigarette in his hand, and he's mostly in shadow. Tell me if you recognize him.'

It was hard to stare unobtrusively. He glanced to the right and caught a glimpse of a tall figure pressed against the wall. He couldn't make out the face properly, but got an impression of a large forehead and a moon-shaped expanse of flesh. He started opening the door on the passenger side, saying, 'I can't see him clearly. Who do you think he is?'

'I dunno. But he looks like the doctor who passed us in the corridor.'

He shot another look to his right. The street was empty. 'Maybe. I'm not sure. What would—'

He never finished the sentence. The explosion ripped apart the night silence and whirled both of them round in time to see the windows on one of the first floor wards cascade out, followed by a firework show of flame and sparks. A wave of black smoke followed. When the roar died down there was the crackling of the fire, mingled with the rising tide of voices, people shouting, as figures poured out of the surrounding buildings.

'My God!' exclaimed William, already halfway across the road. From behind him came the sound of an engine revving up as a car started to move, but his eyes were fixed on the fire ahead. He was climbing the railings to re-enter the compound when she caught up with him.

'Wait for me.'

'Don't be stupid. You can't do anything with that arm. You'll only be in the way. Stay here.'

To his surprise she didn't argue. By the time he got there the compound was alive with lights. He heard the different screams of fire engines and police cars. A crowd had already gathered. The men in uniform were cordoning off the area, and firemen were preparing to hose the blaze. It was clear that whatever had happened they had it under control. There was nothing he could do to help. Halfway back down the slope she met him, her face tense with questions.

'I don't know,' he said, guiding her back across the street. 'The blast was limited to one building. It seems to have more or less blown itself out. There were doctors and nurses everywhere. The last thing they needed was amateurs. Whatever it was, we can read about it in tomorrow's papers.'

Inside the car she leaned back and closed her eyes, looking suddenly grey with tiredness. William drove towards the roundabout. Another police car passed, siren screeching. He found his heart was making more noise than ever. My God, what a night. She directed him towards Hornsey Rise. For a while they drove in silence.

'Wonder if it was gas,' he said. 'If it comes out there was negligence, it'll play straight into the hands of your Health Not Wealth friends. You'd better get that wrist better in time for the demo.'

There was a pause. 'Fuckers,' she muttered. Then aloud, 'I wonder if anyone was hurt.'

'If they were, they chose the right place. No doubt your errant doctor got right back in there – if indeed it was him out having a quiet smoke. I didn't notice him in the compound, did you?'

She was staring out at the road ahead. 'No, I didn't. Oh – you have to take a right here, by the pillarbox. Then it's the fourth house on the left.'

William pulled up outside a darkened terrace with a cat sitting on the ground floor window ledge. He turned to her. 'Well, Josephine . . . the end of a long night. I hope you feel better in the morning.'

She got out, then ducked her head back inside. 'Thanks for the lift. If you go straight on it'll bring you out at Finsbury Park. Go easy on the cyclists. And by the way, the name's Josie, not Josephine. See you.'

He watched her fumble with her keys then enter the house, the cat streaking in after her. Ten seconds later an upstairs light went on.

Two twenty-three on a Saturday morning, according to the dashboard clock. He started the car and headed off. Josie suits her better, he thought, as he turned the corner.

Chapter Two

She woke early. It was a habit she had acquired during a year spent travelling, when the right bus was always the one that left at the crack of dawn. She rolled over, registering that she was still tired, but admitted defeat. She got up. The sky had that soft, hazy quality that comes before heat. It was going to be another baking day. Gingerly she touched her wrist. It hurt, but not as much as before. It could have been worse. In the kitchen the cat was already ordering breakfast loudly.

He turned out to be luckier than her. There was milk in the fridge and a half-full tin of something foul-smelling which he found irresistible. There was no butter or eggs, and the bread had developed little green stains in the middle. A couple of aspirin would do, she had no need of penicillin. She made herself a cup of coffee, picked up the newspaper and went back to bed.

The *Guardian* led on South Africa, where speculation had grown that the continuing riots and sabotage might result in a victory to the extreme right in the coming general election. In the left hand column half way down the front page under the headline EXPLOSION BLASTS LONDON HOSPITAL there was a short, bald account of the bombing, obviously a last-minute insertion. Josie leaned over and switched on the radio. Ten minutes later Radio 4 carried a fuller story. The renal unit at the Royal Highgate Hospital had been badly damaged by an incendiary device. The unit's kidney stone machine, the lithotripter, was completely destroyed, and damage had been caused to the two wards, and to transplant and dialysis equipment. There was one casualty, a security guard named Malcolm O'Grady, now in the intensive care unit of the hospital after an emergency operation. His condition was described as critical. The renal unit, the reporter explained, had been completed two years before but never put into operation because of government restrictions on health service manning levels, according to the north-east Thames Regional Health

Authority. The announcement six months ago that the unit was to be leased to a private hospital group had led to demonstrations and an occupation by members of the Health Not Wealth pressure group.

Josie switched off the radio and got out of bed. Before William contacted her and they went together to do their duty there was something she had to find out. In the living room she stepped over the cat on the way to the phone.

In a more salubrious apartment in West Hampstead two hours later the ten o'clock news broadcast interrupted William's breakfast and significantly re-arranged his day.

Josie's diagnosis had been correct. With the possible exception of the odd parking fine William Stevens was a man who upheld the law. The implication of the news report was clear. It was not a gas leak but a bomb. He was in no doubt that even if what he and Josie had witnessed last night should prove irrelevant, it should nevertheless be reported. It was not a prospect he relished. His life had established a certain order and pattern to which traffic accidents and bomb blasts did not easily accommodate themselves. The day had been mapped out. Squash followed by lunch with an old friend. Better get this over with quickly. He found the scrap of paper on which he'd written Josie's address and phone number. She answered immediately, as though waiting by the phone. He couldn't decide if he was pleased or irritated by the prospect of seeing her again.

She was late by almost half an hour. Reluctantly, William found a phone and informed his squash partner accordingly. When she did arrive, moving swiftly through the crowds outside Archway Road Garden Centre, she looked different. Maybe it was the clothes. She was wearing a skirt and a light cotton jacket. Her hair seemed a tidier halo round her head. The care she had taken amused him. It made her seem more fallible.

'Good morning,' he greeted her. 'How's the wrist?'

'As well as can be expected,' she answered with a deliberate politeness. 'I'm late. The bus took a long time coming.'

No apology, he thought, just the implied accusation that he had deprived her of her bike. 'I almost didn't recognize you. You look different.'

'So do you. Maybe it's the cashmere sweater. We're obviously both dressed to give evidence.'

Interesting, he thought. She's nervous too. Maybe the prospect of police stations had the same effect on everyone, kindling guilt even among the innocent. 'Shall we go in?'

'Are you sure we shouldn't synchronize stories first?'

He frowned. 'Why? We both know what we saw.'

'Yes, but will we be able to stick to the details under torture?'

He stared at her. She clicked her tongue in mock impatience. 'It's all right. It was just a joke, you know . . . about police brutality. Forget it, come on, let's get it over with.'

Inside Highgate police station they discovered they were by no means the only passers-by with something to contribute to the investigation. Half of Holloway, it seemed, had an opinion on the matter. Outside an improvised Incident Room, containing desks, files, telephones, maps, computer terminals and up to thirty police officers, William and Josie waited their turn to give evidence. It's a little like being back in Casualty, William thought, as they stood watching the minutes tick by. Twenty minutes into what should have been his squash game a detective constable ushered them into a small interview room, apologizing for the delay. The place was hardly inviting: just a table, four chairs and a couple of windows high up on a slant. William's nostrils detected a distinct smell of stale sweat.

The young detective sat down opposite them. 'All right, what do you have to tell me?'

There was a moment's pause when William waited, assuming that Josie would take the floor. Nothing happened. Instead she half turned to him expectantly. The sudden deference was not in character. Well, so be it. He told the story rather well, he thought, making it clear and concise. The detective stayed silent, sitting back in his chair, arms folded over his chest. The pose made him look older, giving a solidity and authority to his body that was lacking in his face.

'Let me get this straight,' he said at the end. 'You both saw the doctor pass, and then you' – pointing at Josie – 'went down the corridor further, while you, sir, stayed where you were, right? Miss Ridley, what made you go on?'

'Just curiosity, I suppose. We'd come so far. I thought it might lead to a canteen or something.'

'Are you by nature a curious person?'

She shrugged. 'I don't know. I suppose so.'

'I see.' The phrase was allowed to hang in the air. But the effect, if that was the intention, was lost on William and on Josie, who sat very still, hands on her lap, a picture of quiet, obedient attention. The detective shifted in his seat. 'And the man outside – you're sure it was the same man that you saw in the corridor?'

'Yes.' A well-judged pause. 'Yes, I think I'm sure.'

'You *think* you're sure? But it was you who pointed him out to Mr Stevens?'

'Yes.'

'You were some way away from him.'

'Yes, we were. But his face was quite distinctive. The forehead was very broad.'

'Hmmm. Mr Stevens, how about you? Could you be sure?'

William frowned. 'I don't think one hundred per cent. He certainly looked familiar, but it was only a glance, and as Josie said, the light of the street lamps was not very powerful.'

'I see. And neither of you saw him again, after that moment? Mr Stevens?'

'No.'

'Miss Ridley?'

'No . . . no, I didn't see him. But I did see a car.'

It had been going so well that William was thrown completely off guard. It even took him a second to register what she had said. When he did he looked at her sharply. She turned to him, shrugging, 'I didn't even think about it last night. It was just after you'd run across the road after the blast. Everything was so crazy. My mind was full of what was happening. Then you rushed off to see if you could help, and by the time you'd got back I'd forgotton all about it. There was no reason to connect it with anything, until now.'

The detective sat forward. 'What exactly did you see?'

'It was just after the explosion. I saw a car pull out from a side road and set off down the hill away from us.'

'How far away?'

'Ooh, forty, maybe sixty yards. I don't know. I'm no judge of distance.'

'And what make was it, could you see that?'

Josie made a grimace of apology. 'It was dark-coloured, quite big, I do remember that. Blackish, maybe dark brown or dark blue . . . but I'm not very up on cars. I'm afraid I couldn't possibly tell you what make it was.'

'We'll show you some pictures later. It might jog your memory. What about the registration plate – any memory of that?'

Josie screwed up her eyes as if deep in thought. 'Oooh, it was so fleeting. Maybe an S, and I think there was a one and a nine . . . Sorry, I really don't remember any more.'

'And you, Mr Stevens, you never saw anything after the explosion?'

In his mind William was standing again by the railings staring at the fireworks display. There had been some kind of noise behind him. 'I seem to remember hearing a car, but I didn't look round. There was too much going on in front.'

'Tell me, Miss Ridley, what reason do you have to connect this car with the man you had seen?'

Josie looked blank. 'I'm sorry?'

'The car. This was a residential area – why did you think this particular car was significant?'

Josie glanced at William, then back at the detective constable. 'Well, the timing,' she said, a little flustered. 'The timing was right. The man in the road was gone, then the car started up. I suppose I just put two and two together.'

The detective was frowning, as if he felt addition was the prerogative of his profession and not to be left to amateurs. He picked up a pencil from his desk and moved it around in his fingers. 'All right. So to recap: you both saw a man in the basement walking away from the kidney unit. Then you both think that you might have seen this same man outside the hospital just before the explosion. And after the blast you, Miss Ridley, saw a car driving away, a car that Mr Stevens may or may not have heard. Is that correct?'

'Yes,' they both replied together.

'Good.' He didn't sound as if he meant it. 'One last question . . .' He paused to formulate it. 'Have either of you ever had anything to do with the hospital before?'

William waited for Josie to reply. Eventually she did. It was a firm no.

'And you, Mr Stevens?'

'No, never.'

'Fine. Now, I'm afraid there are a few formalities. First I'm going to need a statement from both of you. And then I'd like you to look at some drawings of faces so that we can get a description. Also some photographs of cars. Excuse me.'

The detective left the room. William turned to Josie and opened his mouth to protest, but she silenced him with an index finger to her lips. He obeyed reluctantly with a look that read, 'O.K., but we'll sort this out later.'

Later turned out to be an hour and a half, during which time they pored over different combinations of hairlines, chins and noses, to say nothing of fifty-seven varieties of car models. The uniformed constable who typed out their statements was clearly no graduate of Pitmans, and when they finally got out into the sunshine William was more than a little irate.

'Well, if you don't mind my saying so, that was a pretty stupid thing to do.'

'What was?'

'Good question. Let's start with the lie you told about never having been to the Royal Highgate before.'

'It wasn't a lie. He asked me if I'd had anything to do with the hospital. I assumed he meant medically. And the answer to that was no.'

'That wasn't what he meant. And you know it.'

'So what if I did? Since it's already clear they're eager to nail this bombing on some lefties, I didn't want to hand them ammunition. They would hardly have believed anything I said if I'd admitted that I went to HNW demos.'

'So how do you think they'll feel when they find out?'

'They won't find out. Unless you tell them, of course.'

'Well, you're the one who's supposed to be politically informed. But I'd have thought they'd keep records on those sort of things. You might well be on file.'

She said nothing.

'And it puts me in a pretty compromised position, knowing you were lying and not being able to say anything. And what about the car? How come you didn't tell me you'd seen a car? I distinctly remember asking you if you'd spotted the man again.'

'I didn't tell you because, believe it or not, I had genuinely forgotten, that's why. Jesus, there were a lot of things going on, if you remember rightly. My hand was hurting and I was tired. It didn't seem important until I thought about it later.'

'Oh come on, Josie. I wasn't born yesterday.'

She whirled on him. 'And just what is that supposed to mean?'

'It means that you must have known last night that that explosion was caused by a bomb.'

'Why must I have known? You didn't. You thought it was a gas leak.'

'Yeah, but I'm not the one connected with Health Not Wealth. I didn't even know there had been threats.'

'Threats! It was all just rhetorical shit. It would have been political suicide for anyone in HNW to pull a stunt like that. It undermines the credibility of the whole movement.'

'So who else would have done it?'

'How should I know?' She shook her head angrily. 'But I'm certainly not going to help the police to blame the wrong people.'

'And that explains the sudden transformation of character just now. I presume the butter-wouldn't-melt-in-her-mouth persona was designed to put them off the scent.'

She scowled. 'I don't like police stations. They give me the creeps. I tend to over-compensate.'

'You're a regular visitor, I take it?'

'Hey, what is this – a cross-examination? Listen, you rang me up, we went to the police, we told them what we saw. Finito. We've fulfilled our obligations as citizens. Unless, of course, you feel committed to going back in to set the record straight about my private political affiliations.'

He regarded her for a moment. There was nothing to be gained from bickering. 'O.K.,' he said in a normal voice. 'Let's leave it there. You told them everything you know, that's the important thing.'

Her stare was still cold.

'No doubt if they need us again they'll get in touch. In which case we'll be seeing each other again.' He extended a hand which with a brief hesitation she shook. 'So goodbye for now. You have my card so you know how to get in touch, don't you?'

'Yes. William Stevens, Personnel Manager, Actonics Ltd, Acton Road, W3 4DB. Telephone number 876 5958.' She recited this with a flourish. 'Close your mouth,' she added sweetly, 'you'll catch flies.'

'That's one hell of a memory you've got.'

'Yes, photographic I believe it's called. I owe most of my academic qualifications to it.'

'Well, it's a shame you didn't get a photographic look at that car number last night.'

The pause was so slight it was hardly there. 'Oh very funny. Ha ha.'

'Josie . . .'

She had already turned and was walking away.

'Josie!'

She tilted her head in the form of a question.

'*Did* you see the number?'

'No. Was that all?'

He shook his head. 'The trouble with you is I don't know whether to believe you or not.'

'I think that's your problem, not mine. Why don't you just go home and forget about it? You've done your duty. Don't bother your head with me doing mine.'

It made sense. Maybe she was right. Or maybe, he thought, I should walk back in there and tell them I think she knows more than she admitted. But she'd simply deny it, and then where would we be? No doubt in the category of suspects rather than witnesses. Even as he considered it he knew he wouldn't do it. For whatever reason he felt some loyalty towards her.

'Well, I'm not going to stand on street corners slugging it out with you,' he said. 'I've said what I have to say. If you get any sudden surges of memory you know where to find me. I'd be happy to accompany you back into the lions' den.'

'Thanks, you really are a gentleman. Now, if you don't mind, I've got to start repairing my transport.'

She strode off down the street. He watched her move. Even her back seemed to emanate a kind of anger. He wondered vaguely if he didn't regard her as a challenge. It crossed his mind he could have offered to help her with the bike. But he wasn't a glutton for punishment. Let her swear at herself for a while. It would probably calm her down. He walked off in the opposite direction. Somehow he knew it was not a final parting.

Chapter Three

The rest of the weekend stretched ahead. He attempted to bring it under control. On the way home he did some shopping and called in at a carwash, feeling better for the deliberate imposition of normality. In the evening he took an old girlfriend to the theatre then went back to her place for a coffee. He could have stayed, the invitation was unspoken but traditional, but he decided against it. He had a lot to do on Sunday and he wanted to get an early start.

By nine thirty he was settled at his desk in the study in front of a window pouring Sunday sunshine onto a couple of files and a jug of coffee. The next few days would bring a series of important meetings at work and he needed, psychologically more than practically, to feel prepared. For him as personnel manager it concerned the most vital of issues - relations with the trade unions.

Actonics was not a new company. Originally it had supplied transistors and other specialized components for radios and televisions, sharing in those far-off boom years for British electronics when the world had yet to hear the name of Sony. By the early seventies the company was in trouble. Entry into the EEC ended protection, and Japanese penetration of the TV market reached the proportions of rape. 1975 found Actonics with a purpose-built factory on a freehold site close to the M4 making a product that was barely profitable. The inevitable happened: the company was taken over. Not, however, by one of those 'asset strippers' whose heyday it then was, but by Tom Hutchins, a rare kind of British businessman - an engineering wizard with entrepreneurial skills to match. Armed with a loan from the National Enterprise Board, he started production of a new microcomputer which by the end of the decade had become the market leader.

This was when William came in. After five years in his previous job with British Steel, carrying out a vigorous - or ruthless, as some people described it - programme of rationalization and redundancies, the prospect of working for a fast-moving firm in the bullish sector of electronics - the Great White Hope of British industry - was irresistible. With the support of the Board he instigated an enlightened regime of personnel management, abolishing the old class-bound practices such as clocking-in, separate canteens and exclusive management perks. New pension and productivity schemes had proved popular, and at the end of four years William had every reason to congratulate himself. However, it now seemed that his very success might prove to be his undoing.

Now that the workforce was so happy and compliant, had not the time come, William's colleagues argued, to get rid of the unions completely? They looked wistfully at the personnel practices of their competitors, mainly new firms and American or Japanese subsidiaries. These had been able to set up on their own terms. Trade union activity was severely restricted. Shop stewards, who once met regularly on the firm's time, were now reduced to getting together in the pub after work. In some companies there was no union recognition, but instead staff associations, organized by management consultants and paid for by the employer. William was urged by the board to move in this direction, by subtle but significant changes in the disputes procedure perhaps, or by making the now weekly meeting with the shop stewards into a monthly occasion.

William's deepest instincts told him to reject all this. He had already negotiated a no-strike agreement – not without difficulty – and beyond that he was not prepared to go. It was true that management held all the cards. Adverse changes in industrial law, four million on the dole, a tough-minded government of the radical right, a hostile or indifferent public – all these conspired to lower the morale of the unions. But William was convinced this power should be exercised with magnanimity. The pendulum would swing, the unions would be back, and they would remember. Union militancy was a sleeping dog, not a broken-backed camel. For management to go on the offensive was senselessly provocative, a squandering of moral capital in a policy of confrontation which, in the past when the boot had been on the other foot, they had bitterly condemned. Invited to address the board, William argued that if the workforce were to believe in industry as a partnership, it was up to management to make the idea a reality. He was overruled.

This placed him in an invidious position. Whatever he did would make him unpopular. If he followed the board's instructions he would compromise a relationship with men and women he had spent years building up. If he resisted he might find himself out of a job. On the face of it, he was presented with an intractable dilemma.

But one he was confident he could crack. William's modesty of manner belied a conceit in his powers of persuasion. The art of personnel management, he thought in his more cynical moments, lay in reconciling conflict by fudging the issue so that all parties believed they had won. He enjoyed his job, he knew he did it well, and he looked forward to the coming negotiation as a challenge rather than a threat.

But he'd need to have his wits about him, and to be thoroughly on top of the facts. He was not then best pleased to discover that after a couple of hours' work his concentration was beginning to falter. Thoughts of hospital corridors and police interview rooms started to nudge their way centre stage. He kept hearing echoes of

Josie's voice asserting one thing and denying another. And always it arrived back at the same question mark. Had she seen more than she'd told? The Sunday papers had done nothing to relieve his anxiety on this score. The bomb, a 'reliable source' had informed the *Sunday Times*, was pretty amateurish in its construction, so known terrorist groups were not suspected. Even without anti-terrorist squad leaks, the rest of Fleet Street had formed the same conclusion. Health Not Wealth was responsible, either through its own members or by attracting to its banner individuals and parties of the loony extremist left. A few dissenting voices blamed the government for provoking the confrontation, but their effect was parenthetical amid the general indignation.

So where did this leave him and Josie? If she had lied to the police about the car number plate, then she could be accused of obstructing the course of justice, and he of abetting her. Yet he still felt inclined to give her the benefit of the doubt. It had been dark, after all, and the car some distance away. He would have been surprised if she had been able to note the number. And what else was there to condemn her for? Certainly she was noisy, angry and aggressive towards authority. But that was hardly a crime. Anyway, he was used to dealing with people he didn't necessarily agree with. If he washed his hands of everyone just because they were difficult, he wouldn't have a job left. And if she was holding something back, surely he, with his skill and experience at inter-personal problem solving, had a much better chance of getting it out of her than the police had.

Only one thing bothered him – no, he wouldn't say bothered, it intrigued him. Would he have felt so involved if it had been a man? It was impossible to imagine him going to so much trouble if a thirteen-stone plumber had ploughed into the side of his car. He might possibly have taken him to the hospital, maybe even have left him a fiver for a taxi, but he would never have stayed with him and driven him home. So, Josie's sex had influenced events. Did that mean he was attracted to her? Surely not. She was not his type. Without the perennial scowl on her face she could conceivably be called attractive. But her manner was all wrong. She was too careless, too extrovert, too self-centred. No, attraction had nothing to do with it. She interested him, that was all, precisely because they were so far apart. The thought made him feel better, and he felt able to cast her from his mind. By Monday, if she hadn't called him he might contact her, just a gentle nudge to see if her memory was progressing. He turned back to his work. Still, he thought a few moments later, it would be interesting to know just what she was thinking about . . .

He would have been disappointed. At that particular moment Josie was asleep, sprawled on a tattered sofa with the cat curled up beside her, a book half-open on her lap, and the telephone stationed nearby.

She had been waiting for the call all weekend. She passed the time with displacement activities. On Saturday she went to bed early, eating a tin of baked beans and watching television until closedown. Then she picked up a book to kill a little more of the night. None of this stopped her thinking. She was not dissatisfied with her performance at the police station. By all means let them run her name through the Hendon computer. All they would come up with was a nine-year-old conviction for possession of marijuana. It would take a great deal of digging to find out more. No, the police did not trouble her. What did were the three numbers and four letters of the dark blue Audi saloon, which lay embedded like studs in her brain. But she could do nothing with them. Not yet anyway. Not till she had the call. She finally slept at three thirty and woke with a start to the ring of the phone six hours later. It was a wrong number. She put down the receiver and settled herself in for a long Sunday.

It was unfortunate that the waiting should fall on this of all days. Sundays for Josie were a traditional disaster area. On the day when others rested, she fretted, fighting a constant battle to keep the hands of the clock moving and the clouds of depression from dumping on her. It was an old antipathy. As a child in the Ridley household Sundays had always been the signal for marital warfare; a large, empty day to be filled with sniping, splintering rows which came to the boil with the roast and vegetables, exploded into the endless afternoon and cooled into ice chips with the evening. A weekly ritual, as sacrosanct as mass in other homes. For the first few months after Mr Ridley packed his bags and left, an unholy quiet descended on the household and the day gaped even wider. Later, when a new father arrived, sensible but insensitive to memories, followed by a smaller version of himself, Sundays again became volatile, this time with Josie herself providing the blue touchpaper, like father like daughter, in sullen memory of the usurped.

Eventually, when she grew old enough to identify the destructive pattern, she attempted to break the curse by working all day, or by making Saturday stretch so far into the night that Sunday hardly existed at all.

But today the sabbath arrived early and found her tied, as if by umbilical cord, to the phone. The morning dragged its heels into the afternoon. She read two books from cover to cover, slept a little, ate, read some more. Finally the evening arrived. And with it a television newsflash. Malcolm O'Grady, aged forty-three, married with two children, had died in the intensive care unit of the Royal Highgate, the hospital where he had worked as a security guard. Josie sat rigid, staring at the screen.

The death changed everything. More than ever, she needed that phone call. That night she slept even worse, the phone by her bed. Then at last, just before ten a.m., it rang. The message was brief, the information too memorable for her to need to write it down. She was due at work at two. Four hours. She grabbed her bag and left the house in a hurry.

Chapter Four

She called William at lunchtime. He was not surprised. Clearly O'Grady's death had put a different complexion on things. Could they, she asked, meet at Highgate police station in the late afternoon? He had been right. She did have something more to tell. The timing was lousy. He had a meeting at four, and although unimportant in itself – it was a committee on the canteen accounts – he disliked on principle getting behind. But he had no option. He re-arranged the meeting. 'I'll be there at five,' he told her.

In the event he was late. She watched him approach, noting his greying, close-cut hair, the slight flamboyance in the stripe of his blue suit, the lined face which gave a more truthful account of his age — thirty-nine — than the lean, almost youthful body. She held out her hand in the formal gesture of greeting.

'Thank you for coming,' she said. 'I appreciate it.'

He picked up a nervousness. 'That's all right. What do you want to do? We can discuss it first, if you like. . .'

'No, it's my problem. I'll handle it.'

Inside the station the bustle and confusion was if anything more pronounced than before. At the desk Josie said, 'We would like to speak to Detective Constable Harrison.’ William was impressed that she recalled the name. He hadn’t.

‘On what business?’

She explained briefly, and they were shown into the same room as before, the detective joining them. He addressed William, ‘I understand you have some further information?’

Josie answered, ‘Yes, I have.’

‘Yes?’

‘It’s about the car I saw outside the hospital on Friday night. I’ve thought hard about it, and I can now remember the number.’

At first William thought the policeman hadn’t heard. He gazed blankly at Josie as if waiting for her to add something. When she didn’t he asked, ‘What was it?’

‘SHX 961Z.’

There was a phone on the desk. He dialled a number. ‘Maureen, would you do me a check on SHX 961Z? Soon as possible. Thanks.’ He put his finger on the cradle and dialled again. ‘DC Harrison here. Could you spare five minutes? I’m in interview room 2 . . . Yes, it is.’

To Josie he explained, ‘I’d like Inspector Gill to hear this.’

‘Hear what? That was it. I’ve told you what I came to say.’

This was ignored, and the three of them sat in an uneasy silence for several minutes before the door opened and another plainclothes man entered. Taller and older, with a sharp nose and thin features, he fixed the witnesses with a hostile stare. The two policemen exchanged a few words in an undertone. William caught Josie’s eye. She didn’t smile back.

Seated next to his colleague, the inspector took command. ‘Miss Ridley, I understand you wish to change your statement. And that you are now prepared to identify the number of the car you claim to have seen on Friday night. Is this so?’

‘Yes.’

‘Three days ago you said, and I quote’ – glancing at a file in front of him – ‘ “The car was fifty yards down the street and moving away from me. It was so fleeting I was unable to make out the number.” This is the statement you signed on Saturday.’

‘That’s correct.’

‘And now you’re saying the opposite. That you were able to read the number plate. You’ve changed your mind, yes? Do you mind telling me why?’

‘It’s really quite simple. I didn’t want to tell you something unless

I was absolutely sure. I went away and thought about it over the weekend, and now I am sure. That was the number. SHX 961Z.'

'But if this number is in your head now, then surely it was already there two days ago. But in fact you said then that you were sure you *didn't* remember it. It is now nearly four days since the bombing. If this car is significant, then our task of finding its driver has been made immeasurably more difficult. You do understand that?'

'I'm sorry. I can see now that it would have been better if I'd spoken up before, but I'm afraid it's just not in my nature to say things unless I'm absolutely sure of them.'

Admirably restrained, William thought. Well done.

'Tell me, has anything happened over the last few days to jog your memory?'

'No.'

'A vivid retrocognitive dream, perhaps? A visit to your local hypnotist?'

The remark came out so bland that it took Josie a moment to register its sarcasm. 'Look, I didn't—'

She was interrupted by the noise of the telephone buzzer. The caller had a lot to say. The inspector listened in silence apart from the occasional grunted acknowledgement. All the time he kept his eye on Josie, managing simultaneously to record the information on a notepad in front of him. Josie dropped her gaze, and stared firmly at a point on the floor. Finally he put the receiver down and regarded her in silence. Her reaction was a rock-like stillness.

'You see, Miss Ridley,' the Inspector continued in a conversational tone, 'where was I? Yes. I want to try and explain to you why I'm still not happy. Let's put it this way. A witness comes forward and tells us something. The next time we talk to him, he says, well, I don't know, maybe that's not what I saw, I've been going over it and well frankly, I'm not so sure now. That kind of thing happens time and time again. We learn to expect it. But in your case it's entirely the opposite. You seem to have become not less but *more* confident.'

The silence demanded a reply. She gave it. 'So?'

'So, I just don't know what to think. Let me tell you about police work. When we appeal for witnesses to come forward we invariably get a huge response, mostly - regrettably - useless. You wouldn't believe the stories we hear. The imagination of the public is extraordinary. People spot villains like they spot UFOs. Sometimes it's innocent – they're just dying to be helpful. Sometimes it's egoism – they see themselves winning medals, rewards, headlines in the *Daily Express,* that sort of thing. And there again, some people can be quite malicious – there's a neighbour they can't stand, so they shop him, never mind the crimes are pure fantasy.'

William could feel Josie's irritation rising. It's bait, he thought. Don't go for it.

'They're the worst of all. Those people who deliberately and consciously set out to mislead us. Pathetic people who confess to crimes they didn't commit. Stupid people who claim they've planted a bomb in the Albert Hall. Vicious people who ring up the victim's family pretending to be the kidnapper— '

'All right, Inspector.' Josie's voice gave away her anger. 'I appreciate the lecture, but I still don't see the point.'

'The point, Miss Ridley, is quite simple. Are you or are you not now telling us the truth? Are you a reliable witness, or someone, for whatever motive, with an over-active imagination?'

She held her ground. 'I've told you the truth. The whole truth and nothing but the truth.'

'So help you God. Fine. Then are you also able to say that the car you saw on Friday night was a dark blue Audi 2000?'

'We've been through this before. It might have been. I'm pretty useless at car types.'

'Which is a shame considering how good you are at numbers. Well, this car is the property of one Mr De Villiers, a company director. I don't suppose either of you have ever heard of him. Mr Stevens?'

'No.'

'Miss Ridley?'

'Of course not. How could I?'

She's lying, William thought suddenly. The inspector did not show what he thought.

'Well, it seems that in this case all your razor-sharp faculties of memory and your public-spirited determination have gone for naught. Mr De Villiers' car was stolen on Friday sometime between eight p.m., when he parked it in Mayfair, and two a.m., when he reported it missing. It was recovered the following morning parked on a double yellow line in Soho. No damage. It was assumed it had been taken for a joyride.'

'What about fingerprints, Inspector, and that kind of thing?' William said, trying to impose some control on the conversation.

'Not taken. Not for a joyride. It's unlikely now that forensics will come up with anything. Of course, had we known on Saturday that it had been spotted at the scene of a crime . . .'

Josie made a move to get up.

'Before you go, Miss Ridley . . .' She sat down again. 'You're not intending to leave the country or anything?'

'No.'

'Because I expect we shall want to speak to you again. And you, Mr Stevens?'

'I'm at your disposal, Inspector.'

Inspector Gill nodded. They were dismissed. As the door closed William could imagine the interchange that followed. 'Maureen, I need another check. Does the computer have anything on a Josephine Ridley? I'll be in my office.' Well, he thought, she's brought it on herself. After all, they're just doing their job.

Outside there was a breeze. He realized how hot and clammy it had been in there. Beside him Josie took a few gulps of air and leaned against the railings, stretching her head back. He regarded her quietly. There was an element of exaggeration in everything she did, as if she kept having to make statements, to convince herself as much as anyone else. He wondered what she was like alone, with just herself as audience. She turned to him suddenly, as if she had just thought of something.

'Are you busy?'

He was. He wanted to get home and shower before going to a meeting at the Institute of Personnel Managers. There was an urgency in Josie's voice, though, that he was reluctant to refuse.

'Not for half an hour or so, why?'

'Can we go for a drink somewhere?'

'Josie.' He held his ground. 'You didn't hide anything this time, did you?'

'No!' she protested. 'At least nothing I should have told them, I promise you. But there are some things I have to sort out in my head, and I need another brain to bat them against.'

Despite himself he was just a little flattered. 'With me? How can you be sure I'll bring the right political perspective to the discussion?'

She clicked her tongue impatiently. 'I need to talk to you because you were there, stupid. You're involved, and you'll know what I'm talking about. And because,' she smiled mockingly, 'when the wind is in the right direction you know a hawk from a handsaw.'

Funny, he thought, despite her hard edges, I do sort of enjoy being surprised by her. I don't know anyone like her. Maybe that's what fascinates me. He failed to register the small warning bell which was sounding somewhere in his head.

'Well?'

'O.K. I'm pretty sure the wind is in a southerly direction. Where shall we go?'

Settled in the corner of a pub surrounded by faded red velvet and gilt mirrors, she nursed a straight scotch, he a half pint. He waited, watching her turn the glass slowly in her hand. It was unlike her not to know where to begin. She looked up at him, frowning.

'I think there's something rotten about this whole thing. And somehow now we're right in the middle of it. Let's go step by step. First, I don't think HNW has anything to do with the bomb—'

'Wait a minute. Step by step, remember. How can you be so sure of that?'

'Hell, William, they're a respectable pressure group. They've got doctors, nurses, consultants, trade union leaders, MPs even.'

'I know that. No one's suggesting they planned it at the annual general meeting. But why not extreme members of the rank and file? There have been threats—'

'Yes, but no action. It doesn't make sense. The Royal Highgate occupation was a success politically. Sure, I know we lost the battle, but it was a moral victory. We gained a lot of popular support. The government is on the run. Now this bombing changes everything. It makes it look as if HNW is packed with underground dangerous extremists - you see, even you think that. It gives the initiative back to the government. For anyone in HNW to have done that would be political suicide.'

'But I thought that was the whole point of terrorism. To undermine the middle ground and force confrontation.'

Josie shook her head. 'No.'

'Why not?'

'Because it still doesn't make sense. No one's claimed responsibility. The aim of terrorism is to gain notoriety. People have to understand who did it and why.'

'I dunno. Seems to me there've been quite a lot of anonymous bombs over the years. Anyway, what about suggestions that it's some other, unconnected group - the IRA, for instance?'

She snorted. 'Oh William, not you too. Since when did the IRA mount an operation without publicly patting themselves on the back afterwards?'

'What about a splinter group? They might be acting independently.'

'And you might be reading the wrong newspapers,' she retorted scornfully.

'Listen. You're the one who asked me to lob you the balls. If you've got something to say, then just come out and say it.'

'O.K. Let me ask you a few questions. Who has most to gain from bombing the kidney unit?'

'You tell me.'

'Put it this way. Who has most to gain from discrediting HNW and the pro-NHS movement in general?'

He paused, resisting the rhetorical bullying. He shrugged. What the hell. 'The government?'

'Well then?'

He suddenly felt very impatient. 'Oh, don't be absurd. Didn't you ever hear the parable of the sledgehammer and the nut? Why should they contemplate doing such a thing? It's not worth it. It would destroy them.'

'Not if they don't get found out it won't. And it is worth it. The government came into power with this thinly disguised vision of dismantling large chunks of the welfare state, in particular the national health service. But it's not working. People resent having to pay for something they're used to getting free. The NHS is really popular. HNW is an expression of that. The government's in trouble. There's an atmosphere of panic. Don't you feel it?'

'Not particularly. At this stage of a parliament it's always like that. You're wanting to make this into a Watergate. Yes, yes, I know that Watergate actually happened. But burglary isn't in quite the same league as bombing. And anyway, this is Britain. I don't think the British government is any more moral than other ones, but I do expect them to be more subtle.'

'William, don't be so naive. They've done things like this before.'

'Oh really? When?'

'What about the department in the Ministry of Defence set up to smear CND?'

'That's propaganda. Within the rules.'

'Oh yeah – and how did they get their information?' I suppose you still think Hilda Morrell fell on her own gardening fork?'

'What?'

'Oh never mind. What about Ulster then? There've been scores of unclaimed bombs and assassinations that make no sense in terms of the interests of those who are supposed to have done them.'

'Like what?'

'Like the 1972 Dublin bombing, the night before there was a crucial vote in the Dail to ban the IRA. The bill was carried. Everyone blamed the IRA. But how could it have been them? They didn't claim it. They'd have been mad to do it, they didn't want to be banned. So who was it?'

'A protestant terrorist organization?'

'More likely a British terrorist organization. Like the army. The SAS. Military Intelligence. MI5. MI6. If they get away with that sort of stuff in Ireland, what's to stop them bringing it all back home?'

'What stops them possibly is that they lack your paranoid imagination. You say the government sanctions these things. Well maybe. You're better informed than I am, but I think you'd agree that it's not only governments that practise disinformation. And even if it's true, there is a war on over there. If you're going to convince me the government would do that in Britain, and over a trivial issue like this one, you're going to have to do a lot better than that.'

Josie fell silent. She ran her finger around the top of her glass, causing a soft, echoing whine, then frowned at the noise, as if unaware of what she'd been doing.

'Your trouble is you've seen too many movies,' he added.

'And you haven't seen enough,' she shot back.

William glanced at his watch. Seven o'clock. He winced. 'Listen, can't all this—'

She put up a hand to silence him. 'What would you say if I told you—' she paused dramatically; it struck him as a device for delaying his departure '— that the man who owns the car is a South African businessman. Someone with embassy connections.'

'I suppose I'd say, "Good heavens!" '

'Well, it's true. He lives in Kensington, and the woman who cleans his flat says he often gets visits from a man in a car with CD numberplates.'

In his solar plexus William registered a sharp twinge, similar to the one he'd felt that night in the basement of the hospital. It was like being in a car with someone driving too fast and not being able to reach the brakes. He made a lunge for the steering wheel. 'How do you know this?'

'I have a friend who knows a tame policeman who will track down car numbers for him. He got me the name and address and I did some snooping this morning.'

'So that was why you suddenly "remembered" the number. You wanted to check out the politics of its owner? And I thought it was because the security guard died last night.'

'It was, partly. I was going to call you this morning, but I thought you'd probably disapprove of private investigation. You see now what it can turn up.'

'Yes, but you're forgetting something. You heard what the police said. The car was stolen. Did you see the South African? Surely you aren't telling me it was the same man?'

'No, he wasn't in. But that stuff about it being stolen was nonsense. Or at the very least tacky. It was reported stolen at two a.m. We saw it before that.'

'Correction. You saw it. Anyway, he had an alibi. He was out to dinner with people.'

'It needn't have been him. He could have lent it to someone.'

'Josie, you're clutching at straws. This is fantastic. You tell me the car belongs to a South African businessman. So what? Would it be any less significant if it had been a Venezuelan ice cream vendor? Leave it to the police. They'll check it out.'

'Boy, your faith in them is touching.'

'Well, I happen to believe that they're as concerned with justice as you are.'

'It might be a different kind of justice.'

'What does that mean?'

'It means that they have their politics too. God, William, what were you doing during the last miners' strike?'

'Oh come on, Josie, what are you saying? That the police were lying when they said they'd checked out De Villiers?'

'No, they just didn't give me the impression they were that interested.'

'If you mean they gave you a hard time, then what did you expect? I wouldn't be surprised if they suspected you of making the whole thing up.' He put up his hands in mock defence to ward off the impending explosion. 'Don't rage at me. It was your own fault they went for you. Why should you expect them to believe that you just forgot the number and then remembered it again? I didn't believe you. And it wasn't true. I'll lay you odds on that your erratic memory has put you straight on their suspects list. That and your "previous connections".'

'And what the fuck does that mean?' Her face was screwed up with anger. 'That you don't believe me either?'

'No, that's not what I mean,' he retorted, disconcerted to note that he was losing his temper too. 'Really, for someone who thinks so much, you're sometimes very stupid. Don't jump so fast. If you say that was the number, then I believe you, although I think you were wrong not to say so on Saturday. But that doesn't mean the man who owns the car is the man who planted the bomb. He probably has nothing to do with it. We don't even know for sure that the man in the car was the same man we saw in the hospital.'

'I know for sure.'

'Well, I don't,' he said more quietly. 'And if it came to it, I would have to say that in court. And you'd be on your own.'

'But you would recognize the man in the basement again?'

'Yes. Yes, I would.'

'Then he's the one we should try and find. That way at least we'd be sure of our story.'

'What's all this "we should" business? I don't understand this obsession you have for running a private campaign of justice. The police have all these facts. Why don't we wait and let them do their job? I hate to suggest it, but they're probably better at it than you are.'

'And what happens if they do nothing? Meanwhile the press and the rest of the media and the government are making hay while the sun shines.'

'Josie, you are not responsible for the world's ills. It's got nothing to do with us. We've done what we could – and in your case probably more. It's not going to endear you to the police if you start doing a Harriet Vane on the job.'

'Who's Harriet Vane?'

'She's . . . oh, never mind, it's not important.'

'So you're telling me you're not willing to help, to go any further? Is that it?'

'Yes, that's what I'm saying.'

'Well then, I'm sorry I've wasted your time.' She got up angrily, causing beer to slop on the table. 'Thanks a lot.'

'Josie!' William's voice penetrated above the level of the bass note of the jukebox. A man at the bar glanced their way. It was a little early in the evening for a lovers' tiff. Josie stopped in her tracks and regarded William coldly. 'You make trouble for yourself, do you know that?' he said. 'I'm not ignoring what you said. I just think it would be utterly reckless to go poking our noses into something the police can handle better than we can. I know you want results *now*. But sometimes that isn't possible. Why not let it rest a few days? If nothing happens by then, we'll talk again.'

'If nothing's happened by then, I'm not going to bother with talking. I'll look for a journalist who's interested in a good story. That'll help break up the consensus of the press.'

He didn't protest. He knew it was useless. A few heads turned as she surged through the bar and out of the door. He sat for a few moments, pondering his unease. Then he remembered. He drove too fast across town in an effort to keep his appointment at the Institute. He was twenty minutes late.

Chapter Five

The meeting, a sub-committee on employment legislation, was some distraction, and afterwards in the pub, swopping anecdotes with his peers about recalcitrant shop stewards and unrealistic managing directors, he had the comfortable feeling of 'here, at least, I am understood'. He went home on a high, sufficient to still his anxiety and take him through to the next day at work.

He had set aside the morning for admin. It did nothing to distract him. He imagined Josie sleuthing round London, stationed outside some large white Kensington townhouse, taking down car numbers and clicking polaroid shots of drivers. But so what? She was an adult. It was her business. Let her go to hell her own way. The thought failed to reassure him. The idea of her sniffing around alone, almost certainly getting herself into more trouble, aroused strong emotion, although whether anger or concern it was difficult to tell. He felt a sense of responsibility towards her, if only to protect himself from being labelled an accomplice.

But what to do? Tell the police about her snooping? Out of the question. She would never speak to him again. Pick up the phone and call her, just to make contact? And say what? That he was sorry about their row? That was absurd. He wasn't sorry. He stood by every word. The very act of calling would be tantamount to an apology. He thought about speaking to someone else, getting some advice. But who? Penny. Of course. Always first choice. He even got as far as dialling her number when he realized it was impossible. He couldn't talk to her. There were too many other things they had to talk about first.

The afternoon brought a meeting with the shop stewards' committee. He found his manner becoming uncharacteristically abrasive. He even swore at one point. There was a silence in the room. Hackles rose. He apologized, kicking himself for the loss of concentration. It wasn't his style. There was a type of personnel manager who believed in the bludgeon, in going around calling spades spades, but they tended to remain personnel managers. William had his sights set on higher things. As they left the room his assistant Bob Spandar commented diplomatically, 'A little more like open warfare today. You've been practising.'

Practising. He certainly had. That took him back to thoughts of his sparring partner. In his outer office his secretary Karen seemed flustered. 'You've had a number of calls. From a woman. She said it was important, but she wouldn't leave a number. Or a name.'

Oh yes?

'She really was quite adamant that she talk to you.' Karen seldom repeated herself. She evidently needed confirmation she had done the right thing. 'She even told me to get you out of the meeting. But you had left word you weren't to be disturbed, and, well, quite frankly, she was really rather rude.'

He smiled. Karen had held her own with more than her fair share of difficult callers. Josie had clearly cracked the thermometer. Don't worry about it, he reassured her. If it was that urgent she would call again.

But she didn't. And neither did she answer his calls at home. He waited in the office till after seven, completing the letters he had set himself to do that morning, and trying Josie's number every twenty minutes or so. Then Laurence Crowther from sales knocked and asked if he fancied a quick drink. William had been planning a quiet evening at home, to get back a little of his own rhythm. But what if the message really had been urgent? He rang home to check his answering machine. No messages. He picked up his jacket and went out to the pub.

There were a couple of others there too, a chap from sales and a line manager from the Birmingham factory, talking shop. It was the kind of conversation he usually took note of. Office politics exerted a bizarre, soap opera-ish fascination over him – provided you didn't allow yourself to become one of the characters – and besides you never know when the gossip might come in handy. But tonight he couldn't keep his mind on the conversation. He went up to the bar to order another round. On a shelf high on the wall the television was on, but soundless, showing a talking head to camera. It was seven thirty. Channel 4 News. Then the screen flashed to a picture of the Royal Highgate Hospital. The barman came over to take his order. He asked for two scotches and a little more volume. The sound rose above the chatter at the bar. Over a shot of a parish church with a coffin being carried through the front doors there were crocodile tears in the reporter's voice:

> The funeral of Malcolm O'Grady, victim of last Friday's bomb attack on the Royal Highgate Hospital, took place today at his local parish church of St Mary's in north London. Outside the church a small group of demonstrators used the occasion to call for government action against the pressure group Health Not Wealth who they believe were implicated in the bombing. Health Not Wealth has denied this, but some of the people here are not satisfied with that.

The camera panned across a group of people bearing the odd placard. William noted 'Democracy before Health', and 'Let the Government Run the Country'. Then there was a cut to a head shot of a well-groomed, middle aged woman, captioned as Mrs Lucy Myers. She addressed the camera as if it were a public meeting:

> We're here today to show our great sympathy and support for Mrs O'Grady and her family. Those responsible for this atrocity must not be allowed to go free. The lesson to be learned from this terrible event is that protest can be allowed to go too far. Health Not Wealth are responsible because they have created a climate of agitation over the last year which has led to this disgraceful act of violence.

The barman brought back William's change, and he picked up his drinks. Josie had been right about one thing. Whoever was behind the bomb, HNW was going to get a rough ride. And with the public, or at least a section of it, baying for blood, the pressure on the police for a conviction must be considerable.

At the table he excused himself. The public phone next to the gents ate his ten pence piece and played her number endlessly. Three-quarters of an hour later he tried again. Still no response. William said goodbye to his colleagues and left.

Driving along Westway he changed his mind. Instead of turning off at Little Venice for the Edgware Road and home, he continued past Regents Park and through Camden towards Hornsey Rise. It took him a while to find her road again. When he finally tracked down the right pillarbox it was after nine o'clock. So much for his quiet evening. He parked up the road fifty yards from the house. As he walked towards it he saw a man coming out of what looked like her front gate. They passed on the pavement. William rang the middle bell and waited. There was no Josie. He hung around on the porch for a while feeling foolish, until a couple came out from the downstairs flat. They looked at him oddly, and he was forced to explain that he had made a date to meet Josie but she was late. He told his tale so well – or it may have been the cut of his suit – they let him in to wait in the hall.

It was a scruffy communal entrance with dust on the surrounds and a few envelopes tossed in a corner, the residue of long gone tenants. The slight smell of damp triggered off a sudden flash of déjà vu. Rooms of one's own. He had lived in houses like this when he had first come down to London. It had seemed such a cause for celebration then. Funny how quickly it became just a stepping stone to something else, with that abrupt transition into orderliness which comes with being an owner-occupier. Josie, no doubt, would label it selling out. It wasn't that simple. Money had made his life more comfortable, but had it changed him that much? Memory was a notoriously sentimentalizing process. Life hadn't been that wonderful, or that carefree, ten years ago. And a mortgage hadn't turned him overnight into a conservative. But of course she wouldn't see that. To her people were either right or wrong. It was a long time since he had felt that kind of passion. It occurred to him fleetingly that he might envy her a little, even if he did see it as naive. But it was hardly enough to give up his life style for. He would stick to his car, let her keep her bicycle. And sure enough there it was, under the stairs, tucked away with its new back wheel in odd contrast to the griminess of the rest of the machine. At first he thought its presence meant she couldn't be far away, but then he remembered the bruised wrist. Wherever she was, she was using public transport.

He climbed the stairs to her landing. As he reached the door the light, operating on a time switch, went off. He pressed it again. It flickered on, then, with an ominous pinging sound, off. He wondered what to do next. It was ridiculous really. For all he knew she might not be coming home tonight. The calls might not have been so urgent. She could be out somewhere with a guy, or at a movie, or anywhere. His concern was over-reaction. He certainly wasn't going to stand any longer in the pitch black. He was about to return downstairs when he heard a rattling of the front door lock. He felt a chill of apprehension, as if it might be someone other than Josie trying to get in. He took a step back into the shadows. The door opened and slammed shut. The steps on the stairs didn't sound like hers. They were slow and cautious. But of course there was no light, the person would have to grope their way up. It must be Josie. He opened his mouth to call her name, then stopped himself. What if it wasn't her? It was already too late. Whoever it was was going to get the fright of their lives. He stepped out of the shadow onto the landing. Their cries clashed in the darkness.

'Jesus Christ, William, you scared the living daylights out of me.'

It wasn't until that moment that he realized how worried he had been for her. There was no chance to tell her.

'How the hell did you get in here anyway?'

He explained.

'Oh great. So much for security around here. Did you show them your claw hammer, or did they let you in unarmed?'

She didn't wait for an answer, but slid the key into the lock and rattled it impatiently. The door fell open and she snapped on a light. It dazzled them both for an instant. He followed her into a rather basic living room. The cat looked up from the only easy chair and stretched out a lazy paw, before re-settling itself with an even greater sense of ownership. Everything normal. Of course. What had he expected? Dead bodies on the rug? He could have been home, reading a book. Stupid to have over-reacted.

'I've been calling you for hours and hours,' he muttered, taking out his annoyance on her. 'Your message said it was urgent. Why on earth didn't you get back to me? You might have realized I'd be worried about you.'

It was only then that he noticed the look in her eyes. A gleam of triumph. Oh my God, he thought. What next?

'Sit down,' she ordered. 'You're not going to believe what I have to tell you.'

That's just what I'm afraid of, he thought. He lowered himself into a sofa that looked dangerously lacking in springs. She perched on the arm of the chair and leaned forwards.

'I'll make it as short as I can, but there's a lot to tell. You ready? "My Day" by Josephine Ridley.'

Chapter Six

'I'll tell it to you exactly as it happened, right? That way you can do your own interpreting. It began this morning first thing, just before nine. I know it was that early because I was due at the hotel at ten, and I had the radio on listening for the weather forecast. I was in the middle of breakfast when the doorbell rang.

'The guy was weird-looking. Tall, a bit stooped, maybe late fifties. His skin was parchment-like, and he had these little lizard flaps stretching between his neck and his chin, the kind of thing people get when they're starting to look old. I remember because I didn't like the look of him. We get a lot of Jehovah's Witnesses around here, only they usually hunt in pairs. Then he introduced himself. He had a classy voice, he sounded much smarter than he looked.

' "Miss Ridley? My name is Detective Inspector Coulton. I wondered if I might have a word with you?"

'I didn't budge. "Do you have any ID?" They're supposed to show it, you know. So he smiled and apologized and flashed his bit of plastic saying he'd leave a card with me at the end of the interview and might we perhaps go inside? So I showed him up here. He sat where you're sitting. I stood by the table. I didn't want him to feel too comfortable.

'It all began very politely. "First of all, Miss Ridley, I would like to thank you for coming forward so swiftly after the incident at the Royal Highgate, and for making such a sustained effort to remember so many details." To which my immediate reaction was, sarcastic bastard - except that he didn't let it show at all in his voice. "Your name has been passed on to me by Highgate CID, but I think I should tell you straight away that I am from a different department - the anti-terrorist branch." Which didn't surprise me in the least, because I'd heard they were a lot of smoothies, and I knew it was only a matter of time till they got their noses into it.

' "We deal, as you probably know, with bombings and crimes of that order, incidents like the Royal Highgate. And I would very much appreciate it if I could check over some details of your statement. In fact, perhaps the simplest thing would be if you could go over the events of Friday night once more in your own words."

'All of which was very nicely put, but since it was well after nine, and I had to be at work within the hour, it wasn't on. So I told him, in the nicest possible way, to stuff it. That they already had two statements from me, and if they needed another then they'd have to make another appointment, because I had a living to make. To which he replied that he quite understood, but as this really was urgent, perhaps I wouldn't mind just answering a few questions, if it didn't take too much time.

'Anyway, to cut a long story short, I might as well have repeated the statement, because we ended up going through the whole thing again. Was I sure I could recognize the man in the corridor? Could I describe him? Was he definitely the same man as I then saw in the car? What was the car number? How much of all this had you seen? blah, blah, blah – the whole lot. Then he said: "Well, I must congratulate you on your first-class powers of observation, Miss Ridley. Maybe I should try and persuade you to join the police force. I could only wish that all witnesses were so meticulous."

'You can imagine my reaction to that! I was standing there thinking, what's all this sweetness and light? What does the guy want from me? So I called his bluff. "This is all very flattering, but what's caused the change in attitude?"

' "I'm sorry?"

' "It's just that the last time I spoke to a policeman he was distinctly more critical of my 'sudden memory recall'."

'Then he made this little placatory gesture. You know, the kind of ambiguous wave of the hand that suggests there might be more to tell, but it's not really his place to tell it. And he says, "Well, I expect they were just doing their job. Perhaps they did over-react a little to what I might imagine was a certain defensiveness on your part?"

'Fucking cheek. So I ignored that one, and asked him if he had any other questions. Which of course he had. He was most concerned to know if I had discussed this business with anyone other than you. I said no. Then he wanted to know if you'd told anyone. I said I couldn't be sure, but you seemed like the sort of person who respected the law and didn't speak unless spoken to – O.K., O.K., only kidding.

'Anyway, we establish all this, and then he started to act really oddly. First he gives this little clearing of the throat, then he spends a lot of time picking cat fluff off his sleeve, while I stand there waiting. Finally he looks me straight in the eye and says: "The reason I hesitate, Miss Ridley, is because what I am about to say is rather delicate. It is not something I would even consider saying to most witnesses, but I am going to take you into my confidence because, quite frankly, this case is too important, and you are too intelligent not to be told the truth."

'Then he leaves this little pause – he was very good at little pauses – and flashes me this Mona Lisa smile. And all I can think of is, I wonder if he can hear my heart beating. For some reason I was really nervous as to what he was going to say.

' "You see, Miss Ridley, what with all the news and media hoo-haa going on around the story, it can sometimes be hard to separate the wood from the trees. We aren't interested in speculation. We aren't interested in theory. First and foremost we are interested in hard facts. And according to your first-hand testimony certain hard facts lead us to certain possible conclusions, and in turn to certain people. The man seen in the hospital corridor, for example. Seen first by both of you, then by you alone outside the building in a car. Obviously both man and car are of great interest to us. Except, as you know, further investigation tells us that the car has in fact been stolen. Which takes us back to square one – a common occurrence, I might add."

' "Except," I pointed out, "that it wasn't reported stolen until *after* the bombing."

' "Of course you're absolutely right!" Another Mona Lisa smile. "But there's something else you might like to know, and that is when we talked to Mr De Villiers – whose alibi was substantiated, by the way – yesterday afternoon he was at pains to point out that we weren't the only people who seemed to be interested in him. Apparently, only a few hours before, a young woman had been at his apartment, asking questions of his cleaner. Interesting, don't you think?"

'This time he makes it a big pause. Presumably it was meant to be the pause that I confess in. We both waited while the silence got longer. Eventually he got tired of waiting and went into the old "just suppose" routine.

' "Now, let's just suppose, for reasons of convenience, that this young woman was in fact you. If that were so, then I could only assume that you had determined for some reason to take a personal interest in the case. Personal enough to have gone to the trouble to find out the name and address of the car owner – how did you do that, by the way? Very clever. Now, if this is indeed the case, then it makes our job considerably more difficult. You see, on paper the issue is clear. The car was stolen. There is no reason for us to pursue that line of questioning any further. But just suppose, once again, that there was more to it than that. Suppose that there were some 'stones' to be turned over. Certainly, I'm sure you'd agree the best people to do the turning would be the police. They would know when, and they would also know how. The worst thing that could happen is that someone else, who understands less about these things, might try to do their job for them. That could be a disaster."

'You see, William, what he was really saying was that we were right. He was more or less admitting that there was something in this car business. There *is* a South African connection! Anyway, he delivers this little speech, and waits for my comment. When I don't say anything he gives it another shot.

' "Maybe I should be more blunt. We both know, Miss Ridley, that you've been what can only be described as 'politically active' in your time, although somewhat less so in recent years. Now I'm sure that you are as eager as we are to find those responsible for this outrage. And you're obviously very concerned lest the blame falls on the wrong shoulders. But I must warn you that it would be extremely counter-productive, not to say dangerous, for you to interfere with the process of justice in any way whatsoever. For instance, it is vitally important to our investigations that certain people do not realize that we are interested in them. It would therefore be disastrous if anything you had seen or heard found its way into the press. I'm sure you understand that."

' "Are you accusing me of something?" I asked.

' "On the contrary, I'm appealing to you. The most important thing for all of us is that these terrorists be apprehended and charged. To achieve that we need your co-operation. That is why I am here to ask you to put aside any traditional – what word may I use? – mistrust, yes mistrust that you might feel towards the police, and to give us your help. And when I say 'us' I might add that not even everyone taking part in the investigation knows precisely what is going on. Which is why I have another request."

' "Which is?"

'That should you by any chance remember or notice anything that you think might help us, however small or insignificant, that you get in touch with me, personally and directly, and with no one else. The fewer people who know, the more likely it is to remain that way."

'William, imagine my glee at that one! A Detective Inspector admitting that some of his own men were less than trustworthy. "You mean even among your own officers?" I asked naively.

' "Put it this way. Some clichés are more useful than others, and we still find it better to be safe than sorry. So . . . I've told you all this because I thought you'd be satisfied with nothing less. And now I must ask you, having heard all that I've come here to say, can I rely on your assistance and, perhaps more important, your silence?" '

Back in the present of the darkened sitting room Josie paused for dramatic effect. 'So,' William chivvied. 'What did you say?'

She shrugged. 'I said the only thing I could say. Fuck it, I didn't want to co-operate with the anti-terrorist squad. But what else could I do? I can recognize a corner when I've been painted into one. I said yes.'

William let out a low whistle. 'My my. Josie Ridley turned police agent. Well done.'

'Well done, my ass. All I can say is it had better not get onto my CV. It'd ruin my political credibility.'

'I doubt it will. What did he say? Was he pleased?'

'I suppose so. He didn't exactly wear his heart on his sleeve. But he did ask for a drink of water. I got the impression he was sort of relieved. Then he thanked me and left, making some crack about how if I ever wanted a job . . . God, you can always tell the fuzz from their lousy sense of humour. Anyway, I was about to call you to tell you what had happened when I caught sight of the clock – by the way, what time is it now?'

'Half past ten. Why?'

'Because we're going to have a visitor before too long, that's why. And you need to hear the whole story before they get here.'

'You mean there's more?'

'Yeah, hold on. O.K. – I caught sight of the clock. I had to move like a bat out of hell, and even then I was forty minutes late. The coach driver was furious. And I couldn't contact you after that. I was stuck on the river with a boatload of Mid-westerners.'

'A boatload of what?' It suddenly occurred to William that in all their conversations he had never actually found out what she did for a living.

'Mid-westerners. The Anglo-American Cultural Appreciation Society of Ohio. Doing the Westminster to Greenwich run. Don't look so astonished. That's how I earn my daily bread. I'm a tour guide.'

It wasn't so astonishing. In fact it fitted. He could imagine her standing at the front of the bus, microphone in hand, haranguing coach loads of unsuspecting tourists with her particular reading of history. If she talked for her living, no wonder conversations with her were like trying to interrupt a lecturer.

'I'm very good at it, I'll have you know. I have a history degree and the London Tourist Board diploma. Americans make interested audiences. They're very keen on history. It comes from not having enough of it themselves. You should come along with me sometimes. I know stuff about London that you've never dreamed of.'

That he could believe. 'How long have you been doing it?'

''Bout eighteen months. I used to do it years ago, before university. Now it's just a convenient way of earning a living for a while. All right, can I get on with the story now?'

'I'm listening.'

'So the river trip finishes and we have lunch in Greenwich. That's when I first tried to call you and got your bloody secretary instead. Then straight after lunch it's the observatory and the museum, which means it's not easy to get to a phone, and even less easy to be polite to little miss noli-me-tangere when I finally do get through. We returned to the hotel just after five, and I set off home. Now, I want you to take a deep breath, William, because the next bit is going to piss you off, but I need to tell it without interruption, O.K.?

'The first fact is pure coincidence. It just so happens that the route to Knightsbridge tube goes right through the back of Kensington, and one of the streets I had to go through was Canning Square. Now, you've probably never heard of Canning Square, neither had I until yesterday morning, but it is in fact the residence of one Mr De Villiers and his shiny blue Audi saloon. So, I'm walking through the square, on the other side from the house, and I'm curious. But the door is closed and there's no sign of the car. The square is fabulous. A big garden in the middle, flowerbeds, sunshine through the trees, the lot. A perfect place to sit and read a newspaper for half an hour on a summer's afternoon. After all, it's slap bang in the middle of rush hour. Why risk suffocation just to get home half an hour early?

'I'm halfway through the Londoner's Diary when a car turns into the square, an Audi saloon no less, and draws up outside the house opposite me. I've got my head behind the newspaper, but I can still manage to get a look at the driver. I've never seen him before. He's a great broomhandle of a man, he has to almost unfold himself out of the driver's seat. Then he takes out a briefcase from the back, locks the car and disappears into the house. Just like that. He doesn't look round, doesn't see anything. Leaving me sitting there. Christ, William, I felt like a real fool. I mean Coulton had told me it wasn't the same man. You knew it, I knew it, I suppose I'd just been hoping there'd be something familiar about him, some clue, some discrepancy, anything. But there wasn't.

'I was feeling pretty pissed off with myself for being so stupid, so I sat there for a while giving myself a hard time, then decided to go home. I was bending down to stuff my newspaper in my bag when – hey presto – out of the corner of my eye I saw the door opening and broomhandle comes out. But now in different clothes, much more casual – only this time he doesn't go to the car, but instead starts walking off towards the end of the square and turns left.

'Well, since that's the direction I have to go anyway, I get up and walk after him. You have to believe me, William, I swear to God at this stage I had no intention of following him. I was just going home. Me and two million other people. Just some of us happened to be going the same way. It's easy enough as far as the tube. The streets are crowded, he's a long way ahead of me, but he's so tall you can spot him in a crowd. Hell, for all I know, if Coulton's that interested, he's probably got a couple of plainclothes men tailing him anyway. At the station I spot him again on the escalator. He turns left at the bottom. That means it's the Piccadilly Line going east. Same as me. When I get to the platform he's nowhere to be seen. The place is chocka with people, he could be anywhere. I stand with my back to the wall. When the train comes it's already full. A few people crush themselves on. The rest of us stay. That's when I spot him, near the edge of the platform. If he'd got on then I'd have lost him for sure. But he waits. The next train isn't much better, but everyone's impatient now and there's a great surge forward when the doors open. I see him move inside as part of the wave, and I smash my way through to the doors. I only just make it, jammed right up against the side.

'For the first six or seven stations I don't get to breathe properly. Then as we get out of central London the spaces between the bodies begin to expand. He's still there, strap-hanging, dead easy to spot because he's so tall. But he can't possibly see me, because I'm such a midget. It's about now that I decided I was going to miss my stop. I mean, it was such a twist of fate, him on my train going my way. There had to be some meaning in it. I don't care what you say, William, if it had been you in that compartment I bet you wouldn't have got off either. Mind you, a lot of people did, because Finsbury Park is the last connecting station with the Victoria Line. By the time the exodus has passed there are spare seats. He takes one of them.

'I keep standing by the door, but I can see his reflection in the glass partition opposite. He sits with his eyes down, only looking up to check stations. Just another tired commuter heading for home. Then just before Arnos Grove – Jesus Christ, I've never been so far north in my life – he gets up and moves to the door at the end of the carriage. The train stops and he gets out. I leave it as long as I dare, then just as the doors are closing I dart out onto the platform. He's already by the Way Out sign and walking fast. I wait till he's out of sight then follow. I get to the bottom of the escalator when he's at the top. I figure I'll catch him up on the street. Except of course I don't have the right ticket. The woman at the booth is so slow, it takes her half an hour to find the change. By the time I get out of the station he's nowhere to be seen.

'I stand there like a dummy. There's no sign, no clue. So in the end I just make an arbitrary decision and start walking to the left. Then I see him, across the road coming out of a florist's shop clutching a large bunch of yellow chrysanthemums. He turns right. So much for casting one's fate to the winds. I cross at the zebra and start following, leaving a big gap between us. It isn't exactly rush hour in Arnos Grove.

'We carry on for a while, maybe half a mile or so, over a major roundabout – or rather under it. I have to wait until I see which exit he's taking, then hurtle through the tunnel to keep up with him. Now we're heading up a hill, and getting into real suburbia. On the right there's a long brick wall, on the left a parade of semis with bay windows and tidy little glass porches. And it's now that I really begin to wonder. My instinct is telling me to carry on, but my brain is getting a little obstreperous. I mean, what the hell is he doing this far into the back of nowhere with a bloody great bunch of flowers in his hand? What if it's some absurd false alarm? For all I know maybe he's off visiting some select suburban brothel – I mean we're in the original sex-and-luncheon-voucher belt. In which case I'm going to look a right idiot standing on a street corner while he slips in through some lace-curtained frontage, only to re-emerge three hours later minus the flowers and a handful of £20 notes. Maybe the chrysanthemums are part of some Genet-type fantasy. But if all this is leading up to a bit on the side, why not find a lady of the night nearer home? Knightsbridge must be crawling with them. No, common sense tells me there has to be an uncommon reason for his being here.

'Then suddenly he disappears. Just like that. I sprint the fifty yards or so between us, and cross the road. And do you know what I find? A damn great set of iron gates with this huge sign reading North London Cemetery.

'All this just to lay a wreath! And that's only the half of it. The place is gigantic. I'm faced with this circular flowerbed with paths leading off in all directions. And broomhandle has vanished. So, it appears, has everyone else. The cemetery is deserted. I feel completely exposed. He's bound to spot me now. What can I do?

'So I'm standing there, paralysed with indecision, when – and I swear this one is really God-given – suddenly there's this bloody great crack of thunder followed by a couple of fat drops of rain. A thunderstorm. Of course. I'd seen the clouds blowing over when I came out of the station, real pot-bellied black ones, but I hadn't given them any thought. Now they really started to dump. It was perfect. Because, like every good tour guide, Josie Ridley always comes prepared, she always travels with a large plastic mac at the bottom of her bag. Don't look so dumb, William. Don't you see? A green, transparent plastic mac? Camouflage. It's big, and it's got a hood, and with it I don't look anything like the girl he might just have seen walking up the hill behind him. I'm a stranger, a common-or-garden necrophile out visiting a few favourite graves. Harold and Maude. Perfect. So I put it on, put my head down and started walking.

'Not that I knew where I was going. I picked the outside path because it gave me a good view, and followed it round for a while. God, it was weird. The whole place was so still, so quiet. And at first it was all really well-groomed and tidy, neat borders and trimmed grass, but as I got further from the entrance it started to get more scrubby and wild, long grass and weeds on old graves.

'Then there's the tombstones. This place has been swallowing corpses for centuries. Some of the stones are so old and blackened that you can't read the inscriptions, but there are others, more elaborate – life-sized virgins with faces half-eroded by the weather, archangels in white-streaked stone. It's funny, when I was a kid I used to really get off on cemeteries, I thought they had a kind of faded romanticism about them, raw history. But not this one. This one just enveloped you. It was all so lost and cold. And the rain was pissing down and my skin was all clammy from the plastic. I could feel myself starting to get freaked.

'There was a clump of trees off to the right, and I stood under them to get some shelter. Then I spotted him. I saw the chrysanthemums first. A great splash of yellow on a bench about forty yards away through the trees, with him sitting next to them, getting wet. He had his back to me, but even so it wasn't easy to get any closer. There was just open ground between us, a long stretch of bodies. But there was a new grave just off to the left, piled high with flowers, and from there I could get quite a good view of the bench. I kept my head well down and made for it. I crouched behind the flowers and waited for a bit. Then I looked up. And ducked immediately.

'He had a visitor. Another figure was approaching, dressed for summer with a newspaper held over his head as a rain shield. I couldn't see him properly – all I could tell was he was average height, and average build, everything else was rain-soaked. Just as he was nearing the bench the rain slackened. He removed the newspaper and shook it carefully. I had my head down on my chest. Most of my body was obscured by the flowers. I doubt he was aware I was there at all. If he was, it didn't seem to worry him. He was by the bench now. Through the edge of my hood I saw him pick up the flowers and sit down. Then he looked up.

'I can still see him on the back of my eyelids. The great moon face, the wedge of forehead. The man with the white coat and the blue car. It was him, William, no question about it. The bomber.'

Chapter Seven

William had neither moved nor spoken for three-quarters of an hour. His left leg was numb and the loose spring in the chair seemed intent on coiling into his right thigh. But he knew better than to interrupt a storyteller, particularly one who relished it as much as Josie evidently did. Her eyes were shining with pleasure, her face slightly flushed. The silence grew longer. He dared to interpret it: it was time to ask a question.

'What did he do?' he prompted.

'Not a lot. They sat together for about five minutes, talking, animated but voices low. I could hear nothing but the slight buzz of the words. Then eventually they both got up and left.' She paused. 'But not before I had taken some pictures of them.'

'You what?'

'I took some pictures. I had the Rollei in my bag. I often take it when I'm guiding. You sometimes get some great photos. It's small, automatic, and it takes classy shots. It was perfect. I didn't have to do anything. The rain had almost stopped, the sky was getting lighter, they were deep in conversation, in three-quarter profile to me. All I had to do was scoop it out of my bag, hold it between my hands so no one could see it, bring it eye to eye, and just click away.'

'You just happened to have it with you, did you?'

'Sure.'

'Weren't you scared?'

She smiled weakly. 'Are you kidding? I was fucking terrified. I was shaking so much I could hardly point the camera. By the time I got back it in the bag I couldn't move. I just stayed doubled up in prayer, counting up to three hundred before I dared risk a look. The bench was empty. They had both gone. The clouds had blown over, the sun was shining on the raindrops. The miracle was complete. I stood up, brushed the earth from my knees and headed for the exit.'

It was her adventure. He was just a passenger. She was bubbling over with the thrill of it. The way she told it made it exotic, almost baroque. Had it really been like that, or had she spiced it up, elaborating the dialogue, inventing details? She had given her all in the performance, and even though he couldn't fully share that pleasure, he hadn't the heart to take it away from her.

'My God, Josie, you must have more lives than a cat. Didn't it occur to you how dangerous it was? No wonder Coulton was so determined to keep you out of it. He'll be furious when he hears this.'

'He already has. I rang him from the pub over the road from the cemetery as soon as I got in. I had to talk to someone. You'd already left work, and I wasn't going to tell your bloody answering machine.'

'What was his reaction?'

'I think he was pretty impressed.'

'Was he angry?'

'I'm not sure. He certainly put the fear of God into me though. He was super cool and super efficient. Asked a lot of questions as to where exactly I was, and told me I had to stay there. That I mustn't leave the pub, that I should make sure there were always people around me, I shouldn't even go to the loo, and I should speak to no one. Not even you. And that he would come and get me. It might take a couple of hours, but whatever I did I wasn't to budge. So I sat and I sat and I sat, and after about an hour and a half the barman came out and asked if there was a Josie Ridley in the house. He said he'd had a guy on the phone, name of Coulton, saying there'd been a change of plan and he wouldn't be able to meet me there after all. I was to order a taxi from the pub, go straight home and wait for him there, and he'd join me at midnight. The barman was pretty miffed. He wanted to know how come this guy had been able to find his ex-directory personal number just to leave a message for his girlfriend. Christ, I walked away from the bar feeling like Coulton's bloody mistress. There was only one snag to this great scheme of things. I didn't have enough money for a cab. I only had four pounds cash, it wouldn't have got me to Golders Green. So I had to take the tube after all. I spent the whole time looking over my shoulder. Now you know why I jumped so high when you stepped out of the shadows on the landing.' She rubbed her hand over her face. 'And that, as they say, is that. Finito. The whole story.'

William stared at her for a moment, then down at the carpet. What did he feel? It wasn't that he didn't believe her. It was incredible, but there were no warning bells in his gut telling him it wasn't true. It all fitted in with the atmosphere of the day, the sense of unease in his head. No, it wasn't that he didn't believe her. It was just that he wasn't ready. It was like day-dreaming in the covers when suddenly there's eighty miles an hour of cricket ball hurtling towards you. It had occurred to him while she was talking that everything in this crazy saga, from the moment she had smashed into the side of his car four nights ago, had been moving at her pace. He wanted to grab hold of it with both hands and force it to slow down so that he could look at it and think about it without that sense of being rushed.

'Well?' she said.

He was being asked for his opinion. He had no opinion. He struggled to concentrate. 'I wonder why he didn't send a car for you. If he seemed so concerned about your safety.'

It was the first thought that came into his head. She dismissed it with an impatient shrug of the hand. He tried again. 'Are you absolutely sure it was the man in the hospital?'

'Of course. The photo will show it.'

'You were some distance away. And it was raining.'

'William!' It was loud enough to warrant the word shout. 'Don't be so fucking obstinate.'

He didn't react.

She shook her head, more in sorrow than anger. 'I'm sorry . . . but you're so frustrating. You know what I'm saying is true, it's just that you can't let yourself believe it because it messes up your sense of order, it means that you have to get involved.' She sighed. 'But you are involved, like it or not, and all the wishing in the world isn't going to make it go away.' She leaned over and touched his hand. The gesture was so unexpected it unnerved him.

'All right,' he said quietly. 'I believe you.'

'Thank God for that.' She let her head drop, rubbing the back of her neck, as if the effort of talking had exhausted her. She shivered.

'What's wrong?'

'Nothing.' Her eyes were closed. 'I'm just tired. Or maybe I've caught a chill from the rain.'

Yes, she did look drawn, and less invincible than his picture of her. What a strange woman. He tried to imagine what the day must have been like for her. He couldn't. He stood up. 'Which way is the kitchen? I'll make some coffee.'

'I think I'd prefer scotch.'

'Have both.'

'O.K.'

She wandered into the kitchen, leaning against the door frame as William picked up the electric kettle. The cat followed, interested to see if he was to be included in the refreshments. 'Coulton stood here this morning. Just like this,' she said, fingering the lintel. 'You know, I'm still surprised he didn't get in touch with you. After all, you're a witness too.'

Having filled the kettle under the tap, William put it down on the stainless steel draining board. Josie idly watched the domestic procedure, her mind half elsewhere. The cat leaped up on the worktop and rubbed against William's hip. He stroked its head, running his fingers down till they reached the fleabite scars at the back of its neck. Selfconscious of its blemishes, the cat pulled away, flicking its tail in annoyance. William flipped on the wall socket switch and folded his arms, waiting for the kettle to boil.

'My God,' she snorted. 'Can you imagine how the shit's going to hit the fan when this gets out – "South African Connection in Hospital Bomb Attack"? The closer it gets, the more rotten it smells.'

It was difficult to work out the exact sequence of what happened next. There was a hiss from the kettle, a huge squawk from the cat. Hair standing on end, he arched his back for an instant, then charged, terrified, out of the open window. He clattered rapidly over the roof tiles of the rear extension before disappearing into the garden. All that was left was the acrid odour of burnt tail.

'What the fuck . .?'

Josie rushed to the window and peered into the darkness. William unfolded his arms, moved a step away, and stared down at the kettle. She came and joined him.

'He's all right,' he said. 'He wouldn't have been able to run away if he wasn't.'

'What happened?'

'Your kettle,' he said, 'seems to be live.'

'What?'

William had spoken calmly, but his next action was rather less confident. With a swift flick he turned off the wall socket switch and snatched out the plug, dropping it instantly. Then he returned to the crossed-arms position, as if only there would he be safe from electrical assault.

Josie still hadn't quite grasped it. 'You mean . . .'

'I mean if one of us had touched the kettle, we would have had a nasty shock.'

'It would have killed us?' Her voice rose, incredulous.

'No, I don't think so. We'd have let go, like the cat did. Painful but not fatal.'

He bent down and looked at the kettle. She noticed that even though it was now unplugged, he avoided touching it. He moved round, examining it from all angles. 'Aaah,' he muttered.

'What do you mean, aaah?'

'Look.' he pointed at the underside of the black bakelite handle.

'Look at what?'

He brought his finger to half an inch from the handle and traced a line. 'There. See that?' A thin piece of bare wire ran from the metal shell of the kettle up underneath the handle. 'If someone got hold of the handle –' He demonstrated with a bent hand '– with the power on, then you'd get a shock from this wire.' He made his hand quiver. Josie winced. 'Your hand automatically contracts, you wouldn't be able to let go, the current would keep going through you—'

'Till you're dead?'

'Yes, I suppose so. Specially if you're alone, no one else to switch off. You're in the act of filling it, the other hand on the tap, on the steel drainer, water all round, the perfect conductor, the current passes through your heart—'

'Shut up!' she cried. 'I don't want to hear about it.'

She started pacing the kitchen, every so often going to the window and calling without avail for the cat. Having transferred his panic to Josie, William was filled with the spirit of inquiry. He wanted to know how it had been done. Using a potato peeler from the drawer he unscrewed the socket into the kettle and checked the wiring. Nothing unusual. Then the plug. Ditto. Finally he turned his attention to the wall socket.

'For Christ's sake, William. What are you doing?'

'It's O.K. I'll take care. I won't touch anything metal.'

He removed the white front of the socket and peered within. 'I think I've got it,' he said. 'See those wires? That one should be the earth. And that one should be the live. But they're not in the right place. Have you had the back off this?'

'Are you kidding? Of course not.'

He nodded slowly. 'That means someone has been here and switched them round.'

It was difficult for the imagination to penetrate the calm explanation. They stood staring at each other, in a look that changed from incomprehension to suppressed terror. Freeze frame. It was William who broke the spell, who finally said, 'Josie, it looks like someone was trying to kill you.'

She stayed still for a few seconds more, frowning as if trying to solve a puzzle, then flung herself out of the kitchen with a kind of long howl. It echoed through the flat. He rushed after her into the bedroom, where she threw open a cupboard, pulled down a canvas bag, and started stuffing bits of clothing into it.

'Hey, what are you doing? Slow down.'

'What do you think I'm doing?' She didn't look up. The voice spat out between clenched teeth. 'I'm getting out of here.'

He took a step towards her. 'I think you should sit down. Have a drink. You've had a shock.'

'Too right I've had a shock.' She glared up at him. 'Don't patronize me.'

'I'm not patronizing you. I'm trying to communicate with you. Hold on . . . just for a moment so we can think this out.'

'Whatever thinking we have to do, we can do it somewhere else. I have to get out of here.'

'But what about Coulton? He'll be here any minute.'

The question brought her frenzied activity to a halt. 'For what? To issue the death certificate?'

'What do you mean?'

'Oh, come on. Who else could it be? Who else knows what I saw today? Who else made sure I didn't come home immediately? That I sat in some pub in the sticks for two hours so my flat was empty for someone to get in here and set up the fireworks. Everything was normal in there this morning. I made tea. I was still alive afterwards. Christ, he even asked me for a glass of water and came and stood in the kitchen while I poured it. All so he could check out my kitchen. It has to be him.'

'But why should a police officer try to murder his chief witness?'

She was pulling a T-shirt out of a drawer, but the sleeve got caught up with some other garments. She stopped and stared at the tangle of clothes. Then she smiled, but with her mouth not her eyes. 'Jesus, I'm so stupid,' she said, almost under her breath. Then to William, 'He wasn't a policeman. I didn't meet him at any police station.'

'But he had ID?'

'False.'

'He left you his card.'

'So what? It was just a card. It was nothing official.'

'But he knew all about us. That's what you said.'

She was thinking fast now, re-running tapes in her head. 'Yeah, he knew a lot of it, maybe all, I don't know. But he did ask me to check details, and sometimes he asked questions rather than getting me to confirm statements - as if he genuinely didn't know the answers. I thought that was interview technique. Maybe I did tell him more. Or maybe he just wanted to find out how much I knew, how dangerous I was. And I played right into his hands. Christ!'

William made a decision. He moved towards the door. 'Well, there's one way of finding out.'

'What are you going to do? She flew after him and stood in the doorway to block his path.

'I'm going to call Highgate police.'

'Why?'

'To report an attempted murder.'

'No.' The word spat in his face. 'Don't be crazy. It was talking to the police that got us into this mess in the first place. If we tell the police now, it'll go straight back to Coulton.'

'The fact that there's a leak doesn't mean the whole police force is out to kill us. Be reasonable, Josie. They'll give us protection. That's their job.'

She didn't answer, but resumed her packing, taking out her anger and panic on a snagging zip.

'All right. Not the police then. So what are we going to do?'

'I don't know yet. But whatever it is, we're not going to do it here. They'll probably send someone along in a while to check that the rewiring lit up the right torso. I don't intend to be around for that.'

'We'll go to my house,' he said. 'We can spend the night there and decide what to do in the morning.'

She regarded him with a scorn that bordered on disbelief. 'And how do you know your bedside light hasn't been reconnected to Battersea power station too?'

'Why should anyone go for me? It was you that recognized the guy at the cemetery.'

She smiled grimly. 'Yes, and it was me that told Coulton you were the only person I'd been in contact with.'

He swallowed, but his throat seemed to have temporarily closed up. 'Oh great,' was all he said.

There was a moment's silence. Then the doorbell rang. Josie jumped like a startled rabbit. William went rigid, his stomach executing a messy backflip. Her last remark had taken its toll. He had no reassurance left to give.

'What shall we do?' His voice encountered some resistance getting out of his mouth.

She put down her bag and put a finger across her lips. She hurried into the sitting room, crushed herself against the wall by the window and peeped out. Nothing unusual. The doorbell rang again. She returned to the bedroom and picked up her bag.

'Come on,' she said. 'Let's get out of here.'

'How?'

'Through the back door and over the gardens. Where's your car?'

'About fifty yards down the road.'

'O.K. We'll work that out when we get to it.'

She closed the flat door silently behind them. At the bottom of the stairs through the frosted panel they could see the silhouette of two figures. All that was lacking was the homburgs, William thought, as they crept around the banister and out through the back passage to the garden door. She slid the bolt silently and turned the key in the lock. Outside she locked it behind them. The garden was a wilderness of willow herb and nettles, the end of it obscured by trees. An abandoned fridge glowed ghostly white, half covered by ivy. The neglect extended to the back wall, which was crumbling and breached in a couple of places. He followed her, canvas bag bouncing on her back as she pulled herself over lumps of masonry and jumped down the other side. Incongruously he remembered an old newspaper story about Koo Stark, having to pick her way through neighbours' gardens in high heels and evening dress to avoid hungry photographers outside her front door. Every picture tells a story, he thought, as he scuffed his new shoes on a concealed brick. From somewhere outside his body he was observing the scene – figures scuttling through the garden twilight, crouching and panting. He was feeling a little crazy. They ran across a small communal square of garden, over two more walls, and finally out through a narrow passage that brought them back into the real world of orange street lamps and men walking their dogs.

Under the lamppost her face looked jaundiced too. 'You double back and see if it's safe to pick up the car. I'll meet you at the station.'

'Wait a minute.' He grabbed her arm. 'Which station?'

'Finsbury Park.'

'Will you be O.K., at this hour?'

She smiled bleakly. 'I'd say the dangers are relative, wouldn't you? See you in ten minutes.'

There was no one on Josie's street. They could be sitting in parked cars. He didn't wait to make sure. He jumped into his car and drove off.

It took him five minutes to work out Finsbury Park's one way system. When he drew up outside the station he spotted her immediately. She was sheltering in the shadows of the entrance hall, looking for all the world like the kind of girl TV producers make award-winning documentaries about. He leaned over and opened the passenger door.

It was gone midnight when they reached West Hampstead. Most of Gardenia Road was settled behind closed curtains. As they approached it Josie said, 'Don't stop. Drive past as slowly as you dare without being conspicuous. You check to the right and I'll check to the left.'

They passed a Volkswagen camper, his neighbour John's Toyota, and across the street from his house a Renault 4 van. It was unfamiliar to him. Its lights were off, but he could clearly make out the shape of a man in the driving seat. William craned his neck to take a look at his flat. From the darkness of his living room there was a brief flash - a torchlight?

She saw it too. 'There's someone up there,' she hissed. 'Get the fuck out of here.'

In his mirror William thought he saw the Renault switch on its headlights. Somewhere inside his head a small voice said, 'This is it, William. This is really it.' He put his foot down on the accelerator and left home behind him.

Chapter Eight

Revving up in second gear, William careered through the familiar maze of West Hampstead. A smart right turn into West End Lane elicited a horn blast from an outraged truckdriver. Josie was turned in her seat, looking out the rear window. 'I think we're O.K. now,' she said. 'I can't see anyone following.'

'Maybe.'

He dared not take his eyes off the road. The steering wheel was like rubber in his hands, and he didn't trust his sense of perspective. Cars loomed towards him, then passed. To his surprise he managed to miss them. I'm in shock, he thought. I shouldn't be driving this car. I'm going to hit something.

'Look out!' Josie shouted.

A red traffic light was staring at him accusingly. He regarded it in shocked indecision, noting the moderation of colour from dark red in the centre to near orange on the outside. Then his body took over. He jabbed at the foot brake and the car abruptly halted, tyres whingeing, its nose tipping forward. It was lurched to the left and pointed slightly towards the kerb.

The brakes are out of balance, William noted. Must get them seen to.

He glanced across at Josie. She had been thrown half out of her seat. 'Sorry,' he said. Then, 'Put your seat belt on.' She didn't move. 'We don't want to draw attention to ourselves.'

'Well, for a start you could try driving more carefully.' She pulled the belt across her.

They continued in silence for a few minutes. 'Where are we going?' she asked.

William didn't answer. He was peering into the mirror. 'What about that hatchback?'

'What is a hatchback?'

'The BMW,' he snapped. 'He's been with us for some time.'

'William, I wouldn't know a BMW from a doubledecker bus.'

'Two cars behind.'

They had turned off Finchley Road up the three lane highway leading to the M1, and the car in question now took the opportunity of overtaking them. Inside it a man and a woman were engaged in what might have been a row. Watching the car speed into the distance, Josie said, 'I think we're all right now. Seems to me you're over-reacting a little.'

'Oh, that's a good one, coming from you.'

She tried again. 'Why don't we pull over? Then we can check if anyone is following. If not, we can decide what to do. We can't go on driving all night.'

He stopped the car in a lay-by. For a while they just sat there watching the cars go by. With each passing vehicle they felt a buffet of air vibrate the car. Neither spoke. Then, without looking directly at him she leaned over and put a hand on his arm, squeezing it slightly. He looked at the hand, small and rather grubby with dirt underneath the nails. If it was meant as a gesture of reassurance she gave herself away – the fingers were trembling. He put his own hand on top of hers and returned the pressure. He felt her give a little and was afraid to speak for fear of breaking the silent communication.

'We're all right,' he said at last.

She nodded. 'I know.'

Only then did he look across at her. 'What now? Any ideas?'

She shrugged.

'Friends?' he suggested.

'Do you have any friends you could tell this to?'

'O.K. A hotel then, just for tonight?'

'I think that's the safest.'

'Do you know any?'

At any other time it would have been a funny question. 'What about Kings Cross?' she said.

'Kings Cross?'

'Sure, there are lots of places there.'

'Isn't that a bit extreme?' Visions of badly-lit, rubbish-strewn side streets ran through William's mind. Pushers and prostitutes in alternate doorways, and a steady stream of cars kerb-crawling.

'I wouldn't say that. It's where a lot of younger tourists go. I should know.'

William wondered what kind of tourists Josie knew. 'O.K.,' he said. They drove south towards the centre of town. From Euston they went down towards Southampton Row and glided past a couple of hotels with battered neon signs announcing single rooms at £30 and doubles at £45.

'This isn't Kings Cross,' William complained, 'It's Russell Square.'

'So? Don't be so pedantic. Take your pick.'

He stopped outside a place that looked a little smarter, and called itself the Walton. Josie glanced at the concrete and glass exterior. The plate-glass front showed a garishly decorated reception area, with glossy potted plants and minions in American-style uniform.

'Bit flash, isn't it?' she said.

'Flash? I'd call it tacky.'

'That's what I meant. I suppose it'll do.'

William turned off the square and parked in a side street. Josie didn't move.

'What's the matter?'

'I don't like it.'

He looked round. It was a quiet street with a few other parked cars. 'It's a single yellow line. We'll be leaving before nine. What's the problem?'

'It could be spotted.' Her voice was stubborn and she didn't look at him. 'If there's an alert out on us, then all it takes is a copper passing on his beat.'

William suppressed a sigh. 'What do you suggest then?'

'There's a multi-storey a little down the road. It's small but it's open all night. If you go round the block you'll come to it.'

A little down the road turned out to be a quarter of a mile. He parked, and they walked to the hotel in silence. Entering the lobby, he was absurdly conscious of not having a bag of any kind. The receptionist, hemmed in her booth by two large constructions of plastic flowers, looked bored and tired. She watched them approach with minimal interest. Obviously not husband and wife. Boss and secretary? Businessman and pick-up? These two were harder to place than most.

'Do you have any rooms?' William asked.

'Yes sir. A double?'

'Two singles,' Josie replied in a voice that would have cut through car wreckage. The receptionist stared at her. William's eyes flickered skywards in exasperation. Anonymity was obviously not one of Josie's strong points. The receptionist recovered first: she had the benefit of a script. 'A single room is thirty pounds for the night, without breakfast.'

'That's fine,' William said quickly, pre-empting any further eruptions. 'We'll pay now, if that's all right, as we may be leaving very early in the morning.'

He took out his wallet. American Express? Perhaps better not. He was beginning to get the hang of this. He counted out the cash and she handed him two keys.

The porter was a little too small for his uniform. He led William and Josie into the lift, where they stood on opposite sides, leaning against the walls. He looked across at her. Her head was bowed on her chest and her eyes were closed. She looked young and almost vulnerable. He wondered what it was in her that made her so aggressive at any hint of protection. What was she frightened of? Surely everyone needs comfort sometimes. The porter was staring resolutely at the steel doors, distancing himself from his charges. He pressed the button for the fourth floor. Nothing happened. After over a century, William thought, when will they invent a lift that works when you tell it to? The porter jabbed again, and with an obstreperous lurch the lift took off. William glanced at Josie. She frowned back, then her face unexpectedly creased into a grin. Her eyes laughed too. He returned her smile, first automatically, then spontaneously, affected by her rare moment of openness. His eyebrows asked, what's the joke? She shook her head. The porter's back glared at them. I wonder what he makes of us, William thought. A dirty-night couple in separate rooms. What is the world coming to?

On the fourth floor the porter abandoned them outside their two rooms. William gave him a tip to make up for the fact that Josie had refused to let him carry her bag. The corridor smelled of dusty carpet and stale air. They were suddenly awkward.

'What now?'

'We sleep,' she said coldly.

'I know that,' he said, irritated. There was something perverse in the way she consistently misinterpreted him. 'I mean afterwards.'

'I don't know. Let's talk about it tomorrow. I'm really tired now. I can't think any more.'

'O.K. Will you be all right?'

She nodded.

'What time tomorrow?'

'Whoever wakes first, wakes the other.'

'All right. Goodnight, Josie. Sleep well.'

She smiled wanly. 'Yeah. Like the dead.' She dragged her small, burdensome body into her room and closed the door.

Inside his room William rated the facilities in a score up to ten. It was an automatic appraisal, born from years of practice on business trips. Fitted carpet, large plate-glass window with heavy curtains, twin beds, armchair, bath and shower cubicle with shampoo and bubble bath sachets. Radio but no television, and the desk light didn't work. Seven out of ten. He turned on the shower experimentally. Scalding hot and strong pressure. Not bad. He undressed. It was a reflex with him to take showers in hotels. Why, he didn't know. He had a shower at home but rarely used it, preferring a bath.

He stayed under the water a long time, sitting down against the tiles and allowing the water bullets to bounce off his head. It was an American-style shower, fierce and full. As long as I stay here, he told himself, I don't have to think. It was the kind of pact he often made with himself, a conscious method of compartmentalizing his life to cope with stress. He had seen what happened, by way of ulcers and heart disease, to those colleagues who failed to find such techniques. The blast of water beat out the worst of his anxieties. In bed the slide show of the day began. He anticipated a few sleepless hours of analysing, evaluating, seeking order out of the chaos of events. Instead he fell asleep immediately.

Four doors down Josie found it not so simple. To begin with she was not at ease with the room. It gave her the creeps. It was the kind of place where you ought to be someone else but you could never work out who. This was not the time for hotel paranoia. She sat on one of the beds, moved to an armchair, then across to the desk. She caught sight of herself in the mirror. The day had taken its toll. She scowled and looked away. At the window she stared at the deserted street below. The summer shower had left the surfaces shiny. Behind a flickering belisha beacon the neon sign for a restaurant pulsed black to red. Film noir territory, trenchcoats and the bulge in the pocket that didn't mean the guy was pleased to see you. Mean streets. In daylight on any other day it would have been just another London thoroughfare. She drew the curtains and turned away.

In the bathroom she splashed cold water on her face and watched the whirlpool of water disappear down the plughole. Undressing, she folded her clothes with untypical care and laid them over the back of the armchair. Of the two beds, she chose the one next to the wall and nearest the door. She stripped off the blankets and slid in. The cool, stiff, hotel linen crinkled and creaked under her. She reached out for the light switch above her and pressed it. The room went dark. She closed her eyes. The world span.

Twenty minutes later she admitted defeat, sitting up abruptly and blinking in the darkness. As her vision began to penetrate the charcoal air she made out the forms of the furniture and the large square glow from the window. She got up, drew back the curtains and sat for a while in the armchair. Gradually she began to feel better. The room gained a life of its own, moving with the regular pulse of the neon sign, now a dim red, now a soft black. She closed her eyes and put her head back against the chair. This time she stayed in control of the pictures in her brain. After half an hour she climbed back into bed, curling up, her back to the window. She stared at the wall, watching the shadows lighten and thicken in tune with the darkness. She felt herself travelling through it, heading for the edge of a cliff in the far distance, beyond which was total blackness. She understood the cliff was sleep. She never remembered reaching it.

William woke with a start. A police siren was sounding, and he listened to it grow and peak and fade gradually into silence. Not so his anxiety. Through the fuzz of sleep he again went over the last few days. It felt like a story, an anecdote overheard on a train, rather than something actually lived through. He remembered the shock and fear, the moments of panic in her flat and later in the car – he remembered these things, but he couldn't feel them. It was a fact not an experience. He had once had a dream of someone repeatedly killing him. The knife flashed, he watched it make contact with his body, about to penetrate, he waited wondering what it would be like to be mutilated, to be dead. But nothing happened. Then the whole thing repeated – the knife, the anticipation. The dream was like an elaborate tape loop. It couldn't advance but only repeat itself. It left him feeling nothing, no fear, only the cool question – why am I not dead? Now there was a similar remoteness, a similar abstract curiosity: what will happen next?

It was quiet outside. Glimmerings of light in the distance. What time did that make it? Four o'clock? In his imagination dawn was always four o' clock. Some childhood trigger of early morning fishing with his dad. Or was that a remnant of borrowed memory from a working-class novel? William wasn't too interested in his early recollections.

A blackbird started up in the Square. 'Blackbird singing at the dead of night . . .' What must Americans have made of a lyric like that when they don't have blackbirds over there, at least not our kind of blackbird? William's mind wandered, increasingly vague. He remembered the summer the white album came out, sitting in the university library trying to wrench his mind off a girl who looked like Patti Boyd. Those years were ring-dated by Beatles albums, for him and a whole generation. Josie probably wouldn't even remember 'Sergeant Pepper', except as folk history. She would have made her transition to the discordant strains of the Stranglers. No wonder she was so abrasive. He remembered the night he and Penny went to the Everly Brothers' comeback concert. In the interval she had said . . .

Whatever it was she had said was lost, for William fell into a deep sleep. The next thing he knew, someone was assaulting him, shaking him and calling his name. He sat bolt upright.

Chapter Nine

'It's O.K. It's only me – Josie.'

He fell back silently, closed his eyes, opened them again. She was still there; no good hoping for a change of reality.

'What is it?'

'It's morning.'

She was fully clothed and aggressively alert. 'Sleep?' he said, for want of anything better.

'A bit. You?'

'More than I expected.'

'Good. In which case how about getting up? We have things to decide.'

In self-defence he kick-started his brain. It began to work. 'How did you get in here?'

'Through the door. It appears you didn't lock it. You're lucky it was me. It could have been anyone.'

' "Anyone" might have knocked.' He must have been tired, to leave a hotel room unlocked. But weren't they supposed to be self-locking? He considered whether to report it to the management.

'Look, we don't have much time. There's a lot to be done.'

'Not before breakfast there isn't.'

'William!'

'Josie, if we're going to spend any more time together, you are going to have to learn to stop guiding the tour. I want a shower and something to eat. Then I'll talk. Not before. So if you'll just make an exit for a few minutes, I'll see you when I'm ready.'

She sat back and pulled a face, mocking his sudden attempt at authority, but after a moment she got up. 'I'll be in the coffee shop,' she announced curtly. The door closed abruptly behind her.

The coffee shop was a relentless mixture of green and white plastic with baskets of fake plants hanging from the ceiling and Barry Manilow oozing from what looked like strategic air vents. William sat in front of an English breakfast, his stomach grinding with hunger at the smell of it. He dug his knife through the egg into the piece of toast, spurting yellow onto the bacon. Josie was opposite, picking at a croissant and waiting, in capital letters. For the first four mouthfuls he studiously ignored her, then feeling revived he looked up.

'We have to leave town,' she announced in a the-world-is-round tone of voice.

He shook his head, swallowing hard. 'That's too fast. What we have to do, it seems to me, is work out what the hell is going on. First analysis, then planning. Action comes last. So, go ahead. Tell me your version of what happened last night.' Overnight he had planned his strategy. Problems are problems, some more impenetrable than others, but surely one ought to be able to apply the same tools to all of them.

She made a noise of evident impatience, but began in a measured, quiet voice. 'O.K. Fact number one. Last night someone broke into my flat and rewired the kitchen in a way that was designed to kill me and very nearly did kill you. And it seems highly likely from what we saw that something similar was planned for your flat.' She paused, waiting for his agreement. He nodded and she continued. 'It therefore seems obvious to me that if we just meekly go back into our normal lives something similar will happen again. Maybe you find that hard to believe. Maybe you think that something that scares the shit out of you in the middle of the night must, in the cold light of day, have a perfectly rational explanation. That—'

'Wait a minute. If I'm going to disagree, I'll tell you. As it happens, I do think that someone was trying to hurt you.'

'In which case you must see that if we're going to get anywhere sorting this out, the first thing to do is to get the hell out of London.'

He shook his head. 'No, that's the bit I don't follow. If we have any decisions to make, why can't we sit here until we've made them? I don't see the need to emigrate.'

'Because,' she said, with considerably less patience. 'Listen. Someone tried to kill us, right? Why? It can only be that we saw something we shouldn't have. O.K? Now apart from us, the only people who know what we saw are the police. Therefore the people who tried to kill us either are the police, or have access to the same information as the police. And if they have access to police information, we're going to have to assume they have access to police facilities to track us down. That means anything normal that we do – go home, go to work, drive your car, use credit cards – can lead them to us.'

William thought about this. It had a certain logic. But then so did their innocence. 'Yes, but . . . We're not criminals. You seem to be forgetting – we haven't done anything.'

'Can we be sure of that?'

'What does that mean?'

'They might think we have. How do you know they don't?'

'Hold on a minute.' He felt himself slipping through the cracks in the meanings of words. 'Never mind that. Surely the point is that whatever they think, it's not going to help them to believe us if we run away. Innocent people don't do that.'

'So what's your suggestion? That we just go back to everyday living and wait for someone to take another shot at us?'

He slowly buttered another piece of toast, less because he was still hungry than to impose his pace on the conversation. She waited. 'According to your argument,' he resumed, 'these things have happened because we – or you – know something that someone didn't want us to know.'

'Right.'

'So what happens if we share this knowledge? There would then be no point in eliminating us.'

It was her turn to consider. 'All right, go on. Who do we tell?'

'A solicitor.'

'A solicitor!' The word came back at him dipped in scorn. 'And how would that help? What would he do about it?'

'He could act for us while we stayed out of sight. He would know everything we knew and —'

'William, the police know everything we know. It's not the facts that matter, it's that we're witnesses. It's us who can stand up in court and say, "Yes, your honour, that was the man I saw." Telling a solicitor makes absolutely no difference. He'd just play it by the book, and he'd be the only one who did.'

'But he could hold affidavits from us in case of trouble.'

'Yeah, and a fat lot of good they'd be if we're slabbed out in the morgue.'

'I still say it makes sense. At the very least he could force the police to investigate what happened in our flats last night.'

'Oh, don't be so naive. What would the police find in our flats? I'll tell you. Sweet fuck all. What do you think those two lumpen shadows at the front door were there for? To check the pulse on the body, and, if there was any problem, to put everything straight. There'd be nothing to investigate at the flats. All that would happen is that we'd look like idiots, or, worse, suspects, and we'd still be in danger.'

'Oh come on. I hardly think someone would try and harm us after we'd made such a fuss. It would be too obvious.'

'Of course it would. But then who could possibly be held responsible if two weeks later one of us happened to walk under a bus? Or committed suicide leaving a note saying we'd lied to the police? If you want to take that risk, fine, go ahead. I probably won't make it to the funeral but I'll send a wreath.'

'All right. Not a solicitor. What about a private investigator?'

'A private eye! Really - and who do you have in mind? Philip Marlowe? How many private eyes do you know? Let alone ones you could trust with something like this. Someone with political nous, someone prepared to snoop on the police themselves and with the connections to do it - and most of all, someone who doesn't think we're nuts. I hate to disillusion you, but most private detectives spend their lives taking dirty pictures of wayward wives. Anyway, how much do you think they charge?'

'O.K. O.K. Do you have a better idea?'

'I say if we talk to anyone it should be a journalist.'

'Why a journalist?'

'Because there's more to this than we understand. A good journalist would be the perfect person to ferret out information. And because journalists were precisely the people Coulton didn't want us to talk to.'

'I don't suppose you have anyone in mind?' he asked drily.

'As a matter of fact I do.'

'Who?'

'A guy called Josh Barnes. He's with the *Daily Post.* If he could get the story he'd put it where everyone would see it.'

And she accuses me of being a romantic, he thought impatiently. Private eye, supersleuth. What's the difference? And who is this man anyway? 'I've never heard of him. How do you know him?'

'He's an old mate.'

'Is he good?'

'Yes, he is.'

'How old is he?'

'Oh, for Christ's sake. He's the same age as me. Fourteen next birthday. What's that got to do with it?'

'Where do you know him from?'

'Sure you don't want to tie me up and stick matchsticks under my fingernails? We used to work together, all right? He ran a kind of underground press office for the Rock Against Racism campaign. He used to process stuff into manageable form to get it into the tabloids. Got to know a lot of people. Then he went into the wilderness for a while, working on local newspapers up north. He's been back here for three, maybe four years. His name's on a lot of local government stuff. He bust a couple of big corruption deals in the midlands – the kind of thing I expect you don't read.'

Despite himself William was amused. 'Quite right. I never get past the sports pages. So you're sure this guy has the right connections, with the police?'

It was her turn to smile. 'How do you think I got the name and address of Mr De Villiers? Yeah, I'm sure. And he's safe. Good at squirming his way into places. And if you don't know who he is, then they won't either.'

William frowned. This 'they' concept was giving him a little trouble. He didn't see the world in such clear-cut terms. He wished she would find another word to describe the opposition. He took a sip of coffee. It was cold. At the next table a group of flaxen-haired teenage girls were laughing and chattering in a language that might have been Norwegian. He glanced round the room. The two businessmen who had been seated in the corner, eating their breakfasts to the rhythm of the turned pages of the *Financial Times*, had gone. The changed human environment gave him an odd feeling, as if he too were now on holiday. He remembered he had an appointment at ten with – who was it?. It didn't matter, it was after ten now anyway. He felt a twinge of panic. Up till now this had been in his own time. But for William Stevens, personnel manager of Actonics Ltd, Wednesday July 12th was a working day, just like any other.

She interrupted his thoughts. 'Well?'

Her bullying irritated him, and exacerbated his unease. He wanted to get up, walk out, hail a taxi and go to the office as if nothing had happened, leaving her to go it alone. But it was too big a decision to be made on such capricious emotions. So on what basis was the choice to be made? Either he left or he stayed. The dilemma was simple, the consequences obscure. He needed to be better informed. If he did go with her to the journalist, at least they would get a second and, hopefully, objective opinion. Then if he wasn't convinced he could opt out and go his own way. When in doubt, defer.

'All right, I'll speak to him.'

'Good, I knew you'd see sense.'

'Don't push it.'

She stood up. 'I'll go and phone him.'

'I need to make a call too. Work. Tell them I might not be in today.'

'Oh yes. You must. Absolutely vital.'

They paid the bill and returned to the hotel lobby where four out of the five pay-phone booths were occupied. Josie took the fifth as if it were her birthright. Rather than wait, William strolled through the hotel out onto the street. The day was wilfully normal. The sunlight made nonsense of death threats and conspiracies. He stared as people with briefcases and bags strode purposefully towards offices and shops, crossing streets still clogged with rush-hour traffic. Standing there, watching the world go by, he couldn't help feeling absurd, like the victim of a monstrous practical joke. Surely there was still a possibility that the wiring had been carelessness, an accident rather than premeditated murder, that the light in his flat had been reflected from somewhere else, the car parked there by chance. People didn't just kill people. Not for so little reason. Not in the real world. You're the wrong person for this, William, he thought. It should have happened to someone else. He returned to the lobby. There were three booths free. He hesitated, then picked up the phone.

They met outside. She took one look at his face. 'What's wrong? What is it?'

He took a breath. 'Someone's been trying to get me at the office.'

'Who?'

'Didn't leave a name. He just said he'd call back. And Karen said a man arrived to see me – as soon as the building opened. Said it was personal and that I would be expecting him.'

'What did you tell her?'

'That there was a family crisis I had to attend to. I told her to cancel my appointments for two days.' He was distracted. Over Josie's shoulder he watched a man with a briefcase hailing a taxi. It felt like a scene glimpsed down the wrong end of a telescope. Reality had become the illusion. The joke was on him. I'd better start getting used to it, he thought. She was talking to him:

'William!'

'Sorry.'

'You haven't heard a word, have you? I said I got through to

Josh. He's interested. He's meeting us in an hour, at the Tower of London.'

'The Tower of London?'

'Yes, why not? it's not that far and it'll be swarming with tourists. Do you have a better idea?'

No, he thought. Right at this moment I have no ideas at all.

Chapter Ten

'And that's why it's called Traitors' Gate. I'm amazed you didn't know that. I would have thought a good British company like yours would have encouraged their employees to cultivate a sense of national heritage.'

They were standing on the embankment by the Tower, which was dense with people. For ten minutes she had been doing all the talking. He was having trouble with the listening.

'What does he look like? It must be a while since you last saw him.'

'I'll recognize him. Don't worry.'

'You're sure he knows where to come?'

'Third cannon on the right if you're approaching from the west. The one next to the telescope and opposite Traitors' Gate. I'd say that was pretty hard to miss, wouldn't you? Relax, he'll be here. Do you know the only person who sailed in through Traitors' Gate and out again safely?'

'What?'

'Traitors' Gate. The only one who survived it? English monarch. Virgo intacta.'

She's enjoying herself, he thought. She knows we're in trouble and she's having a good time. Or is it how she copes with fear? Everyone has their own way.

'Really William, how can you know so little about your own history? Elizabeth the First, the Virgin Queen – like hell she was. You should read the evidence of the chambermaids who changed the linen the nights when Dudley stayed the year after her coronation. Talk about laundry and history. It's where she first met Dudley, you know, the Tower. They were both prisoners. She came in the Gate in 1554 – just after the second rebellion against Bloody Mary. She was here for months. In a room in the Queen's House, the one that Henry built for her mother Anne Boleyn. The only time the poor woman ever used it was when she was imprisoned there awaiting her execution. Just imagine it. Elizabeth was barely twenty. Under suspicion of treason and spending her days looking out on the place her mother was beheaded twenty years before. Mind you, she wasn't exactly short on her own cabaret. She must have watched a queue of nobles losing their heads. Including that anaemic Lady Jane Grey – you know, the nine days' queen. I've ofter wondered if that's where the phrase comes from – nine days' wonder. She was a real wimp. The classic victim of a father-in-law's ambition. No wonder when Elizabeth got out she vowed never to marry. Boy, was she one of nature's survivors. Do you know the day she died – she was nearly eighty – she got out of bed and danced? Probably terrified the shit out of the grim reaper. Amazing. Hey, normally people have to pay for this, you know. Here you are, getting it all for free, and you're not even listening.'

That wasn't true. Despite his anxiety William found himself caught up in the narrative. 'You know a lot about her. Is that just part of the job?'

'What do you think? No, she's special. I had my first-ever crush on her. Before the gym teacher even. By the time I was fourteen I'd read everything there was to read about her. Most of it romantic bullshit, of course. Although the bit about the sheets is supposed to have had scholastic verification. The longest relationship in my life – me and Elizabeth. The first ardour got a bit dampened by years of academic grind, but it never snuffed out that initial passion. She's extraordinary. The original woman in a man's world. And she comes out of it having more balls than the lot of them.'

Perfect, he thought sourly. I start my one and only experience as an outlaw in the company of a woman who models herself on Elizabeth the First. Still, it could have been worse. It could have been Boadicea. Wise to change the subject.

'He's late,' he said and they both fell silent.

Across the river the sun shot silver weave into the water and the heat sat hazy on the surface. In front of them a toddler made a run for a flock of pigeons grown fat on tourists' sandwiches. The birds waited until the last possible moment, then flapped lazy wings to get airborne. Everyone around them had time to kill. I should relax, he thought. Anxiety won't turn the world any faster.

'There he is.'

William's eyes followed her finger. The man walking purposefully towards them was shorter than he would have liked. With curly fair hair and architects' glasses, even the suit didn't help assuage the impression of an aging boy scout. I must give him a chance. Policemen and doctors have all got younger at the same rate, why not journalists too?

Josh embraced Josie warmly. He took a step back and held her at arms' length. 'You haven't changed a bit. Whose blood are you drinking every night?'

'You have. What's with the suit?'

'You know me. Dedicated follower of fashion. When in Rome – it's better not to look like a Carthaginian. Hello, you must be William.' He held out his arm. It was a firm, serious handshake and a direct gaze. William was reassured. 'Josh Barnes.'

'It's good of you to come so quickly.'

'It sounded important. Shall we find somewhere a little quieter to talk? I gather you're the guide now, Josie. Lead the way.'

Low tide under Tower Bridge. They sat on the steps talking into the small cassette recorder that Josh placed between them. He interrupted little, only, it seemed to William, where embellishment or clarification was relevant. He became most animated when they got to the story of the kettle.

'You're absolutely sure, Josie, that you didn't at some point have a go at mending the kettle?'

'Who do you think I am, handywoman around the house? Of course not. And anyway, what about the wall socket?'

'Some people do all manner of things when all that's wrong is a blown fuse.'

'Joshua, give me a break. I'm not an idiot.'

He smiled. 'No, but you are a woman. And if by chance the device had worked, that would no doubt have been the verdict of the inquest. Inadequate knowledge of electrics. Common fault among the weaker sex. Bad luck. Tragic even, but clearly Misadventure. Very clever.'

'God, I wonder what they were planning for you, William. Something more sophisticated, I expect. Accidental Death of a Personnel Manager. Maybe you would have got caught in a shredding machine.'

William enjoyed the joke. Joshua, however, did not laugh. 'We shouldn't jump to too many conclusions. There's no proof of what they were doing in William's flat. Yes, I know you both saw lights there, but the strength of your story until now is that you actually witnessed things, beyond a shadow of doubt. But by that time in the evening you were both tired, scared and on the move past a flat two floors up. Something as fleeting as a torch beam would have trouble holding up as evidence. You'd need more than that.'

'You think I should go back and check my flat?'

'No, it would have been removed by now. We might not be able to prove anything but, painful though it is, I think we should assume the worst until we can assume better.'

He fell silent. Josie resumed the story and brought it up to the present. Joshua leaned over and turned off the tape recorder. William wondered what he was feeling. Excitement, fear, apprehension? Maybe it's all part of the job. He caught Josie's eye. She smiled at him. He smiled back. Strange, he thought, I came to this meeting an atheist. Yet in the retelling I have become a believer. In convincing Joshua I have convinced myself. Maybe she knew that would happen.

'Jesus,' he said at last, 'I don't know what to say. You're right. Whatever you've run into, most of it is still underwater. We could sit here till doomsday speculating how deep it goes, but the answers would still be theory. But I'll tell you one thing for sure. It can't be printed. Not as it stands. It needs much more substantiation.'

'What, even with the photos?'

'Josie, unless you've taken lessons from Bill Brandt since we last met, and if you were as far away as you said you were, then those pictures aren't really going to prove anything. At that distance in the rain he'd be lucky if his own mother recognized him.'

'Well, Coulton seemed to think they were important enough to kill for.'

'Maybe. Or maybe he thought you were just too much trouble altogether. The photos put a greater price on your head though, I grant you that.'

'So what can you do?'

'Ask a few questions. About Mr De Villiers for a start. Then there's Coulton's exclusive phone number, although frankly I'll be surprised if I get an answer. And Mrs O'Grady.'

'The security guard's widow. What's she got to do with it?'

He shrugged. 'Maybe bugger all. But it's worth a try. When he was in intensive care, no journalist could get within miles of him. Which is not unusual. But there was always a policeman outside the room. Obviously they were looking forward to him regaining consciousness. So, give me a couple of days.'

'And in the meantime?'

'If I were you I'd go to ground for a bit. If the kettle story is what it appears, then I see no reason to set yourself up for any further target practice.'

'What about the police?' William felt Josie's scornful rumblings beside him, but Joshua at least took the question seriously.

'If it were me, I wouldn't. Not for the moment anyway. There's clearly a leak the size of a river up at Highgate, and until you know who is telling what to whom, and why, you have no guarantee your evidence will stay confidential. No . . . don't expose yourselves.'

'Could it have been one of the officers we talked to, do you think?'

'Listen. You made statements, right? You were in contact with a number of officers. More still saw your statements or were in a position to run off a copy. Then there's gossip. A big case like this, they talk about it all the time. In the canteen. In the pub. It could have been any of fifty people high up or low down. It wouldn't necessarily have to be a police officer, just someone who moved in the right circles.'

'So the police might not even be involved?'

'Only unwittingly. By any objective analysis the police are on the side of the establishment. Of course, that's not how they see themselves. The bias is unconscious, except in a few cases. The majority, I'm sure, think they're neutral. They pride themselves on being fair, balanced. Just like the BBC. If you're inside it's not all that difficult to mistake consensus for balance. I'm surprised Josie hasn't lectured you on that. It used to be one of her favourite party pieces.

'As for Coulton,' Josh continued, 'he obviously knew how to handle himself like a policeman. Not everyone leaves the force just to retire to the cottage and the rose garden. The openings for ex-coppers with a healthy appetite and weak scruples are many and various. It might be worth checking out.' He stood up, slipping the tape recorder into his pocket. 'So do you two know where you're going? I suggest you stick together. At least for me it's easier to find you that way.'

William and Josie looked at each other. She shrugged.

'Can I make a suggestion?' Joshua directed the remark at her. 'I happened to make contact with an old mutual friend the other day. He did me a favour. Got me an expensive exclusive interview for a magazine, just as good friends should. He was asking after you . . .'

She dropped her eyes. 'Pass.'

'He spoke of you very fondly. I think he misses the Jiminy Cricket in you. Anyway, you know he has acquired a little pied-à-terre in the country?'

'Meldon.'

'Right. Well, he's very generous with it. Even offered me a weekend. I'm sure if you needed somewhere - quiet, isolated, no neighbours -'

Josie shifted on the stone step, still avoiding him. 'I don't think so, Josh. But thanks all the same.'

'O.K., I'm not pushing. I'm just telling you that it's there. As far as I'm concerned it doesn't matter where you go. Just so long as you keep in touch, and get out of London.'

'What about the car?'

'We can't use the car,' Josie said. 'It's hot.'

William ignored her and looked to Joshua, who shook his head. 'I have to agree. My instinct would be to leave it. No point making yourself obvious.'

'Well, I can't leave it where it is.'

'William!' The car clearly was not Josie's primary concern.

'Not in an NCP car park. It'll cost a fortune.'

'Where do you live?' Joshua said, pouring oil on troubled waters.

'West Hampstead.'

'Give me the keys. I'll pick it up and deliver it home for you. Park it somewhere, but not too near. That way, if it comes to their attention they'll assume that you're somewhere around, which of course you won't be.'

William admired the compromise. He held out the keys. Josie also gave Josh the film and Coulton's calling card.

'When shall we call you?' she asked.

'Let's say midnight tonight, all right?' Josh leaned a hand down to William. 'Good luck.'

'Yes, and thanks a lot.'

Josh grinned. 'I haven't done anything yet. Save the thanks till we get some results.' He punched Josie affectionately on the shoulder. 'Look after each other. And try to relax a little. There are enough demons around without you two becoming your own worst enemies.'

Good advice, thought William. I hope she heard him.

Joshua left, and for a while they sat in silence. On the other side of the river two boys were beachcombing in the mud. Holidays.

Holiday-makers. The perfect camouflage. 'I think I have the answer,' he said. 'We need somewhere with a lot of people, where we won't be recognized. A place where people are strangers to one another. On holiday, in fact. What could be more normal than a couple spending a few days in a holiday resort?'

She looked at him solemnly, as if preparing the usual scornful response she had for his suggestions. Then she grinned. 'Excellent idea. What shall it be – heads or tails?'

'What?'

'Heads for south. Tails for north. I think it would be symbolic to cast our fate to the winds.'

The ten pence piece spun high in the air. Josie made a grab for it and missed. It clattered down the steps, landing with a soft thud in the mud of the river bed. She clambered down after it. 'Heads,' she announced triumphantly. She pulled a large map out of her voluminous handbag and laid it out between them. He had the distinct sense of being outmanoeuvred once again.

'What else have you got in there, a white rabbit?'

She shrugged. 'I knew you'd come round to seeing it my way. I bought it at the hotel while you were phoning. Do you want to do this, or shall I?'

He made a gesture of surrender. She raised her hand with deliberate ceremony, closed her eyes and pointed her index finger downward. It came to rest on the bottom part of the map. She opened her eyes. Their destination, apparently, was the middle of the English Channel. She drew her finger due north to the nearest settlement. 'Branscombe,' she said. 'Ever heard of it? It looks like it's tumbling into the sea.'

He peered down. 'It's near Lyme Regis. Penny and I went there once. A long, rocky coast. French Lieutenant's Woman country.'

'Oh well, so long as it's cultured. Will it do? Who's Penny?'

Faced with two questions, William opted for the easier one.

'I would have thought so. There are hotels, caravans, that sort of thing.'

'O.K. Branscombe it is then.'

He watched her energetically stuffing the map into her bag. 'You're enjoying this, aren't you?'

She turned to him, hands folded in her lap, a moment of stillness amidst the perpetual motion. 'In a way maybe. How about you?'

'You're not frightened?'

'No. Now that we're actually doing something. It's weird. But maybe that's the secret. You just do what has to be done, and somehow that makes it easier. Don't you think?'

A quick half-smile evaded the question. 'I'll tell you when we've done it. So, how do we get there?'

'I dunno. Train I guess. Or we could go by bus.'

'Bus?'

'Yes, you know, big diesel vehicles with four wheels and lots of windows. People who don't own cars use them to get from one place to another.'

'Josie, has it ever occurred to you that your jokes might not always be funny?'

'Or that you might not have a sense of humour? Come on, you heard what Joshua said – we oppressed must stick together. If you agreed with me more often we wouldn't have this problem. Anyway, I shouldn't worry about it. You appear to have tough enough skin. I vote we find a phone box and ring British Rail. That way we can work out how and when we get there.'

They got up. William felt the back of his shirt stick to his back. In his business suit he didn't feel quite dressed for the occasion. He watched enviously as a boat-load of scantily-dressed tourists passed by, cameras clicking. 'It's getting hotter,' he said.

'Hard to believe it was once so cold that the Thames froze from Barnes to London, isn't it? The ice was so deep people skated and sledged on it. They even held a winter fair with stalls and horses.' She climbed over a railing onto the Embankment.

'I never knew that.'

'Well you wouldn't, would you? It's not your job. Everyone was having such a good time they wouldn't get off when it started to thaw. A couple of boys instituted a skating race to Hammersmith. Both fell in and drowned. There were icebergs floating downriver with horses stranded on them.'

He brushed a piece of dried mud off his trousers. 'It's a pity your knowledge doesn't stretch to the future as well as the past. You might be able to give us a little help with the next few days.'

'Are you really sure you'd want to know?' she said with what seemed like no humour at all.

She entered a phone booth and he waited outside. It was interesting, he thought, how quickly their semi-serious bickering had developed into a way of life; the teasing and prodding acting as a reassurance and a means of contact. It was a fragile transaction but the only one, apparently, available to them. Why? Would real communication actually be such a bloodbath? Maybe. She gave off clear signals of isolation, as if she had been closed up for a long time now and had got to feel at home with it.

'Bus,' she said firmly on leaving the booth. 'It takes four hours to Seaton, just down the coast. There's one leaving in an hour from Victoria coach station. If we move we can make it.'

The tube spewed them out in record time. The coach station was an image of London in evacuation, with people and suitcases jamming the foyer. She was surging towards the booking office when he put his hand on her shoulder. 'Hey, wait a minute. We're going to need cash. How much do you have on you?'

'Not much. A couple of quid.'

'And after last night I don't have much more. We're going to have to draw some. And I suggest we do it here.' She opened her mouth to speak, but he didn't let the words form. 'I know what you're going to say. But since any cheque can potentially be traced, and since Victoria could be the start of a journey by rail, sea or air to almost anywhere, then it seems sensible to do it here, rather than in some sleepy little seaside resort.'

She nodded. 'You're right, I agree. How much do you think we need?'

'To be on the safe side, £500.'

'You can draw that much?'

'With American Express Gold Card, yes. Don't look at me like that. I can't help it if I'm solvent. It's just one of the perks of selling my soul.'

'Don't tell me. You keep it all in Barclays.'

'Bank of Scotland actually. But you'll be pleased to know they are affiliated.'

'Good. In which case that assuages any guilt I have for letting you do the paying. Maybe you could ask for a bank loan. Tell them you need it for a week on the run. Give me the rest of your cash and I'll meet you back here with the tickets.'

He returned from the bank to find her with both arms full of newspapers, attempting to read the middle page of *The Times* while one of the tabloids inched its way to the pavement. He retrieved a page-three nymphet in mid-flight earthwards.

'Fuckers,' she hissed. 'Have you heard the latest? A group of NHS consultants have withdrawn their support for Health Not Wealth claiming the pressure group has got out of hand and could jeopardize the health of the nation. The health of the nation!' she snorted. 'They're just the first bunch of rats to fling themselves overboard, and do it publicly so they can get their names into the paper and people know who to call for a little private practice.'

William took her arm and propelled her towards Departures. 'Listen, you can rant and rave to your heart's content later. But preferably somewhere less public. From now on let's concentrate on getting ourselves on the bus, O.K?'

The departure hall resembled Hyde Park at the beginning of a demonstration, with crowds of people milling around trying to locate the right banner to congregate under. OAPs Against the Bomb would have been the most suitable slogan for this gathering, since the majority of travellers were senior citizens, mostly neat little old women pulling suitcases, like dogs, on leads behind them. 'Shit,' muttered Josie, as one of the offending pets rolled over her toe. In the doorway of the Taunton coach the ticket collector suggested that Josie put her bag in the boot. She refused the offer with an unexpected quiet charm. 'It's called femininity, mate,' she whispered to William, pushing past him to get a seat, 'and I can do it with the best of them when needed.' She settled herself in the window seat and stuck her nose in the *Guardian*.

William glanced at the ticket before putting it in his pocket. He noticed the name written by the clerk: John Reed. My God, he thought, smiling to himself, she really doesn't miss a trick, does she?

Chapter Eleven

It proved a long four hours. Josie gave up on the papers early, her stomach lurching with the stop/go out of London. William closed his eyes and dozed. He awoke on the motorway with the coach speeding exuberantly through the midday heat and the sun pouring in through the windows.

Josie had her nose pressed against the glass, watching mile upon mile of thick, yellow fields. The silence between them was not uncomfortable, but rather a release from the frenetic rushing and gibbering of the morning. They both understood the journey was a temporary time capsule. Nothing could be done until they reached their destination, and nothing could be said with so many ears close by. William rested his head against the seat back, noticing her blurred outline in the reflection of the window pane. Strong forehead; small, pointed chin. Too much hair for too little face. If she had been someone else she might almost have been pretty. But the word was not one he would use to describe her. It was too domesticated for her unstable mix of hot air and anger. Perhaps away from the scene of the crime she might grow quieter.

At Southampton the bus stopped at a shiny new depot with a café attached. They piled out thirsty and cramped, and sat in silence, as if the habit was hard to break. She drank two glasses of orange juice and picked at a dead sandwich asphyxiated by its cellophane wrapper. He had a glass of water and a cup of tea. Both would have been undrinkable in any other situation. After ten minutes the bus driver got up from his seat and walked to the door. William rose too. Josie disappeared in the direction of the ladies'.

He waited by the bus. She was a long time. The driver honked his horn. A few latecomers drifted back. Come on, Josie. Inconspicuous, remember. The driver started the engine. At the same moment she emerged from the building, scampered over and climbed on the bus. There was an air of excitement to her, a new tension. As the bus pulled out she leaned across.

'What is it?'

'I've found something,' she hissed.

'What?'

From her bag she surreptitiously lifted out a small, green plastic folder. A driving licence.

'Whose is it?'

'Mrs Yvonne Pryce's.' She read the name off the front. 'Whoever she is.'

'I don't understand. Where'd you get it?'

'It was in the bin in the ladies' loo. At the bottom. A whole wallet, no money, but this and a library card and a few bits of paper. Someone obviously picked her purse, ripped off the cash and dumped the rest. They didn't need a driving licence. But we might.'

'Well, we certainly can't use that one.'

'Why not?'

'Because it's illegal,' he said, instantly regretting it. 'We wouldn't be insured. If we had an accident we could be liable for huge amounts of money.'

'Not we, William. Me. Don't worry. I'd be the one that was driving.'

'O.K., O.K. Forget it.'

'Oh, for Christ's sake. Didn't your mother ever tell you not to look a gift horse in the mouth? I'm not suggesting we get off the bus and use it now. I'm just saying it might come in handy some time, that's all.'

Some time. There she goes again, he thought, seeing this as a long-term life style. Maybe she doesn't really have a life to go back to. And that's why she feels so at home with all this. Maybe she even – the thought was unworthy, but it stuck. 'What were you doing poking about in the bin in the first place?'

'Mind your own business. Why, do you think I made it up? That what I was really doing was beating the shit out of some old lady in order to rip off her driving licence?'

'That's not what I meant.' They were still whispering. This is ridiculous, he thought. We're probably attracting more attention than by shouting. 'You just seem to get such a kick out of it, that's all. As if you're not taking it seriously. And I find that somewhat disconcerting.'

'Yes, well you would, wouldn't you? What would you like instead – me weeping and wailing the whole time, waiting for you, the man, to make all the decisions? Tough shit William, I'm not your secretary. If it hadn't been for me you'd be lying fried on some marble slab by now, still believing in the goodness of man and the impossibility of conspiracy. We're into this up to our necks and all you can do is worry about whether we're insured. I suggest if you don't like the way I'm handling it, then get off at the next stop and hitch a lift back to your cosy flat and wait for them to come knocking on the door.'

A woman's face peered out at them from between the headrests of the seats in front. Every bus has its lace curtains. William gave her a broad smile. The head disappeared out of sight again. He turned to Josie, who was staring resolutely out of the window, the muscles in her cheek clenched. She's really upset, he thought. He thought for a moment, then said:

'I'm sorry. I didn't mean to start an argument. You're probably right. The driving licence might come in useful. I didn't know you could drive.'

'Yes, and I even check in the mirror before I pull out.'

He left her with the last word, and retired behind a newspaper.

Everything he read in it made him feel worse. The rest of Britain, it seemed, was having no trouble evaluating the events of Friday night. The police were 'pursuing a fruitful line of inquiry', but emphasized that such cases 'take time', whatever that meant. Meanwhile, the closure of a cottage hospital in the north-east (it was not 'cost effective') had been the scene of a violent struggle between HNW protesters and the police. Four demonstrators had been arrested and a policeman taken to hospital with a suspected fractured skull. The health minister had not wasted the opportunity to describe the incident in the Commons as 'deplorable and a travesty of the democratic process'. Violence and condemnation. It was a common pattern over the last few years. When had it started? The miners' strike probably. He could feel this health issue shaping up in the same way, into a titanic struggle in which reasoned negotiation played no part. Professionally it offended him, and threatened him, because in such confrontations the mediator becomes redundant and things are settled - or not settled - above his head. For William this was a disturbing trend, both in politics and in industrial relations.

And in this heightened emotional atmosphere someone had set off a bomb. Just a small explosion to get back public attention. Could it be? It wouldn't be the first time the radical left had misjudged public opinion and got caught, as it were, in its own blast. What if, after all, there was some simple explanation for the car, and the man and the wiring?

He shook his head, as if to get rid of the subversive thoughts beginning to take hold there. He'd made his decision. He had to get on with it. Joshua gave the impression of a man who knew what he was about. Leave it to him. It was only a matter of a day or so. Then surely something would be resolved. He looked out of the window. Cornfields in the sun. Midsummer English glory. At any other time this would have been an amazing journey. He settled back in his seat and tried to enjoy it.

Two hours later the coach pulled into Seaton High Street, just eight minutes behind schedule, having spent the last lap of the journey scurrying between seaside resorts along the coast of Dorset and south Devon. It was late afternoon and Seaton was suffering from acute family fever. The bucket and spade and postcard shops which littered the High Street were bursting with families in various skin shades of lobster. Opposite the bus station stood the main entrance and banqueting hall of Warner's Holiday Camp, a 1950s pleasure dome which had not worn well into the eighties. For William the very sight of it triggered a flood of nightmare memories: family holidays incarcerated in mickey mouse chalets with rain on the window panes, children fighting, parents shouting and the endless debate about what to do. Two weeks of annual hell instantly transmuted into halcyon recollections by his parents. 'But we rowed the whole time, don't you remember?' he had once protested over a group of family snapshots. 'William, how could you say that?' His mother's voice, awash with pained indignation. 'I remember that year as if it were yesterday. We had a grand time. You didn't want to come home.' So much for trying to set the record straight.

Later, at university, he had come upon people whose childhoods had been punctuated by package holidays abroad. For them English seaside resorts were already social history, pickled in the aspic of McGill postcards and Monty Python handkerchief sunhats. But for William it still hurt. Roots could pull you down.

The bus pulled out, leaving them stranded on the forecourt with their meagre luggage. Their eyes met. 'Not here,' he said firmly.

She nodded. 'So, which way is Branscombe?'

The tourist office, it transpired, was at the other end of the High Street. Crossing over a side road, they caught a glimpse of the sea, an unEnglish shade of blue in the sunlight, sparkling behind a row of deck chairs and ice cream stalls. He felt a sudden yearning to swim. London and South African businessmen seemed light years away.

In the tourist office William did the talking, while Josie took an obsessive interest in the pamphlets on hotel tariffs. Yes, Branscombe was, it appeared, smaller and quieter too. No big hotel, and the few bed and breakfasts would probably be full, but there was a big caravan site on the coast. Josie sauntered up behind him and stuck an elbow in his back.

'A caravan,' she said between clenched teeth. The girl at the desk gave them an odd look.

'A caravan,' he smiled. Inwardly he groaned. More images of enforced family fun in claustrophobic conditions. Things were strange enough as they were. Why go out of your way to make them stranger? One thing was clear. Josie must have been a Majorca baby. The girl picked up the phone. Yes, they were in luck. The site had been fully booked, but there had been a couple of last minute cancellations. They would hold a caravan for them . . . What was the name?

'Reed,' said William. 'John and Louise Reed.' He felt Josie's raised eyebrow behind him. That'll teach you to underestimate the establishment, he thought grimly.

John and Louise were directed to the taxi rank across the square. There were buses, yes, but not that frequent, and they didn't go all the way to the site. A taxi wouldn't be that expensive. On the way William bought a change of clothes and a toothbrush. The summer slacks were a little on the large side, but the T-shirt and sneakers fitted. He walked out of the shop carrying his suit in a plastic bag, feeling a new person. Josie greeted him with incredulity. 'You look like a man disguised as a holiday-maker.'

'You fit in well yourself,' he replied.

Branscombe turned out to be an unexpectedly pretty village, reached by a narrow, winding road which no doubt saw its fair share of scraped car sides during an average summer. It nestled in the curve of a hill close to the coast, and was full of thatched cottages, with a pub on the corner surrounded by topiary and oak tables. Its siting had saved it from the commercial massacre of Seaton - the topography allowed space for only a very short High Street - and even at the height of the season it retained an air of gentleness about it. People here, it seemed, did not like to hurry.

It was a different matter on the coast itself. The caravan site sprawled up the slow gradient of a cliff which overhung the beach. At the bottom were a car park, restaurant, shop and the site office. The taxi dumped them outside. There were kids everywhere. Josie was back on form, muttering darkly about the cost of the ride. William ignored her, going into the office to register and collect the keys. He took the let for a week, the shortest time allowed, and paid in cash. It was a curious feeling counting out the twenty-pound notes. He hadn't realized how accustomed he'd become to plastic money. It made him feel like a criminal. Presumably there was a whole sub-culture where bank accounts and credit cards had no value. Outside again, he narrowly missed a small, melting pool of ice cream. A child, sensing his belligerence, got out of his way.

'It's the blue one, near the top of the cliff,' he said, trying to inject some enthusiasm into his voice. 'He says it's a bit of a climb, but it has a beautiful view and a lot of privacy.'

'Great,' she said, striding out towards the cliff path. 'Let's go and check it out.'

It was indeed a bit of a climb, and by the time they reached it they were both panting. The view was also beautiful. At the back of the caravan the cliff fell off towards the ocean, a long, hazy blue line along the horizon. There was no one else in sight. It was not, however, all good news. The caravan looked as if it had been there for some time and had caught more than its fair share of salt sea gales. The lock was rusty. It took a number of minutes and as many expletives for Josie to get it open. Behind her William stood silently, assaulted by memories he had spent years trying to forget.

The space inside was smaller than he remembered, with barely enough room to swing a baby, and the furnishings – G plan, or maybe even H or I – had taken a pasting from previous occupants. The atmosphere was musty and heavy with heat. He opened the curtains and the windows and the sun came dancing in, picking out patterns with the dust in the air. She sat down on a bench and rested her arm on the formica-topped table, which creaked slightly under her weight. William looked around, fighting to suppress a feeling of being trapped.

'Well,' he said, 'home is where the heart is.'

'Yeah, and it certainly ain't here.'

'It was your idea, remember?'

His evident bad temper seemed to surprise her. 'Don't worry, I'm not getting at you. It's perfect – safe, secluded, anonymous, within easy reach of a public phone, and –' she pointed to a stack of women's magazines on a shelf next to a couple of old green-backed Penguins – 'its own library. How about tea?'

William put his irritation to work, figuring out the water and sanitation, turning on the electricity, while Josie went down to the camp store. By the time she arrived back with a couple of bags of groceries the kettle had already boiled.

'That's another thing I remember,' he said as they were seated again. 'Whatever you do to it, the tea always tastes lousy.'

'You know, there's something I always wanted to know, and now I suppose I'm going to find out – what people actually do in caravans?'

'Change nappies and play Scrabble. We're not typical. The majority of people here will be families. The kids set the pace. It's a competition to find new ways of raising hell.'

Distant shrieks and shouts from further down the hill seemed to confirm this. They listened in silence to the sounds of other peoples' lives. It was already early evening. The sun was sliding in low through the windows. But there was still a chasm of hours until night. How to fill the time? Josie lay back on the bench-settee and propped her head on a cushion. When she spoke, her voice had a welcoming conversational tone to it. Now we're here, it said, we might as well make the best of it.

'So you were a caravan kid, eh? I find it hard to imagine you raising hell.'

'That's because you put too much weight on the trappings. I wasn't always the great conformist you like to picture me as, you know.'

'Don't tell me, you were a leading light in the Tunbridge Wells chapter of Hell's Angels.'

'There you are - second mistake. I don't even come from the south. I was born in Nottinghamshire.'

'Were you?' Her surprise was genuine. 'You don't sound like a northerner.'

'Well, I did once. You can still catch traces of an accent if you listen carefully. Certain words - or so people tell me.'

'Where did it go?'

'Slid in between the cracks of London University and twenty years living down south, I suppose.'

'Slid, or was pushed?'

'Maybe a little of both,' he conceded.

She sipped her tea, then settled herself more comfortably. 'So, you were brought up in Nottingham. Wild child of the north . . . I still can't quite see it. What were you like?'

'Use your imagination. I was a bit of a runt as a kid. Skinny, small for my age. I had to find ways to assert myself. You know, peer-group pressure.'

'And so you became the youngest sociologist on the block and zapped 'em with jargon, right? Go on, seriously, I'm interested.'

'I climbed.'

'What, social ladders?'

'No, I was always a great climber. I was a monkey. I could climb anything. Trees, walls, you name it.'

'And this gave you great cachet, did it?'

'Sure. I once shinned up the outside of a warehouse and in a window. I was supposed to be stealing something, that was the point of it. In fact, I wasn't the least interested in stealing. It was just a gesture. When I got there I had no idea what to take. I finally come out with a grease gun.'

'Whatever that is. And then you descended to loud applause, the young Jimmy Cagney, acknowledged leader of the gang.'

'For about ninety seconds. Then a neighbour came out screaming from the flats opposite. She'd seen everything. We ran like hell.'

'And that was the beginning of a life of crime?'

'Correction. It was the end of a life of crime.'

'You were arrested?'

'No, my father got me out of it. She recognized me and went and told him. He gave the grease gun back and managed to hush it up.'

'So who was he – E.G. Marshall?'

'Not exactly, but he was a respected figure in the community. He was a shop steward.'

'Well well.' That delighted her. Her eyes lit up, determined to extract the maximum mileage from this revelation. 'Son-of-poacher turns gamekeeper. And what does he feel now about your provocative choice of profession?'

'See, that's another thing you're wrong about. Personnel managers aren't necessarily the enemy. Not the good ones anyway. The good ones know it's not in the interests of the company to screw the workforce. Because once the workforce feels screwed, then sooner or later you're in for a lot of trouble. No, the aim is to get a settlement that's accepted as fair. A personnel manager who plays it straight is respected by both sides. Anyway, what makes you so sure you know what my politics are?'

'You voted Labour till 1974, Tory in '79, then SDP in '83 and ever since.'

'Hmmm,' he grunted. 'Almost right.'

'And I still bet if you asked your father what he really thinks, he'd see you as a class traitor – smoothing the road for the profit makers.'

'I can't quite hear him using the jargon.' The reply came a little sharply. 'Anyway, people in glass houses . . . I would have thought exactly the same thing applies to you. Your background is middle class, I take it?'

'Yeah, but the great thing about leaving the middle classes is that you don't have to feel guilty about it.'

'Just complacent?'

She grinned. 'Touché.'

'Anyway, I doubt whether you really have left.'

'Meaning?'

'If you weren't so tied to your bourgeois roots, maybe you wouldn't need to make such a display of your radicalism.'

'Do me a favour,' she grimaced. 'Do you realize how many clichés you use during the course of a day?'

'I have a feeling the same could be said about both of us.' He hadn't intended to stray into the political arena, especially when things had been going so well. He got up and pulled a six-pack of beer out of the carrier bag. They were still cold. He handed her one. She took it and ripped off the pull top, then took a long swig from the can. He watched the act of class betrayal, amused. From his new vantage point leaning against the sink, he said, 'So now your turn. Tell me about your childhood?'

She shrugged. 'There's nothing to tell. You got it in one. Middle-class child suffocated by respectability packs her embryonic socialist ideals in a big red spotted handkerchief, and heads out for the real world, spending a couple of years en route at a redbrick university learning the language.'

'Simple as that?'

She smiled. 'What do you think?'

'Were you born in London?'

'Yep. Born and bred. A desirable little semi in the less salubrious quarter of Shepherds Bush – in the years before the BBC gentrified the place.'

'What about your parents?'

She wrinkled her nose. 'Let's see – how shall I put it? Very nice to me, very unpleasant to each other. I think they were what was known as "an early casualty of our alarming post-war divorce statistics".'

'That was hardly the apogee of respectability.'

'You should have seen what came next.'

'How old were you?'

'Old enough. My mother remarried a couple of years later, when I was in my early teens. They now live in Ruislip.' She handled the word as if it were a soiled dishcloth.

'And your father?'

'He made a lot of money, and then lost it again. It's a habit he has. He lives in the Canary Islands now. Runs a hotel and watering hole on Lanzarote.'

'Alone?'

'Aaah, now that's an interesting one. For the purposes of my mother's morality, yes. There's a lady, but no ring.'

'Do you see him?'

'Not too often. He's one of those men who weren't really cut out to have children. I think it would have been O.K. if I'd come out of the womb fully grown. It was the early stuff he couldn't handle. Can't blame him really.'

She was having a good time, he thought. Bright-eyed, judging every ball and sending it spinning with a deliberate sense of panache. The strangest things, it seemed, turned her on.

'Do I gather that you like your father more than your mother?'

'You gather that I like my stepfather least of all. And since he now lives with my mother, that has, over the years, strained communication somewhat, yes.'

'So you don't see them either?'

'Nope.'

'What would they make of all this?'

She rolled her eyes to heaven. 'God only know. They gave up on me a long time ago. He's a headmaster. She used to be a teacher until he plucked her out of the staffroom to share his life and prejudices. They both have an instinctive - or in his case pathological - regard for authority. Need I say more? This one would crack the thermometer.'

'What about brothers and sisters?'

'One half brother. Fourteen years old. The last I heard he was in line for canonization. Loving, obedient, hard-working - the perfect child. A gift from heaven after me.'

'Sounds to me like a clear case of usurped maternal affection. How old were you when he was born?'

'Aaaah.' She pointed an accusing finger at him. 'I wondered when we'd get to the amateur psychiatrist bit. What's this one - the old politics as a product of upbringing theory? In which case what did your parents do to drive you from the northern nest?'

He took a sip of beer. 'I think I responded to economic climate as much as anything,' he said carefully. 'They always brought me up to believe ability and education gave you the keys of the city.' The truth, but it sounds so pompous, he thought. She's bound to stomp on it.

'Sure, except when you get inside and find the keys don't fit all the doors. Some are still marked By Birth Only. You know, the trouble with your theory is that it's only constructed to fit your set of politics. And your politics have nothing to do with class.

'According to you there's only two sets of people in the world, the fucked and the unfucked. The unfucked, such as yourself, succeed, and the fucked - well, they don't deserve to get anywhere. The only little fly in the ointment is the disturbing rate of increase among the fucked, which of course has nothing to do with anything as political as government policy.'

He detected the signs of conversational escalation and considered diversion tactics. He didn't agree with her views – nor indeed with those she attributed to him – but he had to admit to a certain sneaking admiration for the vigour and tenacity with which she expressed them. He used to enjoy debate. What had happened to him? Maybe he was out of practice. Or maybe he had been spending far too much time with people who agreed with him. Josie was a pain at times, but he did find her, well, yes, stimulating.

He pulled out another beer and handed it to her. 'Let's go back to Eamonn Andrews. What did you do before you were a tour guide?'

She followed him back into neutral territory. 'Not a whole lot. I was abroad, travelling for a while.'

'Where?'

'Oh, here and there. America and further south. Working, moving, travelling for a while.'

'On your own?'

'Yes. Don't sound too impressed. It's not such a big deal any more. You don't have to be Freya Stark to catch a Greyhound these days. And do you know what you're going to say next?'

He shook his head. 'No. Tell me.'

'You're going to tell me that it's interesting how I've never done a proper job in my life. And how I'd maybe learn more about the world if I operated inside it for a while.'

'To which your reply would be?'

'That you don't need to do something to know it's fucked. And that I'm getting hungry. Maybe we should stop this interrogation in favour of supper. We'll both argue better on full stomachs.'

In the event he offered to cook while she went for a walk. He fried up some onions and bacon for an omelette. The stove spat and smoked so much that he was forced to open the door to let in some air. Outside it was a fiery sunset. He turned off the heat, took his beer and sat on the caravan steps. Clouds of midges danced in front of him. He thought about his father. It was true they didn't talk much about what he did. But then he didn't go home all that often. If his father had been disappointed, he had never let it show. He already had one son following in his footsteps. Probably he'd expected one or the other of them to make the move away. He tried to imagine having a conversation about it, but the picture wouldn't come. He'd never talked that way to his father. Probably the old man would be as embarrassed as he would. It would be like discussing his private life. They never talked about that either.

Except maybe for a comment a couple of years ago – about when he was going to settle down. But that had been his mother. Just after he had met Penny and they had gone home for a weekend. He'd sidestepped the question, and talked about the need to consolidate work first. No more was said, but the next time he and Penny went up they stayed in a hotel to avoid the question of separate bedrooms. He wondered how Josie would have dealt with such a situation. The thought made him smile. Confrontation versus compromise. Maybe they were both a little blind to the virtues of the other. He remembered her comment about her family – 'This one would crack the thermometer'. What about his parents? What about Penny? It didn't bear thinking about. He got up and went back to the stove. By the time she got back the meal was ready.

'Where did you go?'

'To the beach. I came back via the phone booth. Called Joshua but he wasn't in.'

'He did say late tonight.'

'Yeah, I know. It was just a thought.'

He brought the food to the table and they ate, splitting another beer between them. She was quieter than before, either that or more distracted.

'You tired?' he asked at last.

She shrugged, not looking up from her plate. 'A bit. I was wondering what was happening in London. What card Coulton's going to play next.'

'We'll know soon enough. Look on the bright side. Maybe Joshua will have come up with some answers. Tomorrow night by this time we might be home and dry.'

She glanced at him and frowned. Then with an unexpected seriousness in her voice she said, 'We really are different, William. Do you know that?'

'Yes,' he replied, matching her tone. 'But that doesn't mean we can't find some middle ground, does it?'

She shook her head. 'It'll always be temporary, that's all. You'll always go on believing the best, and I'll go on believing the worst. The trouble with you is you're more interested in your ambition than in finding out the truth. Think about what you just said. You still wish in your heart of hearts that this whole thing was just some terrible mistake that would go away leaving you free to step back where you were before.'

'And what's so terrible about that? What exactly is so contemptible about normality?'

'I'll tell you what's so terrible. It's about complacency. You don't have any doubts, William. You just fit in. You do your "good job", manage people so that no one causes any trouble - so the status quo continues unruffled. You're a conservative - in the original sense of the word. You may be more enlightened than most of them, but that's still what you are. You want to keep things as they are. I want to change them. We're on different sides of a chasm. It's as simple as that.'

'And as far as you're concerned the chasm has got nothing to do with your fear of fitting in?'

'It isn't about fear. It's about anger.'

'Anger versus complacency, eh Josie? Is that it? And you say it's me who sees things in black and white.'

They sat grimly across the formica top. Neither of them spoke. Eventually she got up and took his plate. He tried one last time. 'What's the matter? You afraid you'll catch something from me? A sudden bout of compromise? I shouldn't worry. I think you're immune.'

'Yeah well, why don't we keep our cups and cutlery, just in case?'

She went over and began the washing up. It was almost dark outside. He drew the curtains and looked through the library. One of the old Penguins turned out to be *Rogue Male* by Geoffrey Household. Hardly the best book for assuaging paranoia. He began re-reading it anyway. He had reached the pursuit in the underground when his watch bleeped twelve. She was sitting at the kitchen table flicking aimlessly through the stack of women's magazines.

'You coming?' he said.

She followed him out. They walked through the sleeping site to the phone booth outside the office. She held the door open while he dialled. There was no reply. They waited five minutes, then tried again. So much for their progress report. In this case no news was not good news.

Back in the caravan William pulled out the sofa to form a double bed. Josie took a tightly rolled sleeping bag out of her bag. 'Where do you want to sleep?' she asked.

'I don't mind. You choose.'

'O.K. I'll take the single. You stay there.'

She went to the sink to brush her teeth, and he lay on the bed with his back to her, reading. When he looked round she was already in the bag, curled away from him with her eyes closed.

'You sure you don't want a sheet?' he said. 'You might be too hot in there.'

'I'm fine,' she said, not opening her eyes. 'Whoever wakes first calls Josh, right? Goodnight.'

He turned out the light, pulled off his trousers and T-shirt and tucked a sheet around him. The bed was unexpectedly comfortable. He lay for a while watching the tin roof, until he felt drowsy and turned over on his side. In the bunk on the other side of the room Josie opened her eyes and blinked in the darkness.

Chapter Twelve

In London Joshua was on his way home. A hundred feet underground somewhere between Monument and Tower Hill his watch bleeped twelve. That meant he would miss their call. Maybe, under the circumstances, that was no bad thing. At least they would sleep well tonight. On his lap tomorrow's edition carried two inches of newsprint that would have brought insomnia.

The story wasn't written by Josh. His own contribution to the enlightenment of the nation was to be found near the bottom of page five, under the headline 'Tighten your bottles'. It was about the last ditch attempt by dairy companies to save, through retrenchment and an aggressive marketing campaign, that threatened species, the British milkman. To write those hundred words had taken him a couple of dozen phone calls and most of the day. In between, he pursued the Highgate story. It had been a frustrating experience.

First Coulton. He lit a cigarette and dialled the number on the card. It did not exist. A long, high whine drilled into his ear. Number unobtainable. The operator confirmed. The number had been disconnected. When? He knew the answer to that. Some time between eleven last night and now. Why? The operator couldn't tell him. He would have to go through to accounts. Joshua didn't bother. Brick wall. Surprise surprise.

He studied the card Josie had given him. Plain white, with Chief Inspector Coulton, Anti-terrorist Branch printed on it. Nothing else. The telephone number had been added later, written by hand.

For his next inquiry Joshua would need a cover story. He thought for a moment, then rang Scotland Yard.

'Press Office.'

'Hello, this is the *Daily Post*. We were doing a story about –'

'Can I have your name please?'

He'd hoped they wouldn't ask that, knowing they probably would; it was routine. He was tempted to impersonate one of the crime people, but you never knew, they might recognize the voice.

'Barnes. I was interviewing one of your officers a week ago, and I inadvertently went off with his fountain pen. It seems to be quite a special pen, embossed with his name, a presentation, and I'd like to send it back to him. I wonder if you could tell me where he's attached?'

'Why don't you contact the station where you met him?'

Joshua allowed a slight do-you-think-I-haven't-thought-of-that? tone to enter his voice. 'I'll tell you. It was down at Fords. A story about policemen on the picket lines, effects on the family, that sort of thing. I checked with Dagenham. They've never heard of him. He must have been with a unit from elsewhere in the Met.'

'O.K. Hold on a minute.' There had in fact been such a story in the *Post*, though Joshua hadn't worked on it. 'What's the name?'

Joshua told him, and waited.

'We have a WPC Coulton at Edgware. Presumably not your man. A Sergeant Coulton, traffic duty in Westminster. That's all. Sure the spelling's right? In that case, you could try City Police, or Kent or Essex. All right?'

So much for Coulton. Joshua gave up, and applied himself to De Villiers.

It ought to have been more promising. De Villiers was, unlike Coulton, a real person with the address of a house where he actually lived. It was ex-directory, not that Joshua had expected any different. He didn't really want to talk to De Villiers, he wanted someone to tell him about him. The foreign desk gave high priority to South Africa. Peter Wilkinson had good enough contacts to have got himself banned from visiting. But Peter was not in the office. He was on leave and no one was answering his home phone number. De Villiers, Joshua recalled, was a businessman. There might be a listing in the Institute of Directors or some such reference book, and he could check for old cuttings in the library. But that would take a couple of hours, and the plight of Britain's milkmen called. He decided to do that first thing in the morning.

Next Mrs O'Grady. Here British Telecom was much more helpful. The green London directory yielded a harvest of nine M. O'Gradys. He went through the list. He was obviously not the first journalist to have done so. The woman who answered the fourth number had no trouble expressing her feelings on the matter.

'Look. You're the tenth person I've had ringing up in the last two days. My husband is a chartered surveyor. He is alive and well and he has absolutely nothing to do with the Royal Highgate Hospital. I daresay you're another newspaperman looking to pester the poor woman. If I were her I wouldn't answer the phone.'

The real Mrs O'Grady had apparently taken her advice. Working on the assumption that O'Grady had lived near his work, Joshua narrowed the quest down to two possible numbers. He called them on the hour, every hour. At four the N16 number answered. Millicent O'Grady was a middle-aged sounding woman, widowed ten years ago, chatty. Joshua extracted himself smoothly. That left the NW5 address. At five he got a response. It was a girl's voice. He asked to speak to Mrs Malcolm O'Grady. She left the phone, and in the background he heard angry voices but no actual words. A moment later the girl returned.

'Mam isn't in. Goodbye.' The line went dead.

He dialled the number again. It rang and rang. He imagined the telephone on a hall table, the girl standing watching it, her mother at the kitchen table staring into space, shutters down to block out the sound. It was a really shitty job sometimes, being a journalist. Thank God he didn't work for one of the down-market tabloids. In the battle of wills she won. He put down the phone and thought of how she must be feeling. He rolled a piece of headed letter paper into the typewriter. Maybe a little gentle formality would not go amiss. A letter of introduction before the finger on the doorbell. His shift didn't start till midday tomorrow. He could arrive at the O'Grady's minutes after the postman.

Tomorrow. That left today. Afternoon turned into early evening. He completed the milk story and wondered what to do next. He counted the stubs in the ashtray. Seventeen. So much for his attempt to cut down. Seventeen in six hours. £2 a day. £14 a week. £728 a year. Three return airline tickets to new York. A trip down the Nile. It was all a question of relative needs. He lit another. Maybe he should call it quits, go home and wait for their call. It was almost eight o'clock.

He was about to leave when he noticed a buzz in the office.

'What's up?' he asked Bill Maitland on the news desk.

'Press Conference. Scotland Yard.'

James Norton, a crime reporter who had been covering the bombing, was among those leaving. Joshua tagged along. It wasn't his story. On the other hand he had a press card and his shift was ended. No one was going to question what he was doing there.

He sat at the back and took down the statement in shorthand. When he heard it, he realized that all along he'd been expecting it. But had she?

Back at the office he slipped out for a pizza, then picked up the first edition soon after eleven, and headed for home. He slept badly and awoke at six, waiting for the call.

It came at eight thirty. He was sitting with a cup of coffee looking down at the small, blurred face on the front page. 'Girl Wanted for Questioning in Highgate Bomb Attack.' After the pips the edge in William's voice gave him away. He too had read it.

'Hello – Joshua? Thank God you're there. Have you seen the papers?'

'Yeah, I was there when they wrote the story. It came through late last night. That's why I missed your call. There was a last-minute press conference to make the morning papers.'

'What happened?'

'You know as much as I do. You've seen the statement. All I can tell you is they sounded very pleased with themselves. As if they know what they're doing. They're not saying what they've got, but they certainly gave the impression it was worth having.'

'But they're not accusing her directly. They just want her for questioning.'

'Cold comfort, William. We all know what those words mean.'

'But why her?'

'Your guess is as good as mine. I don't know what they know. How is she?'

'How do you expect? A mixture of ice and fire; really scared and trying to cover up with anger. I can't talk to her. I don't know what to say. How about you? Have you found anything?'

Joshua briefly described the brick walls. He could feel William's spirits falling. 'Listen, it's par for the course. I hardly expected the answers to fall into my lap. I'm going to try to see Mrs O'Grady today. This latest news might make her more receptive. And there's bound to be more on De Villiers. Give me another day.'

'So you don't think she should go to the police?'

'Do you?'

'I don't know. It just seems crazy not to do something. The longer she doesn't come forward, the more it looks as if she's got something to hide.'

'Try telling her that.'

'I have,' he said with feeling.

'Well, I think like it or not it's her decision. Where are you?'

William explained.

'That's good. Stay where you are. And keep her out of sight. If you were both staying in a caravan with no direct access to news, you could always claim ignorance later.'

'Yes, but how much later?'

'I can't answer that, William. Listen, let's get to the end of today and see where we are. I'll have the photos back by then. Then we might really be in business. Look after her. Tell her not to worry. It'll be O.K.'

'I'll tell her. But it's easier said than done. I'll call you later. Maybe around six or seven. Good luck.'

'You too.'

William put the receiver down. What next? Back up the hill into the lion's den? He did not relish the idea. The day so far had been terrible.

Not that the night had been much better. He had slept in broken sections, a city dweller unnerved by the rustling silence of the countryside. Each time he surfaced he had the impression of a similar restlessness coming from her. In the first light of dawn he awoke with a feeling of being watched – Josie in her T-shirt sitting on the edge of her bed, regarding him anxiously. He flashed in and out of sleep. She was gone. It could have been a dream. Or a premonition of the morning.

He was pulled out of sleep by the sound of rapid machine-gun fire above him. Startled, he opened his eyes. Nothing. Then it came again, from right above his head, the staccato pattern of a bird running back and forth across the tin roof. A movement caught his eye. Josie, up and dressed and drinking a cup of tea. She went over and poured him some too, putting the cup on the floor beside him. 'I'm going to the phone box,' she said.

'Give me a minute. I'll come with you.'

She waited. It was almost eight o'clock. He switched on the radio for the news. He was dressed and standing by the sink when the voice from the box made its solemn announcement. At first he found it hard to take in. He stood transfixed, hearing her name and description, but thinking all the while they were talking about someone else. There must be some mistake. When finally he shook himself back into reality and pressed the off-switch, plunging them into silence again, the air was already charged with her vibrations. She had not moved, she was sitting exactly as before, eyes fixed on the formica top in front of her, but something had changed, there was a frozen quality to her body. He had known then that nothing he might say would penetrate.

Nevertheless he had to try. 'There must be an explanation for it,' he said gently, sitting down opposite her and putting his hand over hers. She did not respond. When she did lift her head, she looked as if someone had slapped her. In the second before the anger broke he knew she was frightened.

'I can't believe it,' she said, her voice hoarse and a grim little smile stretching her lips. 'I can't believe it. I've been set up.' The fire grew. 'They've set me up. Of course. Jesus, I ought to have known. If they can't get me one way they'll get me another.'

He thought of things he might say to comfort her, but his instinct told him not to try. It wasn't words that were needed, it was action. 'Josie,' he said firmly. 'Before anything else we have to call Joshua. Whatever this is all about, he'll be bound to know more than we do. It's pointless working yourself up into a state until we know all the facts.' Her look told him just how naive she thought he was, but he persevered. 'There could be any number of explanations. Don't jump to conclusions, not yet. Let's talk to Joshua first. Are you going to stay here, or are you going to come with me?'

The next glance heralded the return of the ice age.

'In the circumstances coming with you might be a trifle brainless, wouldn't you say? Since it's highly likely that by now my picture is plastered all over the dailies. I think I'd prefer to wait a little before I go out and give myself up.'

He still couldn't quite grasp it. What if the newspaper stand on the camp site really was a gallery of Josies? It didn't bear thinking about. He laced his shoes quickly and headed for the door. 'Don't worry,' he said as he left. 'We're in this together, remember that.'

The face that stared out at him from the row of newspapers in the camp shop was small and fuzzy, cropped down from a larger picture to single her out. It looked nothing like her at all. She could have walked into the store that very moment and bought up every paper on the rack and no one would have recognized her. Surely? It didn't make him feel any better. Neither did the phone call to Joshua. It seemed the only people who were getting anywhere were the police. 'We are very anxious to talk to anyone who knows her whereabouts.' That meant him. And by now they must know that he too was not to be found. The man waiting in his office yesterday morning – he imagined a figure in a summer raincoat flicking open an ID card and Karen's face lighting up with astonishment. He heard her babbling something about mysterious phone calls from a woman in a callbox who wouldn't leave her name, and then Mr Stevens's sudden indisposition. He watched in horror the whispered conversations, the rumour and speculation, from the shop floor of Actonics up to the board room, the canteens and loos . . .

He left the telephone booth behind, fleeing from the vision back up the hill to the safety of the caravan.

She had moved from the table and now huddled in a corner of the divan, the curtains drawn again. 'Look after her, William.' It was going to be like pulling teeth. She started up as he entered.

'It's all right. It's only me.' He tossed the papers down in front of her. She fell upon them greedily, scouring the photographs. 'We've nothing to worry about,' he said lightly. 'Your own mother wouldn't recognize you. You look like something that followed Charles Manson.'

'What did Joshua say?'

He told her, softening the bit about the police confidence, making the very lack of progress sound hopeful.

'And the photos?'

'He's picking them up today. We'll just have to wait.'

He moved to the window and started to pull back the curtain.

'No. Don't open them,' she snapped. 'Someone might see us.'

He sighed. 'Josie, there's no one here. We're right at the top of the damn cliff. On our own. We're safe. And I'm not going to sit all day incarcerated in this tin furnace without some fresh air.'

She said nothing. He drew back the curtains. The sunshine blasted in. She scowled and looked away.

'Well,' he said with more patience than he felt. 'I'm going to make breakfast. We'll both feel better when we've eaten.'

Not so. The meal passed in total silence. She ate a few mouthfuls, then pushed her plate away from her and sat back watching him sullenly. It was like having a defiant child in the room, careless with its energies, deliberately out to antagonize. Equally deliberately he ignored her. After breakfast they retired to opposite sides of the caravan, like sparring partners limbering up for the next round. He read the papers. There was nothing of much interest. The business pages made him feel homesick. Later, how would he account for his absence? He hadn't done anything wrong. Oh yes? he thought gloomily. Only obstructed the course of justice, that's all. He put the paper down hurriedly. No comfort there. He found her staring at him.

'Listen,' he said quietly. 'I know how you must feel. But I think you should try and relax. There's nothing we can do, and the next twenty-four hours are going to be purgatory if you keep winding yourself up like this.'

'It's not your face on the front page.'

No, not purgatory. Hell. He took a deep breath. 'Well, let's talk about why it isn't. Clearly that disturbs you no end. What do you think they've got on you that they haven't got on me?'

'How should I know? Maybe it's your respectability. They obviously think I'm some closet revolutionary who planted the bomb and just took you along for good cover. "Innocent Businessman Duped by Astrid Proll." Take your pick. There are a number of reasons.'

'But why should they be so eager to pin something on *you*?'

'What do you mean?'

'I don't know. I just wondered if there might be anything about you that aroused their suspicions?'

'What are you trying to say, William? Spit it out.'

It was now or never. 'I'm asking you if you've ever been in trouble with the police before?'

She snorted a laugh. 'Of course. I might have known. Did I really forget to mention that I'd done four years for GBH?'

'I'm serious, Josie.'

'Yeah, and so am I. So much for trust and solidarity. Well, since you already feel you know, I might as well tell you. I once hit a policeman during an anti-National Front rally.'

'What happened?'

'He hit me back and in the commotion I got away. But if it makes you feel any better, it was clearly a crime. I would have been done for it if he'd caught me. Come to think of it, I thought that inspector looked familiar. Probably this whole thing is some elaborate form of police revenge. In which case there's nothing more to worry about – you might as well catch the next train back to your precious Actonics, and I'll slip into the nearest town and give myself up.'

'Josie, don't be so defensive. Tearing bits of flesh off one another isn't going to help either of us. We're in this together, remember?'

'Are we?'

There it was. The beginnings of the wedge between them. There was a small but nasty silence. Maybe they would do better after a little separation.

'Would you prefer to be on your own for a while?'

She stared at him. 'Well, I'm not going anywhere, if that's what you mean.'

He stood up. 'O.K. then, I will. I'll go down to the café. Have a cup of tea, go for a walk. Will you be all right?'

'Oh sure. I'll arrange a coffee morning. Invite all the ladies on the hill.'

Enough, he thought. Enough. Why did everything have to be said in capital letters. No wonder you're a loner. No one can take the insults. 'Very well then. I'll leave you to it.' He walked towards the door.

'Fine.'

The word whizzed across the room fast and hard. He turned his back before it hit him. 'I'll probably be a couple of hours.' He closed the door quickly so as not to hear her reply.

Down at the shop it was midsummer madness. Women heaved overflowing boxes out of the doors while fathers stayed outside bribing children with ice cream cones. In the café he ordered a pot of tea, but was forced to share the table with a mother and child. The latter spent most of the meal regurgitating his scrambled egg and grinning, mouth full, in his direction. At the best of times William was not the greatest fan of the under-fives. And this was far from the best of times.

He paid his bill and left. He started walking, no matter where, just to get away from the people. Everyone else was heading for the beach. He took the opposite path, towards the track that rose up from the camp site over the hill inland.

For the first twenty minutes he went at it hard, sweating out his frustration, concentrating on the rhythm of his steps and nothing else. The hill flattened out, and he was rewarded with a spectacular view out over the cliffs to bays and promontories stretching twenty miles to the south west. The scenery did not soothe him. If he'd hoped the exercise would settle his anger, he was mistaken. If anything it fuelled it further. At the root of it was the feeling that he had been manipulated. Somehow, against his better judgement, he had allowed her to pull him into this vortex of trouble. She had managed to make him feel responsible for her, protective of her, gullible to her paranoias. And what had he gained? The threat of violence, the possibility of arrest, and the ruin of his professional credibility. And had she appreciated his sacrifice? Not at all. Her thoughts were entirely for her own skin. She wasn't interested in him, and neither did she care to make any attempt to control her own moods. It was insupportable.

He turned his face from the shining sea and plodded onwards. His shirt was sticking to his armpits. It was incredibly hot. Yet another scorching, magnificent day, the kind that makes you forget the customary dreariness of the English summer. It had been hot that very first evening on Archway roundabout, he recalled. In fact, with the exception of the thunderstorm two nights ago, it had been like this for weeks. The hottest summer, the weathermen must be saying because they always did, since records began. The thought did nothing to uplift him.

The path turned inland, through a copse of hawthorn. He was moving less frantically now, but his mind was still in the caravan, not on the uneven surface of the narrow path. Suddenly he was gone, stumbling on a loose stone and pitching headlong. His hand, outstretched to save him from bruising, landed in a thistle. He lay there, scratched and cursing.

Eventually the fit of spleen passed, and he found himself quieter, released from the manic energy of the walk. He began to feel less possessed. He found he had no inclination to get up. He pulled himself into a more comfortable position, hoisting his head onto a conveniently smooth ridge of grass just off the path. Lassitude took over. It was restful here, his body moulded by the ground and shielded from the direct sun by an overhanging tree. He unbuttoned his shirt and let his hands fall back onto the ground. What a sight he would make should anyone chance along. It struck him as a metaphor for his situation: legless, exposed and out of control. Right now it didn't seem to matter. He looked absurd, but so what? Life was absurd. Why put all our energy into trying to pretend otherwise?

Philosophical detachment led to a quieter logic. How had he got himself into this? When he looked back over the past few days, no single act could be blamed. At each point his decisions had been reasonable. Yet they couldn't have been, because here he was, standing outside the world and looking in at it through a glass wall, divided, in exile.

Except of course that she wouldn't see it that way. This very dislocation would strike her as familiar. She could afford to take time off from normal life to follow the random thread of adventure. And adventure it was for her, she was relishing every minute, even those when she was scared out of her wits. After all, she had nothing to lose. But what about him? What was in it for him? Why should it be he that was left holding her hand while she baited the dragon?

He felt like a mechanic who, having assembled the parts in strict accordance with the instructions, finds the machine stubbornly refuses to work. He was determined to get to the bottom of the contradiction. Surely there had to be a moment when he had made a mistake, when, if he'd acted differently, things would have gone another way? He thought back to that strange morning in the hotel café. His instinct then had been that it would be wrong to run away. The answer, he'd been sure, lay in proper help. But his suggestion had been ridiculed. 'A solicitor! God, you're so naive, William.' So instead there was Joshua – an ear to the ground but hearing nothing. And now they were as deeply implicated as they had ever been – in fact, more so. A solicitor would have been different. They would have known their rights. They would be in some contact with the law. Their truth would have been in his hands before the magistrate signed the warrant. There would have been proof of their goodwill. Yes, it should have been a solicitor. He should have held out against her raging.

But maybe it wasn't too late. What if he went and talked to someone? The very idea made him feel in control again. He looked at his watch. Twelve forty-five. He would not return yet. Better to let the ashes of her anger cool a little. He turned over in the grass, making himself more comfortable. His resolution relaxed him. He began to envisage himself sitting opposite Peter Marshall in his cosy office in Holborn, sipping tea and sorting out strategy. Perhaps there was a road back to reality. He stretched, turned over on his side and closed his eyes.

The next thing he knew it was late afternoon and the sun had travelled westwards, pushing tree shadows ahead of it and causing light streams to run over his eyes. He sat up abruptly, guilty at the ease of his slumber and the memory of Josie in her hot little cave. He got up and brushed his clothes down. On the way back he passed the phone booth. Worth seeing if Josh was back. The phone rang a long time. He was about to hang up when a voice answered. It sounded out of breath.

'I just got in,' he explained. 'I heard the phone from outside the door. You're early.'

'Any news?'

At the other end of the line he thought he detected a slight hesitation, but maybe it was just a clutching for breath. 'I've picked up the photos. They're not good. You can see two people in the foreground, sure, but it's dark and the rain blurs things.'

'We wouldn't recognize him?'

'*You* might. But you'd be hard pushed to use them as evidence.'

It should have been depressing, but instead it offered William the relief of confirmation. She has to go to the police, he thought. Or at least, I have to go to my solicitor. Joshua continued talking. He would, he said, keep trying to reach Mrs O'Grady and to find out more about De Villiers. There were South African émigrés to contact, the African National Congress, Anti-Apartheid, and so on. William found his optimism a little strained.

'So we still have to wait?'

'Unless you have a better idea.'

William opened his mouth, then closed it again. Joshua wouldn't approve, and he didn't feel like discussing it. 'I'll call you tomorrow. Late maybe. All right?'

'O.K. How are things your end?'

'I've been on better holidays.'

'Don't let her get you down. Her bark is worse than her bite.'

'Thanks for telling me.'

Inside the caravan it was hot and stuffy. She was lying face down on the bed, sleeping apparently. He fixed himself some cheese on toast, moving carefully so as not to disturb her. When he sat down on the sofa she faced him, knees drawn up, hands clasping her stomach. He had the uncomfortable feeling she hadn't been asleep after all, just waiting.

'Was it nice out there?'

The pleasantry cost her, he could see. He resolved to tackle this gently. After all, he wasn't the only one to have had a day to think.

'Great.'

'What did you do?'

'I went for a walk and fell asleep on the grass.'

'Sounds idyllic.'

'How about you?'

'As you see.'

'Are you all right?'

'Oh yes,' she said airily. She was being ironic? Reproachful? Or simply self-contained? 'I just need to eat, that's all.'

'Can I get you something?'

'That's O.K. I'll do it myself.'

She stood, a bit painfully, made herself some milky coffee and returned to the bed. She sat cross-legged, cup and saucer beside her. William waited for it to tip over, spilling hot coffee over the sheet and her bare legs. For some reason it didn't.

'Josie, I've something to tell you. I've spoken to Joshua again.'

She frowned, as if she smelled the bad news on his breath. 'What did he say?'

He told her. She listened in silence, her eyes on his face. When he finished the look continued. 'And?'

'And what?'

'And you've something else to tell me, I think.'

She was unnervingly quiet, the stillness more threatening than any agitation. He reviewed his decision and found it correct. So why the reluctance? It could only be attributed to cowardice. Come on, William. Say it.

'Yes, I have. I've come to a decision.'

'Oh yes? And am I privileged to know what it is?'

Knives rustled in the undergrowth. This was not to be without bloodshed. He wrapped his cloak of selfrighteousness a little more tightly around him, and explained. He thought he did it rather well. At the end her face was impenetrable. He waited for the volcano to blow. After what seemed an age, he prompted:

'Josie?'

'You fucker,' she said softly. Her head whipped upwards. 'Just because it's not your head on the block. Just because . . .' She broke off, her voice trembling.

'Josie,' he said firmly. 'I'm only going to get some advice—'

'Advice!' The word exploded into the no-man's-land between bed and chair. 'Jesus, you're priceless. Advice from your solicitor. And what does he usually do for a living? Conveyancing? Divorce suits? Jobs for the boys? He probably wouldn't recognize a fit-up if they delivered it to him registered mail. You don't need to see him. I can tell you what he'll say. That we should go to the police. He'll tell you just what you want to hear. You don't want advice, William, you want an excuse for turning me in. Why bother with the journey? Why not shop me here and now? You still don't understand what we've stumbled into, do you? You just won't listen to the facts. You're so convinced the world is the way you see it that you really can't consider the possibility it might be otherwise. Well, I can. And I'm not trading my vision for yours. I don't suppose you remember the Angry Brigade. The police need a conviction. I doubt whether it matters if it's the right person. People go to jail every day for crimes they didn't commit. Why should you give a fuck so long as it's not you? And it isn't you. And that's just what your precious solicitor will tell you too.'

'Josie, I'm not going to give you up to the police.'

'So you say. Why should I trust you? You don't trust me.'

'That's nonsense. All I'm saying is there are limitations to our knowledge. There must be things I haven't thought of, that you and Joshua haven't thought of, for God's sake. It's a lawyer's job to do that. And he's good at his job.'

'Your faith is touching. But I don't believe you. You won't come back.'

'Don't be ridiculous. I'm not your father—' He stopped in mid-sentence. But the damage was done.

'Listen,' she shouted. The coffee slopped over the bed. She didn't notice. 'Don't start throwing your patronizing little home truths at me. My father! It's you that's been treating me like a child, from the first moment we met. Placating me, trying to "manage" me, to get me to grow up and see things the way "adults" do - i.e. people like you. It's been painfully obvious that's the only way you can handle women who have the audacity to challenge you. What the fuck do you mean - you're not my father? It's you that appointed yourself to that sanctimonious role, as a method of not having to take me seriously. If you don't want to be a father, the answer's simple - stop behaving like one.'

He knew he shouldn't join in. But he couldn't help it. 'All right, Josie. I will stop. But let's make it a deal. You stop behaving like a child every time someone dares to contradict you, and I'll stop feeling like I have to look after you. How dare you manipulate me into protecting you and then turn round and accuse me of being over-protective? It's monstrous.'

'Oh, don't be so fucking pompous.'

'Well, that's it. Fine. I resign. I will not be responsible for you any more. From now on we're just two adults on our own. And for politeness' sake, adult to adult, I'll tell you what I'm doing, so you can arrange your plans accordingly. Tomorrow I'm going to London to see my solicitor.'

'Fine.'

'Yes, fine. And tomorrow night I'll be back to tell you what he said.'

'Do as you please. Whether I'll be here when you get back is another matter.'

Chapter Thirteen

The wristwatch alarm was set for six. At five William was already staring at the ceiling, anticipating the day ahead, and before half past he was up and dressing carefully, so as not to disturb her. He wore his suit, taking toothbrush and razor with him. He could wash on the train. It would help mark the passage from outside the circumference back inside the circle.

He was about to scribble a note when he glanced towards her sleeping form. Except of course she wasn't asleep. He should have expected it. One way or another he was never alone with her. She was lying on her side, sleeping bag drawn up close, two fingers poking out to gather the folds close to her neck. The face was blank. He leaned his head to one side so their faces met at the same angle.

'Bye,' he whispered. 'I'll see you later.'

Her answer was to turn over and face the wall. He opened the door and stepped out into the light of day.

It was another misty, soft, summer morning, alive with the promise of heat. On the cliff in the distance a track-suited youth was failing to control a young retriever, man and dog in loud non-communication. William's spirits lifted. Behind him in the claustrophobia of the caravan lay confusion and anxiety; in front, equal uncertainty but at least the comfort of action being taken. A re-entry into the real world.

From the phone booth he called the taxi number which boasted service night and day. A sleepy voice answered. They agreed to meet by the crossroads in the village. In half an hour he was at Axminster station among a handful of commuters, gazing down the line into the distance, as the train hooted its gleeful passage through the Axe valley. His first-class day return bought him access to one of the old-fashioned separate compartments. It was not hard to find an empty one. He sat with his back to the engine. The train heaved forward. His eyes itched with lack of sleep. He closed them.

At Yeovil he was awakened by the sound of the door opening and two young executives coming in. He sat up and pulled a newspaper out of a plastic bag. Yesterday's, but no matter. They were smart: tidy haircuts and smooth leather briefcases. He felt their appraisal of him. The uniform was right, but he must strike them as oddly dishevelled. He hid behind his newspaper and they gradually lost interest. Snatches of their conversation penetrated during the next half hour.

'... But the plant's redundant. Hopelessly undercapitalized ... Should have gone to the market five years ago ... ten, more like. The MD's a clown ... gather the company secretary's a good man . . . What could he do? Management structure's top heavy. And geriatric ... So – a wholesale clearout? ... Only way. It'll take the wind out of the unions' sails ... We'll have to let go fifteen hundred, wouldn't you say? ... More like two thousand. Furniture market's dead ... What about kitchen fittings? That might be viable. Slimmed down, of course ... Redundancy payments? I think it'll have to be liquidation ... Poor bastards.'

Accountancy-babble. Two brash young men, intent on restructuring the world. He imagined Josie entering like an avenging angel, clawing through their received ideologies, no room for mercy or doubt. Their voices droned on. He left them to it.

Around Andover, washed and shaved, he passed a leisurely breakfast in the buffet car, and by ten he was at Waterloo. Back in London's instant familiarity he felt jaunty, again in control. Out on the concourse he headed for the nearest clump of phone booths. Then came the first shock. Peter Marshall, his solicitor, was on holiday.

'Mr Stevens, are you still there?'

'Yes, I'm here.'

'This is Julia Hitchens, Mr Marshall's assistant. I believe we met last year. Is there anything I can do? Or can I pass you on to one of the other partners?'

William thought about it. He imagined relating the situation to some elderly, incredulous lawyer whom he'd never met before. No. He had banked on Peter. They were friends. They understood each other. How bloody stupid of him not to have checked. He made one last stab.

'Is there any way I can reach him, do you know?' Peter had recently married into a not unwealthy family. There had been talk of a house in the country, he seemed to recall.

'No, I'm afraid he's travelling in the Algarve. He isn't due back for another two weeks, and we have no way of reaching him. I'm so sorry. If there's—'

'No. No, that's all right. It wasn't that important. I'll call again when he gets back, thanks.'

He replaced the receiver, wondering what to do next. Joshua? There was no point. There would be no fresh news overnight. And anyway, he'd talked to Josh already. His feet directed him towards the station bar. He had taken it for granted that Peter would see him. He realized with a touch of panic how out of touch with reality his thought processes had become. Suddenly, even more than before, he needed to confide in someone. Someone he could trust absolutely, and who knew him well enough not to suppose he was crazy.

A double brandy later his mind was made up. He returned to the phone booth and dialled a familiar number. It rang twice. He could see the phone on her sideboard. She would shake her head in that special way to dislodge a lock of hair before putting the receiver to her ear. It rang three times. She answered.

'Hello Penny,' he said. 'It's William.'

William had known Penny Koscinski for three years. It was the longest sexual relationship of his life. They met when she had just emerged from a painful semi-marriage. She was vehemently independent, determined to avoid the patterns to which she attributed past failures. This attitude had suited him very well. 'You know I'm not going to be faithful to you,' she declared the first time they went to bed. 'I should hope not,' he retorted. And he meant it. He had his own reasons for setting limits, based on a fear of possession rather than rejection. If you give too much, a small voice at the back of his head told him, you will have nothing left for yourself. An ex-lover had once put it more cruelly. 'You'll always keep an eye open for something better. You figure if you commit yourself now, you'll miss out later. One day you'll wake up and find that she – whoever she is – never actually turned up, and the rest of the world got tired of waiting for you.' Maybe there was something in that, but the butt end of affairs always disgorge some bitter half truths: it would be a very insecure man indeed who chose to believe all of them. And William was not insecure. He saw his reticence not as an emotional limitation, but more a statement of self-containment. He'd given it a lot of thought, and could make out a strong intellectual case for it. In the old days Penny had often agreed with it.

It had made a strong bond between them, but one that by its nature was temporary. Eventually one of them would see it not as a balance but a compromise, and that one was bound to be Penny, because her reserve was a matter of circumstance, not character. Once her memory of pain had lifted, so would her fear. She would ask more of life, and therefore of him. If he'd thought about it more, he would have seen it coming, but for a while he was just too busy feeling good. Certainly the crisis took its time arriving. They had perfect companionship, good sex, physical ease and an intellectual parity. They enjoyed the same things, and they seldom rowed. At first it was hard for her to pin down her frustration. 'But where are we going, William?' she asked in fifty different ways. 'It's a mystery tour,' he'd reply. 'Why ask me? I'm only the other passenger.'

She began to realize that what for her was only a stage on the journey was for him the destination. Her restlessness became insistent.

'So what is it you want?' he would ask.

'I don't know. But not this.'

'Do you want us to live together, is that it?'

'Sometimes. But it's not as simple as that.'

'Or to have children?'

'It crosses my mind.'

'I thought you'd decided you never wanted that.'

'Maybe I did. People change. It's not a crime.'

'Well, is that it? Is that the problem?'

'I don't think so, no. Not necessarily. There isn't just *one* answer. I may not want those things. I just need to feel they're possible. That you're open to the possibility of change. And you're not. You're closed, William. Do you know how closed you are?'

With each discussion more cracks in the ice began to show. Where once they could tease each other out of moods, now there were frozen silences and edges of anger. There were still moments of closeness, but they were never lasting. 'I've never been further with anyone else,' he told her. 'Yes,' she replied, 'but I have.'

It seemed like the end. They didn't want to admit failure, but nor could either of them find within them a way of carrying on. They decided at last on a temporary separation.

Until this day William had not seen or spoken to Penny for seven weeks.

At one he presented himself outside her flat. She lived in the upper maisonette of a Holland Park terrace, bought outright with money inherited on the death of her parents five years before. With its chocolate brown frontage, white woodwork and shiny black ironwork, it was very pretty - or ostentatiously chic - William never could decide which.

He rang the bell, the answerphone buzzed and the door yawned open. He was left to find his own way upstairs. She was waiting for him on the landing.

'Hello, William.'

She stood three feet away, beyond his reach. She looked good, as if she had made an effort for him. But then didn't she always look like that? Seven weeks apart and five days in Josie's company seemed to have blurred his memory.

'I'm sorry,' he said. 'Did I drag you home from work?'

'No, I was coming anyway. There isn't a lot on at the moment. You're not working today either?'

' . . . Er, no.'

He followed her into the sitting room. They sat at opposite ends of the sofa, a splendid 1930s chesterfield, recently re-upholstered. He noticed a few new acquisitions: an oak chest, a small Chinese lacquer table.

'Very nice,' he said.

'It's just stock.'

Penny worked in the antiques trade, which enabled her to grace the apartment with an ever-changing collection of exquisite period pieces. He had always marvelled at how she managed to live in such volatile surroundings. The furniture and objects he owned held a kind of stubborn importance for him, a statement of who he was and his roots in London. He put a lot of thought into the things he bought, and he needed to regard them as permanent. Penny used to mock this quality in him, playfully deriding it as an example of his northern homeliness coming out. The front room syndrome, she called it. He envied her more casual approach, knowing he would never share it. He understood the envy. She came from a moneyed family, central European émigrés who had got out when you could still take your assets with you. They had proved they could survive anywhere. She was brought up to believe that you didn't need the security of possessions to give you status. His parents would have

been shaken by her easy attitude to such things. When they'd met her he'd made sure it was on their ground not hers. He needn't have worried. They had liked her. Of course. She was very likeable.

She sat still now, waiting.

'What have you been doing?' he asked.

'Reading Proust. Planning a world trip. Reconstructing my life. Nothing special. How about you?'

'The same. Work. Actonics are opening a new factory in the midlands next year. They want me to switch to general management and go up and run it.'

'The chance you've been waiting for. Want to go?'

'No idea.'

She was turned slightly away from him, and he noticed her profile: the beginnings of the double chin he used to tease her about, the straight back, almost too stiff to take it as poise, the familiar slim fingers resting on her pressed cotton skirt. How conventionally she dresses, he thought. I never noticed.

'What is it, William?'

Now that he was back in Penny's home the caravan seemed another lifetime. Did it tempt him, that other reality? It was difficult to say. LBJ, as he had nicknamed it - Life Before Josie. How could he possibly begin to explain?

'Why have you come? Tell me,' she persisted.

She seemed so calm, so attentive. He was drawn to it. 'I need your help.' The words came tumbling out, too fast, odd sounding.

'Something's wrong. Is it your parents?'

'No, no, it's nothing to do with them. Although –' It was useless trying to preface it. He plunged in. 'Does the name Josephine Ridley mean anything to you?'

She thought for a moment. 'No.'

'It's been in the headlines recently.'

Her look was mildly chastening, saying, you know I don't read the papers much. Then: 'Oh yes, I think I saw it on the news on TV. Some kind of terrorist, isn't she?'

He winced. 'Not exactly. I've been with her for the past two days.'

'What?'

He repeated it. Still she had trouble. 'With her?'

'Yes.'

'But where?'

'On the run.' The words sounded comic and melodramatic amidst the rugs and the clocks.

'I think you'd better start at the beginning.'

He told the whole story. She said nothing at first. Her body seemed more relaxed, the backbone less held and rigid. It seemed to him she was having trouble finding the right words. Her tension had been replaced by something else, a kind of sadness almost.

'You realize you've probably broken the law?'

'Accessory after the fact. Obstructing the police. Harbouring a fugitive. These words have gone through my head. I know.'

'You should be talking to your solicitor, not to me.'

'I can't. He's away. On holiday.'

'There are others.'

'Yes, but— '

'But you didn't know how they'd react. So that's why you came to me. Old lovers make good friends. I could be insulted, you know. Substitute counsellor. Free legal advice.' There was a sudden bitterness in her voice. But mixed with something else. Now he recognized it. He should have seen it before. Propelled by his own need, he'd forgotten hers. She was hurt.

He reached out and grasped her hand. It was the first time they'd touched. There was no response to his pressure, just a slight frown. 'Penny,' he said. She avoided his eyes. He moved towards her impulsively and took her in his arms. She stayed rigid in his embrace. He continued to hold her, willing her to give in. A warmth finally returned to her. He kissed her. She dug her nails into his back, not to hurt him but to tell him how much she hurt herself. The gesture was not necessary. He understood.

'I'm sorry. I was insensitive. I didn't think.'

'I know.'

They leaned back against the sofa. He kept his arms round her. Outside, an ice cream van entered the street and broke the spell. She extracted herself gently and moved away a little, creating a space between them.

'I have to say this . . .' she began.

He waited.

'I know you're in trouble, and that this isn't what you need from me right now, but nevertheless I have to say it. When you rang and said you wanted to talk to me, I thought . . . I don't know what I thought . . . I expected – a lot of things went through my head about what you'd say, what we'd talk about – but none of them had anything to do with this.'

'I know. I was stupid.'

'It's all right. It's finished now. I just needed to say it. But there's something I have to ask you. This woman . . .' She hesitated, feeling her way. 'Who is she?'

'You mean, are we lovers? No, we're not.'

She waited for him to realize the inappropriateness of his response. 'If you were,' she continued, 'you'd hardly come to me for advice, would you? That's not what I'm asking. But there's something I don't understand. This story. If you hadn't told me yourself I would never have believed it. And even as you were telling me, there was something odd. You were distancing yourself. It was as if it had happened to someone else, not you.'

William's eyes drifted to the ceiling. He registered a small crack running from the moulding in the centre to the cornice above the window. Funny, he thought. I never saw that before. He had a flash fantasy of himself on a stepladder holding a jar of Polyfilla and a knife, with Penny below, gazing up at him. I should never have come here, he thought.

'William?'

'What?'

'Come back.'

'I'm sorry. You're right. That is how I feel. I don't understand it. At every single moment it felt like I was doing the right thing. But, looking back at the whole sequence of events—'

'Look, this woman—'

'Josie.'

'Josie. Do you trust her?'

'I don't know.'

'Who is she? Tell me about her.'

'Well, for a start, I don't believe she's a liar. Not about important things. If she tells me she's seen something, then I do believe she thinks she's seen it.'

'But that doesn't make her right.'

'No.'

'Do you like her? I suppose you must.'

'In a way. After forty-eight hours virtually non-stop in someone's company, if you don't get to hate them, you do end up fond of them. She's not easy though. She's aggressive, touchy, bigoted, domineering . . .'

'Sounds charming.'

'Actually she is, in her own way. It's funny. I feel protective towards her. She's very bright, but she's also quite lost.'

'And are you sure she doesn't want you to get lost with her?'

'No, I'm not sure.'

'And this man Joshua. You don't sound to me as if you had a great deal of faith in his ability to come up with any answers.'

He shrugged. 'I don't know. At the time it seemed like a good idea. But now . . .' His voice trailed away.

'Look.' Her tone was gentle, but firm. 'I don't pretend to understand this any better than you do. The suggestion is that the police have been trying to kill you?'

'More or less. Not the police as such, but a conspiracy that may include police officers, yes.'

'But that's ridiculous.'

'I agree it sounds ridiculous. But for her the logic is irrefutable.'

'For her? And what about for you? William, you came to me for advice. Well, I have advice to give. But I don't know if you're going to want to hear it. From where I stand, there's only one thing you can do.'

Is this why I came? he thought. To get her to convince me, to provide an alternative to Josie? He knew what she would say. She knew he knew.

She waited for him to think this through, then she said, 'Listen, I won't tell anyone, even if I'm asked. But for your sake, and hers too, I think you should go to the police.'

He nodded slowly. She seemed to be saying what he had known all along. Whatever Josie would have replied now, he could no longer hear it.

Chapter Fourteen

He had said he would return. If she believed him, she had nothing to worry about. If she didn't, then she should have left already. She had allowed herself the comfort of belief. Still, the day was far from easy.

In the tin box on the hill Josie was fast running out of displacement activities. In the hours since William had left she had failed to read three books, cleaned the caravan from top to bottom, drunk three cups of coffee and played ten games of solitaire. When she caught herself cheating she knew it was time to stop. It was hot. Through the back window she looked out longingly over the ocean.

The very sight made her feel hotter. She ran cold water into the sink and put her face under the stream. Standing with a towel in front of the mirror she heard once again that description of herself, spoken in perfect vowel formation by a succession of BBC newsreaders: 'A young woman in her twenties. Five foot three. Dark curly hair. Green eyes.'

On the other hand, the face in the mirror looked older than twenty-eight. There were charcoal shadows under the eyes, and she could see lines she hadn't noticed before, the beginnings of gravity tugging at the corners of the mouth. What a lot gravity has to do with the way we age, she thought with surprise. A little less and we'd all stay baby-faced into senility; a little more and we'd grow old like liquid rubber, globules of flesh stretching and sliding downwards until our cheeks rolled onto our collarbones and our breasts reached our knees. The picture conjured up was like a vision from an all-American meat comic, and absurd enough to make her smile. The face in the mirror immediately defied gravity. She felt better for the wonder of it. And from the fact that some things were still funny. It also gave her an idea. If gravity could age her, then maybe there were other tricks to be played.

She stood up straight. Five foot three. There was nothing to be done about that. But so what? Probably a good ten per cent of the beach down there were five foot three-ers. It was not sufficient reason for them to go around making citizens' arrests of one another.

Dark, curly hair. Marie Antoinette went white overnight during the storming of the Tuilleries. Josie Ridley just slept badly. She picked up a handful of hair. Heavy, coarse, irrepressible. She saw an image of herself with her head over the sink, a bottle of peroxide in one hand, combing in a river of fizzing bleach until she emerged, head like a ripe cornfield, hard, yellow and stiff all over, like the mug-shot of Myra Hyndley that hard-nosed newspaper editors kept on file, ready to prejudice another generation of readers when the idea of parole came up again. No, no bleach. Freaks attract as much attention as criminals.

What about a scarf? She had one in her bag. She scooped up her hair, dragging it back and securing it as best she could with a shoe lace. Then the green and white scarf, which she knotted and pulled low over her forehead. Presto. No dark curly hair. Someone older and more serious looked back at her. She blinked. Still 'ole green eyes. She reached into her bag again. The sunglasses covered everything. Eyes, eyebrows and a good portion of her nose. The woman in the mirror was a stranger - Madeleine Stanford, perhaps, or a Martha Someone-or-other. Josie Ridley? The one with dark curly hair and green eyes? Haven't seen her on this beach.

Savouring an obscure sense of triumph, she armed herself with a book and a towel and made her bid for freedom.

Down at the water's edge she dodged waves and picked her way along the shingle. After a quarter of a mile she was out of the urban sprawl and into the open countryside of the real sun-worshippers. She chose an empty spot, stripped to her underwear and lay down on her stomach. She glanced first to one side, then to the other. No one was looking. She closed her eyes. The sun covered her with a sheet of hot air. She listened to the hissing of the ocean. The glare burnt into her brain and sucked out the bad humours. Blinded by the light, she thought, the song tracking through her mind as the sunspots played on her sealed eyelids. Then after a while she thought nothing.

And so on grimy English sands Josie slept, whiling away a sixth of her waiting day. The sun got to work on a new colour coding for her back, as the sea crept steadily towards her.

She awoke suddenly. A few inches from her nose, so close that the vision was blurred, she registered a pair of small, cherub-fat feet, podgy toes half buried in the sand, and the trace of a wobble where the feet joined miniature tree trunk legs. From somewhere above came the sound of a small cow chewing the cud. Startled, she flipped over onto her back, squinting against the white glare of the sun, and made out a round, downy-haired head and large, solemn eyes. He, or maybe she, must have been a year to eighteen months old, the age when walking is still a novelty that sometimes works and sometimes doesn't, and standing still for any length of time is a distinct hazard. Josie glanced around. There were fewer people on the beach now, and no obvious parent to be seen. She rose slowly, putting her weight on one elbow so she was almost level with the little face. Gently does it Josie, Whatever you do, don't make it cry.

'Hello,' she said.

Gulliver spoke, and the wind thus created knocked a dozen Lilliputians into the sand. The child sat suddenly, far too suddenly for it to have been intentional. It blinked a few times, as if to take in the unexpected rebellion of its legs, and crinkled its face just in case this should prove the moment to cry. Instead, it reached out a pink, grabby fist towards Josie's face. She turned her head to avoid losing a handful of cheek, and the fingers closed around the edge of the scarf. She pulled away, and the grip tightened, catching strands of hair as well as material. She let out an involuntary yelp which the baby took as encouragement. With a strength out of all proportion to its size, it yanked, and the scarf, plus a few uprooted hairs, came away. The shoelace holding back her hair had worked itself loose as she slept, and she sat now unmasked, dark-curled and green-eyed for all the world to see.

Her hand shot to her head, and she stared in horror as the child waved the scrap of material like a flag, a look not so far removed from adult triumph on its face. Josie took a deep breath and went into battle. With one hand she grasped the little wrist, and with the other started pulling the scarf back. The baby's gurgles subsided immediately. It took one look at her dark face and changed tactics, opening its mouth to let out an explosive yell. Sun-drenched heads lifted off towels to check who was the child molester.

'Shit,' she muttered, and then, 'oh Christ,' as a woman came scurrying along the beach towards them, her face set in familiar mother-worry creases.

Taking advantage of her split second loss in concentration, the baby further secured its grasp on the spoils of war. Josie gave up, letting go of the scarf and slamming on her dark glasses. 'O.K., you little fucker,' she whispered sweetly in its ear, 'you've won. I'm not competing. So why don't you just give it back to the nice lady?'

The mother was upon them. 'Oh dear, I'm so sorry. I only took my eyes off him for a moment, and he was off. I do hope he hasn't been causing trouble.'

Josie opened her mouth to reply, but the woman was already giving her attention to her child, who was now belting it out with renewed vocal violence.

'Jamie . . . Jamieee,' the woman sang in a high-pitched voice almost as glass-shattering as her offspring's. 'What have we been doing with the nice lady's scarf? Come on, give it to Mama . . . yes . . . give it to Mama.'

Not a chance, Jamie indicated, squealing even louder.

'He is all right, isn't he?' Mama said to Josie. 'I mean he didn't hurt himself or anything, did he?'

'Not unless ripping out a handful of my hair caused him any pain,' Josie snapped, then instantly regretted it. She shouldn't be talking to this woman. She shouldn't be here at all. Around them a few people were sitting up watching, enjoying the spectacle of someone else's embarrassment. Josie collected her things together, keeping her head down, making sure not to look at anyone. The mother turned her attention to Jamie, who by now had found a safer place for his spoils, stuffed into his mouth, where dribbles of saliva were turning the cotton a darker shade of green.

'Oh Jamie, that's not very nice, is it? Come on, give Mama the scarf now . . . There's a good boy.'

Josie recognized a familiar stomach-churning which she knew if left unchecked would bring her near to panic. She stood up, pulling up the towel and stuffing her book in her bag. She paused in an agony of indecision. If I walk away now, she thought, it'll only cause a worse scene. There was an alternative. She put down her stuff, saying, 'He's probably upset by my presence. I'll go for a swim and leave you two alone.'

She didn't wait for a reply but walked to the water's edge, holding herself as tall as five foot three could muster and not looking round. The water was cold but she did not flinch, going in straight up to her thighs and, holding her sunglasses on her nose, ducking down to submerge herself. Coming up from the water, her normally bouncing hair was now flattened and sticking to her head. She crouched in the water, watching while the woman soothed and coaxed the soggy rag out of the child's mouth. Jamie, having exhausted the potential of the situation, took defeat gracefully, and allowed himself to be picked up and carried back to the bosom of the family. The woman approached Josie, stopping at the water's edge.

'I really am very sorry,' she called, holding the scarf in her other hand. 'Can I wash it and return it to you?' Where are you staying?'

'No, just leave it there. It's fine.'

'Are you sure?'

'Yes, of course. No problem.' Josie forced her features into a smile. Jesus, why didn't she just go away?

The woman looked dubious for a moment, then nodded. 'Well, I am sorry.' She walked over to Josie's towel to leave the scarf stretched out in the sun to dry. Then she waved, taking Jamie's hand and manipulating it into a floppy salute, and the two disappeared along the beach.

The incident over, people turned to their own affairs. Josie's heartbeat slowed down. She stayed in the water a while longer, then ducked her head again and returned to her towel. The still damp scarf once more in place, Josie left the beach. As she climbed the path, flinging the towel over her shoulder, the tingling on her skin told her that she had, in all ways, stayed too long in the sun. She approached the caravan by a circuitous route, locked herself in and drew the curtains against prying eyes. It was still only four thirty.

Chapter Fifteen

On this, William's third visit to Highgate police station, he enjoyed a pleasantly different reception. The first time he had been one of a multitude of witnesses whose information would be fed into a vast machine, digested, and in all probability crapped out again. On the second occasion he had felt the irritation, if not outright hostility, of his interrogators, directed mainly at Josie but catching him in the wash. But now he found himself miraculously transformed from a nuisance into a VIP. When he telephoned, he was immediately put through to Chief Superintendent Daniels who, addressing him in tones almost of deference, offered to send a car to pick him up. This William declined, sensing the danger in thus compromising his independence.

The room he was shown to was not the bare, functional interview room of previous visits, but carpeted, with comfortable chairs, pictures, plants. Obviously someone's office. Just the place, he reflected, for witnesses of dubious loyalty to be buttered up. He leaned forward in his chair to examine a wall plaque for clues to the room's occupant. The Chief Superintendent himself. He sat back, resisting the reflex to straighten his tie.

A moment later the man in question, or so William assumed, breezed in. Tall, handsome, hardly older than his guest, and wearing a pinstripe that didn't come from Marks & Spencer, he reminded William of a merchant banker. He extended his hand and announced, 'Mr Stevens, how very glad we are to see you. We've been trying to get in touch with you for days.'

'Yes, er . . . I've been away. Staying with friends.'

'Friends?' The word was allowed to hang in the air. 'Well, no wonder we couldn't track you down. Your employers were under the impression you had family business to attend to.' He paused, allowing space for a comment. There was none. 'And by the way,

I'm Detective Superintendent Forsythe. Anti-terrorist Branch. Chief Superintendent Daniels has graciously offered us the use of his office.'

'Oh.'

'Anyway, now that you're here, what can we do for you?'

'Do for me? I thought you said —'

'Mr Stevens, it was you that contacted us. I assume that meant you had something to tell us.'

Expecting to have to justify his absence, William was floored by the sudden change of subject. Without thinking, he said the first thing that entered his head. 'Miss Ridley . . .'

'Yes.'

'You're looking for her.'

'Indeed. Do you know where she is?'

'No.'

'Then?'

'I was with her until Wednesday morning.'

'Wednesday morning. Two days ago?'

'Yes.'

'Carry on.'

'I went round to her house on Tuesday evening.'

'Why?'

The Detective Superintendent's style was becoming apparent. An affability of manner combined with sharp questions and sudden interruptions. William felt simultaneously reassured and disoriented. The very transparency of the technique gave him the confidence to believe he could withstand it. It was important not to feel rushed, he told himself. Not to allow the man's rhythm to be imposed on his.

'Detective Superintendent, I think it would be easier if you could just let me tell the story.'

'I'm sorry. Please continue.'

Once again William ran through the narrative. After first Joshua, then Penny, it was becoming routine. The Superintendent left it to him till he reached the kettle.

'And you're sure that if you had connected the kettle you would have suffered a fatal shock?'

'Almost certainly. Miss Ridley noticed it just in time, luckily.'

'Luckily,' echoed Forsythe, as if the word held the key to the mystery of life. 'And so the logical conclusion to be drawn was that you - or rather she, since it was her flat - was the victim of some conspiracy designed to prevent you communicating the truth?'

'Yes, that was certainly how it appeared at the time.'

'Hmmm. And then what happened?'

William made the rest of the story brief. Their flight across London, the light in his flat, the hotel and finally their parting at Kings Cross station. He said nothing of Joshua. He was here on his own. He had told no one. It involved no one but himself – and Josie, of course, but God knows where she was. The policeman listened, but did not see fit to interrupt again. He appeared, if anything, less interested than before. He can't possibly tell I'm lying, William thought. I have to remember that.

The story finished, the detective continued to look at him for a moment, then nodded slowly. He picked up a briefcase and delved into it, removing a beige file.

'What I'm about to say, Mr Stevens, will come as something of a shock. But I think it's better to be blunt. As a result of our investigations we are convinced that Josephine Ridley is a terrorist.'

He waited. William held his ground, unshocked, but considerably less calm than he would have liked to be.

'I gather that you hold a different opinion of her?'

'That's correct.'

'After what – five days' acquaintance? What makes you so sure?'

William was lost for an answer. Forsythe allowed him to flounder for a time, then moved in.

'Naturally, you see her as just an ordinary member of the public?'

Hardly, William thought.

'But then, a terrorist would not go out of her way to present herself as such?'

William opened his mouth to speak, but was smoothly prevented.

'You're a man of the world, Mr Stevens. A businessman and, I gather, a very good one. A personnel manager, used to weighing up people and handling human problems. You consider yourself – and rightly so, I'm sure – an experienced judge of character. But your experience is in industry – workers, shop stewards, managers. Have you ever come in contact with a terrorist?'

Annoyed at the patronage, William declined to give the policeman the satisfaction of confirming his rhetorical question. Undeterred, the Superintendent continued as if he had.

'Can I suggest, therefore, as one professional to another, that in this matter you allow yourself to be guided by our greater expertise?'

No, thought William, I will not take your word for it. 'By all means. But would you mind telling me on what evidence you have made this judgement?'

'Certainly.' The Superintendent extracted a document from the file and began reading: 'Josephine Stephanie Ridley, born Shepherds Bush, September 13th 1956. This file was opened in 1974, when Miss Ridley was a student at Lancaster University. She was involved in an occupation of the administration block, and was on the students' action committee demanding greater representation and an end to university investment in South Africa.'

William smiled. 'Superintendent, on such evidence you could condemn half the university population, probably myself included.'

The policeman did not acknowledge the joke. 'After university she became involved in the Rock Against Racism and Anti-Nazi League campaigns of the late seventies. It was during this period that she was arrested and convicted of possession of cannabis resin, for which she was fined £50. Her boyfriend was the leader of the pop group –' here he hesitated, like a horse facing a difficult fence, then took a run and cleared it in one – 'Special Branch. Now I don't know how much you know about the Anti-Nazi League?'

William shrugged.

'I'll tell you. The majority of those involved were innocents, but the movement was infiltrated and manipulated by a faction from the extreme left Socialist Workers Party, who used it as a front. We have reason to believe Miss Ridley was one of those. She and her boyfriend, Robert Taggart, then separated, for political reasons. He was, we gather, not considered sufficiently radical. After that she travelled in Central America, in El Salvador and Guatemala, amongst other places. Much of her detailed whereabouts are unknown during this time, but we do know for certain that she had contacts with the guerrilla forces in Nicaragua, and was, in fact, in that country during the overthrow of the Somoza government.'

Amazing, thought William. We could have talked of so many things. Instead we bickered. She had hardly mentioned her travels, had been curiously offhand about them, which was strange considering —

'How do you know all this?'

A smile deflected the question. 'She arrived back in England three years ago. Since then she has kept a surprisingly low political profile. Not at all in keeping with her previous activism. We believe this was deliberate, in order to make her suitable for an assignment such as this one.'

The Superintendent concluded his recitation, closed the file, folded his arms and waited.

'So. It's all circumstantial. What does it prove?'

'It's simply a foundation, Mr Stevens. A foundation which proves that Miss Ridley is exactly the sort of person we might expect to find involved in a leftist conspiracy.'

'But there must be thousands of people with that sort of background. You're not telling me they're all terrorists, are you?'

'No, I'm not.'

'Then why her?'

'Did you know she was interested in the Health Not Wealth campaign?'

'Yes, as a matter of fact I did. She mentioned something about it that first night.'

'And that a former lover of hers, a Martin Croft, was a founder member of the action committee?'

No, thought William. I didn't know that.

'Let me ask you another question. What do you suppose Josephine Ridley was doing near the hospital on that of all nights?'

'I don't know. She told me she was on her way home from the cinema.'

'A cinema which she had attended on her own. No companion to confirm her whereabouts.'

'Well, that's hardly a crime. Are you trying to suggest that she set up the bomb, fled the scene on her bicycle, and then turned around to go back and check if it was still working?'

'No, Mr Stevens, I'm not suggesting that.' He sounded very patient, as if it was just a question of time and that eventually William would acquiesce and the veils would be lifted from his eyes.

'I mean, if you're saying she's a terrorist, she would hardly hang around the scene of the crime, would she?'

'Not unless she had another reason for being there.'

'How do you mean?'

'You and she were involved in an "accident". Her injuries, fortunately not serious, seemed to require medical attention. You took her to the nearest casualty unit, which happened to be the Royal Highgate, and —'

'Wait a minute. That's not the whole story. She didn't want to go to Casualty. It was me who had to insist on it.'

He smiled, as if dealing with an invalid. 'You insisted because you feared she had really hurt herself. I think we can allow a measure of dissembling here. I wonder if perhaps you had been less keen on chivalry, she might not have felt - and shown - proportionately more pain?'

William said nothing. There was nothing to say. You either believed the man or you didn't.

'So, once in the Highgate you somehow got lost and ended up near the kidney unit . . . in the very corridor where you chanced to see a man who seemed to be acting suspiciously. Then when you return to casualty Miss Ridley's injury has mysteriously, not to say miraculously, healed itself, thus allowing you to set off for home. Outside - how the coincidences multiply - just as you reach the car, there he is again, the same man, except you, to her annoyance I'm sure, obstinately maintain your reservations about that. Thirty seconds later - boom. Now clearly it would have been more convincing if instead of going dashing off to try and help you had stayed and witnessed what you were meant to witness - the man getting into a car, its number plainly visible, and driving off. But no matter, for the time being you have seen enough. As the good citizen you are, you felt bound to report your observations to the relevant authority, the police.' He paused. 'I can see you're not totally convinced by this scenario.'

'No, not totally.'

'Let's look at it from another point of view. Imagine for a moment that you'd taken another route home, and had never gone anywhere near Archway roundabout.'

'Yes.'

'And Josephine Ridley had seen all those things without you there.'

'Well, she wouldn't, would she? Not if the accident hadn't happened. Her journey home would have been uneventful.'

'True. But just suppose she had been the only witness.'

'But she wasn't. There was the man in the compound. It's likely he heard the car even if he didn't see it.'

'Well, all I can say is that whoever he is, he clearly doesn't listen to the radio, the television or read newspapers. We have had over three hundred people come forward with information about the Highgate that night, and none of them claims to have been in that particular place and to have seen what Miss Ridley says he would have seen. Let's go back to Miss Ridley. I'll put the question to you again. If she had been the only witness of these events . . ?'

William thought about it, putting himself in their position. 'You might not have believed her,' he said at last.

The policeman smiled. 'We would certainly, once we had checked on her background, have had severe doubts.'

'So?'

'So she needed you. She needed your corroboration. With your support - with your respectability, she knew her testimony would be taken seriously.'

'Are you trying to tell me—'

'That you've been used? Exactly.'

'No. It's preposterous. How could she? How could she have contrived that we pass down that particular corridor—'

'You were deep in conversation. She led you - those were the very words you used in your original statement.' He flicked rapidly through the file and read out, 'Yes, here it is. "Miss Ridley was leading the way. We followed the right fork of the corridor. It wasn't clear where we were, but it seemed sure to lead somewhere." And lead somewhere it certainly did. Right into the path of the man you were supposed to see. Right to the precise spot. She knew the way.'

'But then who—'

'An accomplice, chosen presumably for his resemblance to someone else.'

William became aware of a tightness across his forehead. This man is trying to overturn my reality, he thought. It seemed to have been happening a lot lately. He was not getting used to it. 'Superintendent, the woman ran into my car. She could have been killed.'

'I very much doubt it. You said yourself it wasn't serious. I'm sure the fall was carefully rehearsed.'

'But why me?'

'Why you?' He scanned William up and down as if the answer were self evident. 'You have a Citroen GS, with last year's number plate and a Radio 3 sticker on your side window. All badges of respectability. My guess is that another accomplice spotted you at the roundabout and signalled you as a likely candidate. The right car, the right age, a man on his own - someone who might not be averse to her charm.'

'Charm? Good God, you don't know her.'

'I think you'll find we do, Mr Stevens.'

William considered. The Superintendent's theory was ludicrous, surely? – but every objection he made to it seemed to have been anticipated. It was becoming frustrating. Somewhere there had to be a loophole. 'Wait a minute. If your account is correct, then why didn't she tell you the number of the car straightaway? The delay could only have aroused your suspicion.'

'You're right. It did. But there was a good reason for her not telling us then.'

'Which was?'

'Malcolm O'Grady was still alive.'

'I don't understand.'

Detective Superintendent Forsythe hesitated. He picked up a glass paperweight and balanced it in his hand, while regarding William's face in an apparent attempt to make a similar judgement. Then he made his decision. He replaced the object on the desk and said, 'What I am about to tell you is strictly confidential, and I hope you will regard it as such. But since you have agreed to co-operate fully with the investigation . . .' Had he? 'O'Grady's role is not as simple as you might suppose. In his home town of Peterborough he was known as a political extremist. We have also established that he was involved in petty crime, and on arriving in London he used false references and a pseudonym to obtain this job at the hospital. That, together with his presence on duty on the night of the bombing, suggest to us that he was not altogether innocent.'

'An inside job?'

'If you like to call it that.'

'Why was he killed?'

'Possibly a mistake, an own goal, but more likely as a way of securing his silence. He was not, one imagines, completely trusted.'

'Do they do that sort of thing?' William asked, searching his memory and retrieving news stories of gory murders on Japanese mountainsides. On the other hand, didn't terrorists go to inordinate lengths, hi-jackings and kidnappings, to spring their comrades from jail?

'I assure you they do.'

If the man from the anti-terrorist branch said so, then William felt he had to believe him. But that didn't quite explain Josie. 'What about the cemetery, and Coulton, and the photographs?'

Again the policeman waited for William to work it out for

himself. After a while he prompted. 'Mr Stevens, once again you didn't actually see any of these things. Miss Ridley was alone when she made this alleged journey across London to watch a man plant flowers on a grave and meet a person she claims to have been the bomber. And I'm sure her photographs will show that, although I wonder how clear they will be. I also wonder when they were really taken. You didn't see her holding the camera. Nor did you have the privilege of a visit from this so-called inspector. Don't you find it just a little bit strange, that Miss Ridley should have been so chosen and you so sadly neglected?'

'She made it up?'

'Yes.'

It was true he had never seen or talked to Coulton. And Joshua had told him no such phone number existed. It was also true that the photographs were inconclusive. And the story of trailing De Villiers across London. Now he thought about it, it did seem rather too simple, to have so much good luck on one day.

'What about the wiring?' He didn't want to ask, but the Superintendent would have told him anyway. The answer was as he predicted.

'It wasn't her life at risk. You plugged in the kettle. And what more powerful way to convince you of a conspiracy than by putting you in a situation where you felt your life was in danger. No doubt you're going to point out it was the cat that saved you? How providential. But if it hadn't been the cat, would she not have rushed to your aid and turned off the current herself?'

I don't like you, thought William. Maybe that's why I'm still reluctant to believe you. 'And the men outside the door as we left?'

'Her companions, come to scare you into flight, and afterwards no doubt to replace the original wiring. I have to tell you that when we searched her flat two days ago, with a warrant, we found no sign of the electrics having been tampered with.'

'You're sure.'

'Mr Stevens, it was a particularly thorough search.'

There was a silence. William studied a spot on the carpet where someone had stubbed out a cigarette. He wished suddenly that he smoked.

'But if all this is true, what was the point of it?'

'The point was to lay a false trail. To implicate a South African – and a rather well-chosen South African, I might add, one whose connections leave him, shall we say, open to implication – and to ensure the bombing would be blamed on the wrong people. Now, I don't know your politics, Mr Stevens' – like hell you don't, William thought. If you've checked on Josie, then you've obviously checked on me – 'but as you know the image of South Africa is very poor in some quarters. Especially now. There are many who would like to see the government pushed into action against apartheid, and would use this as an opportunity. Meanwhile all thoughts of a left-wing conspiracy go flying out the window and the real culprits get off scot-free. Fortunately, as yet this hasn't happened.'

'It seems like one hell of a risk she took, bringing herself directly to your attention. If she failed she would expose herself to a conspiracy charge.'

'That's right. That is the charge she's facing.'

'Don't you think that kind of risk would be unacceptable?'

'To you it would be. And to me. But you don't know these people. You don't know their fanaticism.'

Fanaticism. William found the word sticking in his mind. Fanaticism? Josie was neurotic and immature certainly, her hatred of authority was bitter and obsessive, but did that make her a fanatic? Exactly how far would she be prepared to go? I can't answer that question, he thought. My brain says one thing, my gut another.

As he came out of his circle of thought, he found the policeman waiting. 'It is vital that we find her. If you know anything that would help us . . .' The invitation hung in the air. Don't push me, William thought. I need time to consider. I can't betray her. Not just like that.

'Let's go over again what happened after you found the kettle.' Underneath the Superintendent's words the tone said, we have all day, I can go on as long as you can. 'Maybe there's something you've overlooked.'

If he was accusing him of lying it was subtly done. Thankful to be on safe ground for a moment, William said, 'We panicked. Then came the knock on the door and we fled over the back garden. We drove to my flat.' He recalled that night, the thumping in the pit of his stomach. 'I should explain that at this stage I was quite rattled. I'm not sure how far my behaviour was entirely rational.'

'Naturally.'

'We drove past my house and there was a Renault van with a man in the driver's seat, and inside my flat – well, I told you – there really was a light moving, a kind of torch beam. I was sure someone was up there, and it frightened the hell out of me.'

The policeman nodded. 'I'm sure it did. And I'm sure you were right. I'm sure there was someone up there, whose express purpose was to convince you your life was in danger. You're an intelligent man, Mr Stevens, they clearly understood that. Having seen what you did see, you had no alternative but to run. Which of course you did.'

It was hard to resist his reassurance.

'And the hotel you ran to was, I believe, the Walton, off Russell Square.'

He nodded. That Josie had been right about the efficiency of police surveillance was not so much surprising as depressing. He felt the need to make a statement of independence. 'Yes, we spent the night there – separately.'

'I wouldn't have expected any differently, Mr Stevens. And the next morning?'

'We had breakfast together. We discussed what had happened. She said she wanted to contact a journalist and then get out of town. I told her I didn't want to do anything until I'd had some time to think it out.'

'And did she?'

'Did she what?'

'Contact a journalist?'

'I . . . er. I –' He shut up, panicking at the realization he'd been lulled into making a false move. 'I don't know. She went off to make a phone call. She didn't say who to.'

'I see. Then?'

'Then she asked me to drop her off at the station.'

'Kings Cross?'

'Yes.'

'And that was the last time you saw her?'

'Yes, I left her there.' It was such a little lie. How could it possibly be detected after so much truth?

'And what did you do yourself?'

'I took the car back home, and went off to visit friends, as I told you.'

'Oh yes, your friends.' This time the sarcasm was more overt.

'Yes.'

'Their names?'

William was prepared for this question. 'Charles and Linda Bassett.'

'You realize we shall want to visit them?'

'Yes. Unfortunately that won't be possible.'

'Why not?'

'Because they left the country this morning for a touring holiday in Turkey.' That much was true. It wasn't just solicitors who took vacations.

To his surprise Detective Superintendent Forsythe chose not to pursue this line of inquiry. 'And Josephine Ridley gave you no idea of where she might be going?'

'No.'

Another theatrical hesitation. The transparency of the gesture did not prevent William from feeling intimidated. 'Of course you know Miss Ridley is wanted for questioning?'

'That's why I came.'

'And you also know that to withhold information about her could itself incriminate you?'

'I realize that, Superintendent.'

'Perhaps you would like to know why we are convinced she is one of those responsible for this bombing?'

'Haven't you told me?'

'No. What I have told you is circumstantial. But there is also hard evidence. You will recall that I told you Miss Ridley's flat was searched two days ago. What I did not tell you was what we found there. In her bedroom, in a corner under the filing cabinet, there were signs that a floorboard had been recently removed then nailed down again. Underneath we found marks in the dust which indicated that a number of objects had been stored there. These had apparently been removed. However, on further inspection some distance away along the joist we found two items that were apparently overlooked in the haste.'

He reached into his briefcase and brought out a length of what looked like cord, in a plastic bag. William found himself strangely disappointed. He realized he had been quite scared of what it might be. 'Flex?' he said quizzically.

'Yes, flex. Looks ordinary, doesn't it? But not to forensics. They tell me it's identical to the kind used in the Highgate bomb.'

William was aware of too much saliva in his mouth. He swallowed, but the same amount seemed to re-form immediately.

'And this,' the policeman said. This time he withdrew a grubby piece of A4 paper, torn at the corner and with some hieroglyphic marking on it.

It was like being on some stupid TV quiz. 'What is it?'

'It's a photocopy plan of the lower ground floor of the Royal Highgate Hospital. Showing the various entrances to the kidney unit.'

William stared at the two objects in the Superintendent's hands. 'You're sure?' His voice faded away.

'Absolutely.' The policeman's tone was almost gentle. 'I'm sorry. It must hurt to realize you've been duped. If it's any consolation, we believe Josephine Ridley to be a most accomplished operative. From everything you've said, Mr Stevens, I understand you're an intelligent man of considerable loyalty. But you will, I'm sure, appreciate that I have to ask you one more time – where is Josephine Ridley?'

William took a deep breath and began to speak.

Chapter Sixteen

Josie had known for some time now that, given the circumstances, William might betray her. Ever since she had sat in the car with him on the way back from the hospital she had realized that he was not the ideal choice for a fellow witness. His suit, his haircut, his politics were all bound to cause trouble. Josie Ridley was not, by her own admission, a law-abiding citizen. She had, when she thought the bomb might have been planted by the left, lied to the police: first about the car number, later about her knowledge of De Villiers. She had lied to Coulton when she told him she would give up her meddling in the case. And she had lied to William in all manner of ways, from the car number, through her police record, stories of her past life, even down to the cost of repairing her bike. She had lied. Indeed, if someone had come to Josie Ridley's doorstep six months before, and told her that an extremist faction in HNW was planning to blow up the Royal Highgate renal unit rather than let it fall into private hands, and asked her to co-operate, she might or might not have agreed, but she would certainly not have told the police about it. No, clearly not a law-abiding citizen. But nor, on the other hand, was she a terrorist.

Of course, in some ways, she would only have had herself to blame if he thought she was, and on the basis of that decided to betray her. He had asked enough questions, given her enough opportunities; there had been world enough and time for her to convince him of her innocence. A few explanations, a little information volunteered, the removal of the Trespassers Will Be Shot signs – that was all it would have taken. But at the beginning she had not trusted him. And by the time she did it was too late. The boundaries of their relationship had already been forged.

On the other hand, William had been watching. He had seen more than she intended to show, and he had been correct in certain of his diagnoses. He was right to accuse her of being on the outside, of finding it easier not to belong, of having nothing to lose, of feeling the need to provoke. At twenty-eight years of age, Josie was stuck. Somewhere in the last few years she had taken a turning that seemed right at the time, but had the effect of leading her further and further off the track, until her only comfort was to pretend it was where she wanted to be. A mixture of pride and fear made it hard for her to admit the mistake. And she adapted, gradually, until she felt the wilderness was where she belonged. After a while it seemed as if everyone else was on the outside and she was at the centre.

It was cool outside the caravan. The air was silky in the darkness. She was sitting on the steps with a glass of scotch half drunk, staring down at the curve of the hill, waiting, thinking about pasts and futures, and wondering if William would come.

The hours since her return from the beach had crawled by. She had taken them in units of one, celebrating the end of each as a small triumph. At eight she had rewarded herself with a glass of scotch to mark the passage into evening. But it had hit an empty stomach and knocked her sideways. The sun had done the rest. By now her back and shoulders were operating on their own separate thermostats, stretching the skin until it felt one size too small for her body. Her head was fuzzy. What a bloody stupid time to get drunk.

The fresh air had helped. With the sunset came a safety of sorts. The caravan site grew silent. The combination of sun and sea had proved too strong for milk-white English constitutions. Young children had fallen asleep in parents' arms, and the lethargy had proved contagious. She would not be disturbed. Until he arrived. Or until they did.

They. Her faith had faded with the daylight. How long could a visit to a solicitor take? The last train would have reached Axminster half an hour ago. If he was coming, why wasn't he already here? 'Trust me,' he had said. 'I'll be back.' But why should she trust him? He didn't trust her. What really did they have in common but a little fear? And even that was now unequal. It wasn't his face plastered all over the newspapers. When it came down to it, there was no reason why he should protect her. God knows, most of the time it had been little better than an armed truce between them. 'Just what is it, Josie, that makes you feel the need to be so aggressive all the time?' She could see his expression, the mix of anger and exasperation in his face. Why shouldn't he betray her?

She flung the remainder of the scotch into the grass and rubbed her eyes with the back of her hand. Her vision cleared, but the doubts remained. She should have been more careful with him. Used more charm and less anger. But it was not as easy as it sounded. It was one thing to dissemble for an hour or two with a group of American strangers, another thing entirely to keep up a pretence in continuous company. It would have taken more energy than she had to keep pretending she was someone else. And in some ways she didn't have to. He made it very easy for her to be herself. That was the irony of it. Despite the circumstances, or maybe because of them, she felt more herself with William than she had with any man, at least since Rob.

Rob. She shook her head angrily. This was not the time to get into that one. She took hold of the thought and stuffed it to the back of her mind. But it would not be banished so easily. It muscled its way centre stage again, demanding to be considered, as if to say, 'Think about this. Now we're actually analysing how it is that you got yourself into this mess, you might get some answers from considering my story.'

Her skin burned hot in the night air. Maybe William was even now feeling the breeze through an open taxi window half way between here and the station. There was nothing to think about. Everyone has a Rob in their life. The one affair that defies emotional digestion, that is not automatically healed with time. Even after all these years it was impossible to work out just what had happened, even down to which one of them had ended it. He had blamed her, for laying down ultimata that could not be fulfilled, for being unrealistic. How could he leave England now, when finally, after so many years, things were beginning to break for him and the band? For her the question was different. How could he afford to stay, when the compromises were so manifest, the spiritual risks so huge? And how could she stay with him when the only role open to her was that of elevated groupie? So she had left him to the promise of fame and fortune, bought her ticket and got on the plane righteous and strong. But one thing had become clear. As she continued on the road, meeting an endless catalogue of travellers and freaks frying their craniums on drugs and sunshine until they were lucky to know what country they were in, she began to realize that she missed him. But by then England was already a lifetime away and it was too late to go back.

She was away so long the travelling became normal. It made her independent in a way she had never been before. It gave her a sense of herself unconnected with jobs or with men. And it opened her eyes to many things, not least that England was a very small country which knew almost nothing about the rest of the world, much of which was involved in the most desperate of struggles. Some of these she watched from the sidelines. Central America confirmed her politics. It gave her a sense of proportion she had been looking for, and it restored her energy.

None of this helped her fit in any better. In fact it made things worse. It might have been different if she had come back to another England. Instead she arrived home to this brown, unpleasant land in the middle of its third bleak Tory winter. The left had their horns locked in a private death struggle which the press serialized as soap opera, while the rest of the country accepted the imposed diagnosis and took their medicine with all the desperate faith of a terminal patient still unable to believe the truth. There was no place for her. Before she had left, certain of her mates had seen the Tory landslide as just a temporary setback. 'Listen, the only way this country will ever really embrace the left is when it's had a bellyful of the right. In two years' time people will be out on the streets, you'll see.' Two years later the streets were empty. She met friends who asked her what she'd seen, but didn't listen to the answers. She saw Rob, but the reunion was like walking on glass, full of dancing footwork and concealed pain. They had gone to bed together, just for old times' sake, but it hadn't worked. It was just a ritual. Too much damage had been done. He was rich and he was famous, and although these things had not changed him as much as she had predicted, that didn't help because she too was different. When he offered her the job she spat it back in his face, telling him she wasn't yet ready to sell out. But that was only half the truth. The other half was that she wasn't ready to watch him with other women. They had left each other, but the scars refused to fade.

She tried to construct an alternative life based on her recent experiences. She applied for a graduate course at the School of Oriental and African Studies, but had to wait nine months for it to begin. In the interim she filled in her time with Spanish lessons, she read foreign newspapers because they seemed less parochial, and she planned for when she would leave again. But somehow she never made it. Her isolation became a habit. She took up guiding because she needed the money and it didn't tie her down. She lost contact with most of the people she had known before, all of whom were 'doing something' with their lives. And she lost interest in English men, telling herself they were dull and asexual. The few affairs that she had were always begun with an end in view. On balance she was not unhappy, but she knew she was using up her store of energy and nothing was coming in to replace it. She dropped the Spanish lessons and she never made the SOAS course. She tried politics again, testing the water, sitting at the back of a few halls listening to others discussing Nicaraguan solidarity. But she had lost the taste for the endless meetings and wasn't sure any longer what she had to give. She went to a couple of HNW demos, but stayed on the periphery. Mostly she just waited. Sometimes, on the Sundays of her life, she wondered if perhaps she wasn't waiting at the wrong bus stop.

That was why last Friday night had been so important to her. And why, as William had so often pointed out, she had made it her business to get more, rather than less, involved. It was a way out. Or rather, a way back in. She –

SNAP. SSWISH. Down below there was a footstep on the path. Grass and twigs, toasted in the sun to a newspaper crisp, left a clear imprint of sound on the silence. She stood up, her heart thumping. He'd come home. The steps continued, with no attempt at disguise. She had to clench her teeth to avoid calling out his name. Suddenly the noise stopped. A door squeaked open down the hill, then closed again with a metallic bang. Silence. Josie let out her breath and with it a small cry. No William. She looked at her watch. Almost midnight. Who was she kidding?

In the caravan she filled her pockets with ten pence pieces. If there was an innocent reason for William's delay, Joshua would know about it. He was the only contact they had in common. If he had heard nothing, then betrayal must be assumed.

Huddled against the wall of the phone booth with the receiver close to her face, she heard the line connect and then the sound of Josh's voice before the pips drowned him out. She inserted a coin. It wouldn't go. 'Shit,' she muttered. She tried to force the coin into the slot, first one, then another, but succeeded only in bruising her finger. The pips stopped and the line went dead. 'Shit, shit, shit!' Tears of frustration came to her eyes. She slammed down the receiver and tried again. The pattern repeated itself. She had to take in deep breaths to stop herself from crying. She went outside and drank in the salt sea air, steadying herself. Should she take the risk of a reverse charge call? She decided it was worth it. Back in the booth it was an age before the operator answered.

'Who shall I say is calling?'

'Tell him it's Mrs Stevens. Mrs William Stevens.'

The line clicked dead and she waited. And waited. At last the woman's voice returned. 'I'm sorry, caller, but I'm afraid the number you require is an answering machine. Under the circumstances I am unable to connect the call.'

'Oh God.'

Her despair must have communicated itself, because the operator overruled instructions to say, 'I'm sorry. If it's urgent, I can leave a message on the machine. Would you like me to do that?'

Her mind raced. No. She was alone now. She had to be really careful. 'No. No thank you. I'll try again later.' Her voice sounded calmer than her soul.

She surged back up the hill, her eyes squinting into the darkness. There was no time for nerves now. She had to move. Pack a bag, find some real money and get the hell out. To where she didn't know. Maybe the beach, just for tonight. If she used the cliff path and walked a couple of miles, no one would find her. She would grab a few hours' sleep and at first light start off again. Maybe she would make for Meldon. Hire a car on the driving licence - shit, William knew the name. That meant the police would know it too. O.K., take a bus, hitch a lift, walk. Anything. Joshua would help. Tomorrow. She just had to get through the night.

Ahead of her the path was dark and quiet. She began to feel jumpy. What if they had come up the other way? She imagined a small army of police - or worse - creeping along the cliff path from the beach, reaching the caravan, surrounding it in the soft blackness, waiting. She stopped. Maybe she shouldn't go back. It was asking for trouble. But where else could she go without provisions, without money? The ten pence pieces rubbed together in her fist. Not even Richard Hannay could have made it to Derbyshire on sixty pence. No, she had to return to the caravan.

There was no sign of anyone. All she was frightened of was her fear. She forced herself to walk onwards. Fuck you William, she thought. Just you wait . . .

At last she reached the caravan. It appeared in front of her like some old friend, empty, dark, untouched, just as she had left it. She approached slowly, each footfall soft on the earth. The landscape remained still. No sudden explosion of figures from the undergrowth. They had not arrived. Maybe they were still talking. William and his bloody solicitor in a room with an inspector. Or maybe the talking was over and they were on their way. No time to lose.

She was by the steps now. She climbed them lightly, pushed down the handle and let the door fall open in front of her. She took one step forward. Her hand was feeling for the light switch when it happened.

It was a sudden rush of movement coming from the other side of the room. Almost before she heard it she whirled back towards the door, but in the dark misjudged the entrance and caught the top of one eyebrow against the frame. She let out a cry and with one hand clasped to her forehead struggled to get out. Behind her the light snapped on, flooding the caravan and dazzling the other eye with its brightness. I don't want to die, she thought. I don't want to die.

'Josie!'

His voice was shaking with fear. That's what stopped her in her tracks. She turned and saw him, half crouched on the other side of the room, as if ready to spring. The next thing he felt was her catapulting towards him, descending like a harpy, arms flailing. He put up his hands to defend himself against the force of her. She smashed into him, sending both of them spinning backwards onto the floor. The caravan shook. He grabbed at her hands, trying to pin them down.

'You fucker!' The scream caught in her throat. 'You fucker, where the hell—'

He held on to her desperately. She stopped struggling and fell against him. It was then that they both realized with a kind of shock that she was crying.

Chapter Seventeen

In the caravan it was dawn, smudgy and unglamorous, but dawn nevertheless. It slid in through the edges of the curtains and relaxed the intensity of the little sidelight on the table between them. Caught in its half glow were the remains of a meal of sorts. Bread, meat, an apple core, the bottle of scotch.

She was sitting upright, her knees drawn up to her chin and her body encased in a large white shirt forming a tent around her. Above her left eye was a small, livid bruise with a faint line of red where the skin had broken. She pushed her tangled, unruly hair off her face with one hand. She looks almost too young to be up so late, William thought, as he propped his head against the bed and closed his eyes. Her voice prised its way under his eyelids.

'Christ, William, it gets more and more like a bad Borges story. The closer you get to the centre the further away it seems. Why? That's what I don't understand. If it's a police conspiracy, then where do the South Africans fit in? And if it isn't the police then who the hell set me up? Someone somewhere doctored my file, and I just don't believe the South Africans could have done that by themselves. And anyway, why should they even want to on a purely domestic issue like health politics?'

William said nothing. They had been over this ground many times in the last few hours. The fog around the facts was getting thicker rather than thinner.

'And that stuff about bomb-making equipment under the floorboards! I've never heard such theatrical crap. You'd think after the Anne Maguire's bomb-kitchen case they wouldn't dare pull another stunt like that. Do they really believe that "enemies of the state" are so chronically disorganized that they just forget to clear up after themselves? I'm surprised they didn't throw in a couple of grams of cocaine for good measure.'

He opened his eyes. 'They did mention the marijuana,' he said evenly.

She bit her bottom lip. 'Yeah, I know. I'm sorry about that. I had to be safe. I didn't know how you'd react. People can be so touchy when it comes to drugs. I needed you on my side.'

'I suppose it never occurred to you that even pillars of the establishment might have indulged in the odd joint or two. I know I look old to you, but remember – it was my generation that rediscovered the stuff.'

'I seem to have underestimated you in more ways than one.'

She avoided his eyes. The swelling on her forehead looked painful, he thought. He remembered the blind panic with which she had tried to throw herself out of the caravan. 'You really thought I'd bring the police back with me?' he asked quietly.

She frowned. 'I'm not used to trusting people. And I got scared. You would have done the same. Anyway,' she looked up at him, 'I was right to be scared. You came close to it. You did almost believe them . . . Didn't you?'

He visualized the Superintendent's face, with its reassuring half smile, confidently anticipating his collusion. 'Put it this way. It crossed my mind. They made it sound very convincing.'

'So what stopped you?'

The question was as hard to answer now as it had been then. But a lot of things had changed for him in that police station, not all of which he understood. 'I don't know. I just couldn't accept their vision of you, I suppose. Even though all the facts were there, somehow you didn't fit them. It didn't square with your all-over-the-place anger. I kept thinking, if you had been who they said you were, you would have tried harder to hide it.'

She said nothing, but looked troubled.

'Don't be offended. Take it as a back-handed compliment. Even though you lied about some things, I didn't see you as fundamentally dishonest. It didn't feel right.'

She nodded, more to herself than to him. 'Thank you,' she said, with a rare formality. The words were the more valuable because they had so evidently cost her.

'Don't mention it. I was fighting my own battle as well as yours.'

He closed his eyes. Such momentous times, and here he was too tired to appreciate them. Sleep nibbled at his brain. The events of the last few hours began replaying themselves out of sequence in his mind. The face of the truck driver who had given him the lift from Salisbury to Honiton when he missed the last train connection. That sudden panic in the cinema when the window frame had seemed to shrink around his body. The frozen aggression in the police station after the final lie had been spoken.

Detective Superintendent Forsythe's face had closed down. The two men had separated from each other, like hands being withdrawn across a chasm. The lie had been swiftly, although not easily, released. Even as he opened his mouth his better judgement told him to give in, to tell them what they wanted to know. But there was something stronger than judgement at work. The lie, his protection of her, was instinctive. He was almost surprised to hear it. But there it was: firm, sincere. And as soon as it hit the air he felt immediately better. He could breathe again, as if a paralysis had been lifted from him and he was in control again.

He left the station in a patrol car (it was evident this was an offer he could not refuse) which dropped him outside his front door then parked, obviously, a few yards down the street. He had not needed the ostentation of the gesture, he understood quite well he was not to be trusted. In his living room, already a foreign place, he sat and wrote a short note to his parents, telling them he was well but going away for a few days. The letter would confuse them, but if - or rather when - anything happened it would be better than silence. He put a stamp on it and slipped it into his jacket pocket. He thought of ringing Joshua, but he could not trust the phone. He stayed for another hour or so, watching the hands of the clock move, knowing exactly what he was going to do, planning every detail. When he left the house for the tube station he set a pace that the plainclothes man could easily follow. He went to Leicester Square, threading his way through the early evening crowds to the Warner West End complex where he bought a ticket for the new James Bond. The policeman sat eight rows behind him, on the aisle. Together they watched the trailer and the adverts and, as the lights went up for the interval, William left his box of popcorn on the seat and headed quite obviously to the gents loo at the bottom of the screen. It was a door with no exit sign marked. As soon as he got inside he flung himself into action. In the cubicle furthest from the end he bolted the door, stood on the toilet seat and opened the small window above.

The plan had come to him on the journey home in the police car. It was neither inspired nor original, but a simple case of imitation. Eighteen months before, he and Penny had been in this very cinema watching a Paul Newman movie - he could no longer remember which one - when he had gone to the loo. Standing by the urinal he heard scrambling noises and the sound of the window banging, then a voice hissed, 'It's O.K. I'm in.' This toilet door opened and a young punk, gloriously tattered, emerged, dusting down his carefully ripped jeans and looking pleased with himself.

He grinned at William, a kind of triumphant sneer. 'I'm unemployed, mate. Tragic, innit? You tell anyone and I'll push your teeth down your throat,' he announced good-naturedly as he swaggered out. Watching him, the main thought in William's mind was how on earth he'd got his head spikes through the gap. He even went to check the size of the window. The one at the end was for some reason larger, and its catch had rusted free. Back in his seat he related this to Penny. She urged a quiet life. The credits were rolling and the Hollywood version of audacity seemed more compelling.

Now, as he hoisted himself quickly up and pushed his legs out through the gap, his admiration for that audacity increased. The window seemed to have shrunk with time; either that or he was bigger than the youth. In any case he had no accomplice to push him through. There came a dreadful prolonged moment when he couldn't move, and he almost panicked, his mind swamped with images of humiliation and capture, but the banging of the outside toilet door caused a sharp intake of breath and the danger point passed. The threat of pursuit propelled him. Behind him he heard the cubicle door rattle as someone tried the lock. By then he was free enough to jump. The drop was further than he anticipated, and his body jarred on impact. But fear blotted out the temporary pain, and he ran hell-for-leather down the alley and into the crowds, not stopping to check for a pursuer. He plunged in and out of groups and queues, losing himself in the melee of street life. Anyone following him would have needed X-ray eyes. In the Haymarket he came on a cab just dropping a fare. He threw himself into it. 'What's the matter, guv? The old bill after you?' the driver said over his shoulder as they sped down towards Pall Mall. 'No,' said William, recovering his breath. 'I have to catch a train.' He arrived an hour and a half late for the last regular train to Exeter.

He debated with himself whether to stay the night in a hotel or to take the overnight train. But the memory of Josie's face on leaving convinced him. He posted his letter and sat with his collar up at the end of the platform, waiting. At Salisbury it took him twenty minutes to find the right road out of the city, where a lorry driver picked him up almost immediately. It was quite fun really, hitch hiking again after twenty years. They had got on quite well. The driver had even gone out of his way to drop William at Honiton. There his luck ran out. He walked fast, but it still took him over an hour to reach Branscombe. When he struggled up the hill only to find the caravan empty he suffered a moment of sudden anxiety, and began to doubt his instincts in the police station. It was then that the door opened. It had been, quite simply, the most extraordinary day of his life.

He stirred slightly on the sofa and opened his eyes. She was watching him carefully. 'We should sleep,' she said.

'Yes, we should.'

'Then tomorrow morning, first thing, we find somewhere else to stay.'

Another journey, so soon after the last. 'You think we're not safe here?'

'I just think we can't afford to take the risk. The police are going to be pretty pissed off with you. And if your photo hits the front page that'll make two of us too scared to go out. We need somwhere much more isolated.'

He grunted agreement. Both in the same boat, he thought. Two outlaws. Somehow the reality wouldn't penetrate. 'My brain has stopped,' he said. 'Sorry, but I'm going to have to lie down.'

She uncurled herself from the seat and moved the small table to one side. Together they pulled out the sofa to form a bed. She smoothed a sheet over the upholstery and arranged a cushion as a pillow. If he had been less exhausted he would have been surprised by the care taken.

'Maybe we should go to Meldon after all,' she said as she laid out the sleeping bag.

He stretched out on the bed and felt himself slipping towards the crevasse. The name seemed somehow familiar. 'What's Meldon?' he heard himself say.

Josie was forming her usual sleeping position, head resting in the crook of her arm. 'Meldon is a fugitive's paradise,' she said as if the words weighed too much. 'And Yvonne Pryce is going to take us there.'

Chapter Eighteen

The lifts didn't work. One a.m. on a Saturday morning, what did he expect? The doors gaped open, an Out of Order sign slung across them. It could have been worse. At least this time there was no poor bastard stuck between the eighteenth and nineteenth floors. Joshua opened the door to the stairwell and groaned as he contemplated the 380 steps ahead of him. Maybe he could write an article on council block maintenance. Around 365 he heard his phone ringing. He took the last flight two at a time and his key was in the lock when the answer machine clicked on. He heard the beep, then silence. He swore gently under his breath and closed the front door.

There were four messages on the machine. He ran back the tape and listened as he pulled a beer out of the fridge and covered a slab of bread with a doorstep of cheese. The voice of an old girlfriend crackled over the line, cheery and selfconscious, wondering if he was doing anything Saturday night; she had tickets for a band, maybe he would call her.

He smothered the cheese with mayonnaise.

Beep. 'Hello Joshua. This is William. I have to talk to you. I've tried your office. They say you're out. I'll try again later.'

So it had been William ringing the paper. Two phone calls, no name, no number.

Beep. The sound of pips, staccato and frenetic, someone struggling to get a coin in the slot.

Beep. This time nothing. After a few seconds the tape began regurgitating old messages.

He switched off the machine. One call from William, two attempted calls from Josie? Why so much activity? He added it to a long line of unanswered questions. No use fretting. If it was that urgent they would call again. He sat down at the desk and put his feet up. He was knackered. The first part of the day spent running round London, most of the second pushing copy towards a deadline. At least Woodward and Bernstein had only had the one assignment. There had been two of them. And they had had help. Whichever way you looked at it, the breaks had not exactly been flinging themselves in his path these last few days. Coulton was still a mystery: a name and a number, neither of which existed. Mrs O'Grady, when she finally agreed to see him, had been polite and magnificently unforthcoming, and his friends in the Met had developed a severe case of lockjaw (possibly self-inflicted). As for De Villiers, well, up until a few hours ago, the only political connections he had unearthed on him were redder than blue. When he finally got through to Pete Wilkinson, the Africa correspondent had sent him to the back copies of *Anti-Apartheid News*, and there Joshua found out the astounding fact that De

Villiers had arrived in this country after serving ninety days' detention in a South African prison. Not exactly the normal background for a secret service agent.

But Joshua, while not the world's greatest investigative journalist, knew better than to trust second impressions. Working on the basis of *cherchez la voiture*, he had stayed with De Villiers, and late this afternoon, after smashing his head against two days' worth of brick walls, had finally managed to loosen one of the bricks.

From his battered briefcase he took out his miniature cassette recorder and placed it on the desk. He pulled the typewriter towards him. His body made a loud plea that they postpone this till morning. He ignored his body and turned on the tape.

'So, I gather you are looking for Sipho Ntshona. Well, son, I'm afraid I can't help you. Sipho is no longer with us. Now he's workng for the Pan African Congress in New York.'

The voice was muffled. The tape recorder had been sitting in a fold of Joshua's jacket, laid casually on the table in front of them. The words, though, were clear enough, and the sound of them recreated the man. Harry Culverwell, big, stocky, mid-fifties with thinning hair. His South African passport would probably have read 'coloured', although this wasn't immediately evident to the untrained eye. He had welcomed Joshua into his shabby office in Camden Town without ceremony, motioning him to an easy chair. But there had been a certain watchfulness in his scrutiny. No doubt to an editor of *Anti-Apartheid News* any journalist, unless you know their name and copy, should be treated with care. Joshua set about establishing his credentials.

'Well, it was a long shot. The article was written a good few years ago. But Pete Wilkinson suggested I get in touch with you anyway. He thought you might be able to help.'

He flicked his press card, but the name worked better than the plastic. 'Peter? Yes. He's been a good friend to us. Give him my regards. So, what were you looking for from Sipho Ntshona?'

'Some information. On a man called Joe De Villiers.' Culverwell's face registered a flicker of interest. Joshua paused, waiting for comment. None came. 'Ntshona covered De Villiers' arrival in this country six years ago. I wondered if you could bring me up to date?'

'May I ask what is your interest in this man?'

'It's an intelligence story. I have reason to suspect that De Villiers may be connected with South African intelligence, the National Intelligence Service—'

'We still call it BOSS here. The name may have been changed, but the intentions remain the same. BOSS is more evocative.'

'BOSS then. But when I read that De Villiers had been a detainee, it seemed to point the other way. Have you come across him yourself?'

Another pause. This time the sound of a match striking. Culverwell's ashtray had already been overflowing. He took his time answering, then said, 'Yes, we know him. At the beginning, when he first came, we'd see him at parties, meetings, he was on our mailing list . . .'

'And now?'

'Now we don't hear from him any more.'

'He's a spy?'

There was a gesture here. A wave of the hand, maybe yes, maybe no. 'A number of people think so.'

'Do you think so?'

'Circumstantial. De Villiers used to live with a woman called Lily. Lily was a secretary for the ANC. She was caught with her hands in the till. Literally.'

'She stole money?'

'Worse than that. Documents. Someone returned to the office one evening to find Lily bent over a photocopier. That was the last we saw of her. Two months later she turned up in Johannesburg. The star prosecution witness at a terrorist trial.'

'My God. What happened to her?'

'I'm sorry. What was the question?'

At his desk listening to the tape, Joshua smiled. It had been nicely done, he thought. Culverwell's eyes had glazed over, as if he genuinely appeared not to hear the question. Joshua had known better than to pursue it.

'And De Villiers? What was his reaction?'

'Outrage. At Lily. Deceived, rejected, abandoned, betrayed. Of course he hadn't known. How could we suspect otherwise? How could he of all people be a racist - a man living with a black woman?'

'She was black?'

'Zulu.'

'They recruit blacks?'

'Oh, you wouldn't believe it.'

'And then?'

'Then De Villiers lost his credibility. He may have been O.K., but personally I wasn't prepared to risk it.'

'But surely . . . I mean, De Villiers had served detention.'

'That can mean nothing. He probably spent the ninety days reading *Playboy* and playing draughts with the warders. Don't look so surprised, Mr Barnes. It's a classic BOSS ploy for improving their agents' credentials. But on the other hand, De Villiers may be what he claims, because another thing BOSS like to do is to smear exiles, spread it around that so-and-so is a spy, manipulate our paranoia. Some perfectly good people have been ruined like that. Can you imagine what it's like to go through Botha's prisons, electric shocks, years of solitary, living with rats and the screams of other prisoners, only to get out here to freedom and find your friends will have nothing to do with you because they've been led to believe you've been planted on them?'

'I had no idea,' Joshua said, not hiding his surprise.

'Well, it happens.'

'So, De Villiers could be all right?'

'He could be.'

'But you don't think so?'

'Look at it from BOSS's point of view. Let's assume he is one of them. His cover is blown. So, what happens next? How can he be utilized? They do one of two things: they bring him back home, to work in headquarters, or they move him to pastures new. De Villiers used to be a journalist—'

'That's right. On the *Rand Daily Mail*, then on the *Evening Standard* over here.'

'Sure. In the old days, fifteen years ago, BOSS liked to recruit journalists. There are good reasons for that. Journalists are expected to go round asking questions. That's their job. Not only that, but they have expertise, in collating information, making connections, noticing the unusual . . . If you think about it, every journalist is a kind of spy.'

Joshua was acutely aware of the tape recorder whirling soundlessly between them. He couldn't resist glancing at it. But Culverwell softened his words with an ironic half-smile, the first of their interview. He continued, 'But then we got wise. Every journalist who comes out of South Africa now is regarded with a lot of suspicion. So, they spread themselves. After all, BOSS needs intelligence from all kinds of fields – business, trade unions, politics . . .'

'De Villiers is involved in the SDP.' Even the tape's bad quality could not hide the excitement in Joshua's voice.

'There you are.' Harry Culverwell did not sound surprised.

'But why should BOSS be interested in the SDP?'

'Mr Barnes, there is nothing that BOSS aren't interested in. Their appetite for intelligence is vast, their budget astronomical. Nothing is too minute not to warrant their attention. Have you ever written a letter to a newspaper for or against apartheid?'

'Once, when I was a student.'

'Then you're on file.'

Joshua's look must have given away his disbelief. He remembered Culverwell's expression. A kind of shrug – take it or leave it. He said, 'The SDP is a fairly new party, right? Then they need a man in there. The Labour and Liberal parties were sewn up years ago. And as for the Conservatives, they're honorary members.'

'What can he do for them?'

'They need to know who's for them, who's against them, who they can bribe, who they can smear, who to invite, who to exclude. They want advance notice of policy. Even better, someone who can influence policy.'

'De Villiers is doing well then. There are rumours he might be selected to stand at the next election.'

'A member of parliament!' Culverwell guffawed, his faint South African accent coarsening into parody. 'Give the man an Iron Cross!'

There was a small silence on the tape.

'I see,' said Joshua.

'Well, does that answer your question?'

'Yes. Or rather yes and no. So if De Villiers is a BOSS agent, then politics would be his sphere of work. Does that mean he'd confine himself exclusively to that, or might he get involved in other things?'

'Other things?' Culverwell echoed him, the interest evident.

Joshua backed away. 'I don't really have any facts, just suspicions.'

'And you can't print suspicions, is that it? Well, Mr Barnes, I'm afraid I've told you all I know about Mr De Villiers. But if you should feel the need for further assistance, I'm sure I could put you in contact with some people who would be quite interested in what you have to say.'

'Thank you. I'll remember that.'

There came the sound of a chair scraping across the floor. At his desk Joshua hit the stop button. He sat back and stared at nothing in particular.

So De Villiers was a BOSS agent. Of that he now had no doubt. But an agent whose girlfriend was caught in the act? Dumb. Almost as dumb as letting Josie trail him halfway across London to a rendezvous with the bomber. Yet clearly someone trusted De Villiers. Enough to think him right for the job of infiltrating a national political party. Like so many other things, it didn't make sense.

Tomorrow was the weekend. Josie's name was now public property. There was a limit to how long they could stay on the outside. Yet at the moment there was precious little he could do about it. He had nowhere near enough to corroborate a story. He looked up at the notice board above his desk where he had pinned three of Josie's photographs. De Villiers and his associate in blurred half profile in the rain. He could have them blown up. Take them to Culverwell's friends. One side usually keeps a record of the other side's faces. He didn't have much option. Nothing else was moving, and Josie was depending on him. He had to keep chipping at the stone. He turned back to his typewriter and began rewinding the tape recorder.

Chapter Nineteen

They awoke, bedding damp with sweat and sticking to their bodies, to the raucous cries of children whooping a war dance around the caravan. They pulled their complaining bodies out of bed and left the caravan, depositing the key under the step. By ten thirty they were on the road.

Outside Branscombe's only pub Josie rang Joshua. The call woke him, suspended in dreams eighteen floors above London, but he recovered quickly. They exchanged life stories in a minimum of words. If Joshua had feelings about William's behaviour, he kept them to himself. He agreed they were no longer safe where they were, agreed also that their mutual friend's estate would be the perfect answer, but he said he would have to check certain details with the friend himself. They used no names. It was her caution, but he echoed it.

'Don't say it's for me,' she said abruptly.

'O.K., but you might as well face it. It'll be known sooner or later.'

They arranged to talk in the late afternoon, from a service station somewhere between here and there.

From his bench outside the pub William watched her walking back towards him. Something had changed. Even her body language was different. Gone was the tight, hunched creature that had stalked the caravan. Her walk, her energy, even her sense of purpose seemed to have returned. This was the old Josie. He realized he had missed her.

'You look great,' he said. She let her sunglasses slip down her nose and regarded him over the top of them, frowning. 'I mean it. It was always my childhood ambition to be in an adventure movie with Doris Day.'

'Directed by Alfred Hitchcock? You're sick. But you're clearly feeling better.'

On the bus to Axminster she practised her signature, and they constructed a life story for Mrs Pryce and her husband who, alas, was no longer allowed to drive due to an unfortunate encounter with a breathalyzer.

In the event it proved unnecessary. The man in Avis hire didn't know she was a criminal. No doubt he had heard or read about her somewhere, but he was hardly on constant vigil for Josephine Ridley. And even if he had been, Mrs Pryce, in her jaunty headscarf and sunglasses, was obviously just another holiday-maker determined on a little touring. He was, in fact, only too glad of the custom. With this infernal heatwave business had been terrible. It didn't even worry him when she said she would pay by cash. Barclaycard phobia is commoner than is supposed, and, to tell the truth, even his own wife still regarded such bits of plastic as a sophistication designed to trick people into spending more money. The licence was good enough ID. He closed the till on the £175 covering a week's hire and went outside to wave her off. He had to admit later that he had been a trifle surprised when she had taken off like a racing driver. But then, who didn't have fantasies when they got behind the wheel of a car? No, the man from Avis was not hard to fool.

She picked William up in the town square next to the church.

'How was it?'

She grinned. 'A little charm, a lot of money. It was a piece of piss.'

Sweet talking Josie Ridley. Just like old times. 'So – where now?'

'To Derbyshire.' She tested the windscreen wipers. They dragged noisily across the glass. 'And more than that I'm not going to tell you until we arrive. You'll understand why when we get there, I promise you. Trust me.'

This of all times he could hardly refuse. He snapped on his seatbelt and picked up the map.

The journey was long and frustrating. Saturday holiday traffic plus endless roadworks on the motorway meant they spent the best part of the morning staring at a Jesus Saves sticker in the back of a Ford Cortina on the M5. Finally they reached the service station. William bought petrol while she made the call.

She returned with hamburgers and Joshua's latest news. Mrs O'Grady had done a bunk, probably out of London to escape the press.

'And Meldon?'

'Confirmed. The larder's stocked. The caretakers who live down the road are away. We're home and dry.'

And then what? he thought, but not out loud. She stretched, massaging the small of her back with one hand. 'Are you O.K. to drive?' he asked.

'I am. You're not. Mr Pryce drank too much, remember? We're a law-abiding couple. We wouldn't want any trouble with the authorities. If it makes you feel any better, you can do the cooking when we get there.'

'Which will be when?'

She switched on the ignition. 'Before dark if the traffic clears. If not . . .'

Three miles on, the jam unclogged and she put her foot down. Even so, scrupulous attention to speed limits meant it was already dusk when they took a B road out of Bakewell. As they drove through country lanes ragged with summer growth, he tried again. 'So. Now tell me about Meldon.'

'There's nothing to tell. It's just a house which belongs to a friend. It's perfect. Miles and miles from anywhere, and totally isolated and self-contained.'

'And what about the friend?'

'He doesn't usually live here. Hence the caretakers.'

'You mean you have friends with second homes?' It was too much of an invitation to miss.

'Yeah, shocking, isn't it?' she grinned. 'Don't worry. When I knew him he had nothing.'

'Is he safe?'

'I'd say as safe as the houses he owns, all right? Now if you'd just shut up for a moment, I might be able to concentrate on finding the turn-off. By my calculations we should be coming to the gatehouse pretty soon.'

He obeyed orders and they drove in silence. Sure enough, a few minutes later the gables of a late Elizabethan cottage came into view with two large gates next to it. They continued, and half a mile further on a small overgrown entrance presented itself. She took the turning. The road was narrow. The mature trees lining it soon gave way to a sweep of open land and rolling fields on either side. William scoured the horizon for a building. Nothing. She was right. It was isolated. The drive swung unexpectedly to the left and began a long, gentle curve to reveal, against the skyline, the house itself. William gazed ahead in amazement. House was an entirely inadequate description. What he now saw in front of him, rising out of the natural gradient of the land and filling the horizon with its pattern of dark roofs and towers, was something else altogether. He caught his breath.

'My God, Josie. It's a bloody mansion.'

'I told you it'd be worth the wait.'

She drove on slowly. Through the fading light he was able to make out the terraced gardens leading up to the huge brick façade, and above that the criss-cross network of chimneys pointing into the sky like children's building blocks.

'We should park somewhere here off the path, maybe under the trees, and then walk up through the gardens. We can come back tomorrow and check the car's well hidden.'

She drove off the road over some uneven ground to the shelter of some trees where the car would be left out of sight. It seemed an overcautious gesture. It was hard to believe anyone ever came this way, there was such a sense of emptiness to the place. They got out of the car and walked to the drive, where they stood for a moment, just looking. When William spoke, his voice was a half-whisper in response to the silence that seemed to have closed in around them.

'You really don't do anything by halves, do you? Who is he, this "friend" of yours who just happens to own a second home?'

A small noise, maybe a chuckle, broke the silence. 'Use your imagination. How does anyone earn this kind of money quickly? I thought the police would have told you. Rob Taggart, alias Rob Ramasses. A few gold discs, a couple of world tours . . . he's a rock and roll hero, that's all.'

And so they arrived at Meldon, like escapees from romantic fiction, coming upon their Mandalay in the night, its secrets and memories locked away in the moonless darkness. Meldon, where even thirty years before there would have been a small army of servants to greet them, to light their way, carry their bags and provide refreshment before showing them through draughty corridors to warmed bedrooms above.

Instead, these modern trespassers crept their furtive way through a maze of side gardens, across lawns and up steps, by the pencil-beam of a torch, unnerved even by their own footsteps on the gravel, until they reached the path at the side of the house, from where they crossed to the stables and outhouses. Here Joshua's instructions proved perfect. Inside the first barn they followed the torch beam over the straw-strewn floor to a large, retired rain barrel, rusty on its metal hoops and smelling of rotten wood. Gingerly Josie lifted the base and ran her hand over the hard, packed earth. Something fast and many legged ran over her fingers. She persevered. The set of four keys was right at the back. She withdrew her hand rapidly.

Back at the great side door she located the alarm system in the ivy. Using William's cupped hands as a stepladder, she reached up and followed instructions to de-activate it. The rest was child's play.

Their steps echoed on the stone flags as they entered the kitchen, and thence into the main rooms of the house. A few moments later they were standing under the vaulted ceilings of the baronial hall, with its wooden galleries and great oak table in the middle. They were both overawed, she by the realization that all this belonged to the man who only a few years ago was reduced to dodging fare collectors in the underground to save money, and he because yet again he felt out of touch with reality, forced at her pace into what seemed another kind of madness.

'You should have told me,' he said sharply, his voice rising up and fragmenting in the great expanse of the roof. 'I should have been prepared.'

To which she replied, with infuriating simplicity, 'Sorry. I thought you'd enjoy the surprise.'

Chapter Twenty

He was woken by the sun. He stirred into life, blinked a few times and lay still, registering first his surroundings and second the unexpected weight of his body. It felt as if gravity had significantly increased during the night – either that, or he had been drugged. He pulled himself up on a doubled pillow and rubbed his eyes. The room was rainbow-coloured, the sun refracted through leaded windows, spinning light patterns on the floor and walls. He watched in quiet admiration. He was, he realized, feeling much better. He had fallen into bed exhausted, so much so he couldn't sleep. He had lain there for what seemed like hours, ears straining at each creak and groan of the house. To fill the time he had indulged in complaint, grumbling that this was not the place for a secure hideaway, they would have been safer in some characterless, squat cottage on the outskirts of civilization, somewhere more designed for limiting the imagination. And for this of course he blamed Josie, who had once again proved herself the perfect architect of abnormality.

But now he felt better, last night's anger chased away by sleep. He also felt hungry. In fact his stomach felt cavernous, as if he hadn't eaten for weeks. He cast his mind back to the day before, the early rushed breakfast and the limp hamburger at the service station. Already light years away. No wonder his gut was objecting. He leaned over the edge of the bed for his watch and brought it level with his eyes. He stared at it, frowned, turned it round then back again. No, it really was three p.m. He had slept for fourteen hours.

The fact woke him fully. He got out of bed and padded across to the window. The catch was old and it took a moment of fiddling to release it. He gazed out. He had forgotten, if he'd ever known it, that the bedroom overlooked the back of the house. Stretching below, bathed in afternoon sunshine, were the gardens, layer upon layer of them, terracing down into the fields, across a stream and from there over meadows reaching clear to a far horizon. He could see for miles. A room with a view. Whoever had first picked the site for Meldon hadn't missed a trick. It was perfect.

Below him the air was heavy with heat. Everything was still, timeless. Even the sun seemed to have stopped. It seemed churlish even to breathe. Halfway down one of the terraces he caught a glimpse of movement. He darted his head inside, then cautiously peered out again. The figure broke cover. Josie, engaged in an innocent afternoon stroll. He watched her for a moment. There was a carelessness in her wandering, as if she were thinking about something else entirely. Easy, secure, as if she owned the place. How stupid of her to be so obvious. The absurdity of the thought struck him almost immediately. He lifted his eye to the horizon. It was utterly empty. Not a building in sight. Meldon had been constructed for privacy. To see but not be seen, except when they chose. They really were alone. He began to realize that coming here was not such a stupid idea after all. Once again, there had perhaps been method in her madness.

He turned back into the room and felt a wave of hot sunlight on his naked back. Under his feet the rug felt thick and luxurious, like walking on tapestry. There was a warmth to the wood, and to the silence. He dressed slowly, savouring the fact that for once there was no sense of panic, and went down the corridor into the tiled, echoey bathroom, with its fixture of porcelain and brass, high fashion of the 1920s. The water was cold but it did not matter. His toothbrush and a new bar of soap were laid out on the side, with a towel over the chrome bar rail as if the maid had been there just before him. He eyed them with suspicion, rubbing his face vigorously with the towel. Be interesting to see how she squares this with her politics, he thought, as he headed downstairs.

Josie meandered across the rose garden towards the house. She looked up at the yawning hole of the open window on the top floor. So at last William was awake. Maybe his disposition would have improved with the morning.

It had never occurred to Josie that William would not be instantly seduced by Meldon. It seemed impossible that anyone could resist it. She had fallen the first moment she laid eyes on it, six years before. It had been a casual find. They were driving back from a gig in Manchester, wandering through the Peak District, chasing country lanes, avoiding the motorway, stopping when anything caught their eye. Chatsworth Palace was nearby, but they were put off by the line of coaches in the carpark. Meldon they came across by chance, alerted by a half-hidden sign at a road junction. It was high summer, a day as clear as this one only not so hot. They wandered in the house and gardens for hours until the

place emptied around them and a caretaker came to tell ther was closing. Josie wanted to give him the slip, scuttle in behinc of the pews in the chapel or the curtains in the hall, and wait u night to rediscover the place in darkness. A touch of the far fives, Rob dubbed it scornfully as he propelled her towards the But part of her was in earnest. The house left an imprint on imagination, and the atmosphere stayed with them through r of the drive back to London. They fantasized about what it w be like to live in such a place, wondering whether the magic l up through the layers of time would be dissipated by mundanity of everyday living. The conversation ended in fricti most conversations at that time did – although she could no lo remember the exact point where it turned acrimonious.

She could, however, remember exactly her reaction when discovered from the small print in a gossip column that Ramasses had made a bid for the mediaeval mansion, Mel Hall, which was up for sale to counter death duties on Masterton family estate. She was furious, beside herself with r It was partly the gross ostentation of the gesture, and partly the that she felt it, at some level, to be a snipe at her, a finger helc over the ears – 'See, I can do it. I can even buy your dreams n

So much for any vestige of political purity. His occasio well-publicized donations to charity wouldn't even have cove the solicitors' fees on the purchase. Cross-examined by prosecution, his answers would have been predictable. 'There lots of ways of using the system. Buying Meldon prese something that might otherwise have been destroyed. I never I'd do the hair-shirt number. But I still look after my friends. Th that accept help, that is . . .' After this Josie told herself he was a soul, contaminated property. Yet here she was feeling the sa powerful tug towards the house, glad it was still intact, preser by his money. Funny the layers of contradiction in any one tru

She gazed up at the façade, its brick baking in the sunsh What alternative was there for a place like Meldon? Buy it for state and convert it into a welfare centre, an open prison, an people's home? Convert it and destroy the power of it, atmosphere? Maybe it should be left as it was, open all the time people to wander through, free of charge, kept for their ben rather than history's. How long would it last? She recalled how old friend, who had lived for a time in China, had described h the summer palace just outside Peking was always bursting w

Chinese who spent their visits insulting the memory of the Empress who had built for her own pleasure rather than for the benefit of her people. They may have thought the palace lovely, but they had no reverence for it. For them it was an instant history lesson. It was impossible to imagine the British conjuring up such a sense of historical outrage. It would take more than free access to stately homes to bring about such a transformation of political consciousness. Meldon was a contradiction. It was as simple as that. Josie was enough of a realist to appreciate that her politics had pockets of unhappy compromise. She might wish that the kind of society that built Meldon had never existed, but she would find it hard now to agree to the destruction of its product. She didn't want it public property any more than she wanted it private. Romance. Sentiment. It was hard to scrub it all out of a middle-class English soul. William would have a field day with such inconsistencies.

Well, let him. It didn't matter. They were safe here, and there was time to kill. After all, whatever the disagreements, in the end they were in this together. She was no longer outlawed alone. Although she would not easily have admitted it, that - and Meldon - made her feel stronger.

Inside the stone-flagged kitchen she found him sitting at the table, his face stuffed with toast and eggs, a mug of coffee in his hand. She looked at him, remembering the ramrod back, the smart-suited indignation of the man she had met nine days ago. He tried to say something, but bits of toast gummed up the words and he gave up. She nodded politely and poured herself a cup of coffee from the filter machine. She sat opposite him, bare feet against the edge of the table as she tilted the chair back. She watched him eating for a moment, then said:

'You obviously slept well.'

He nodded.

'It's done you good. You look better. The snarl lines have gone from around your mouth.'

He swallowed. This time his stomach did not immediately insist on another mouthful. He could afford to be sociable. 'How about you?'

'I was up early, checking the silver.'

'Didn't you sleep?'

'Yeah, but then the sun came in like butterscotch and stuck to all my senses.'

'What?'

She clicked her tongue. 'I thought you would have recognized it. It's your era. Joni Mitchell – "Chelsea Morning". The girl next door to me at university only had two albums and she played them incessantly.'

'What was the other one?'

'Dylan. "Blood on the Tracks". She had a breakdown in her second year. I was always surprised it took that long. Did you find your towel?'

He nodded. 'And the bread and eggs and coffee. Is this a permanent change of personality or just a ruse to unnerve me?'

'Wait and see.' She smiled sweetly. It made him feel even more insecure. She leaned over and picked up some toast crumbs on the end of her finger.

'Did you get through to Joshua?' he said after a while.

'No.' She frowned. 'Still no answer. Not even the machine.'

'What do you make of that?'

'Well, he said yesterday he was still trying to track down Mrs O'Grady. Maybe there was a tip-off as to where she was staying. She could well be outside London. If that's the case he would have dropped everything and run.'

'What about the answering machine?'

'He might just have forgotten to turn it on. Or he thinks it's a bit tricky for us to leave messages when he's away. Don't worry. He knows we're safe here. If he needs to get in touch, he will. I waited a whole weekend for him to get back to me with the car number. It'll happen. It's only a matter of time.'

William poured himself some more coffee.

'Better than the caravan, yeah?' she said to his back. 'Have you explored yet, or did your stomach come first?'

'I was hungry,' he muttered.

'So what did you think of the view from your window?'

'Remarkable. It felt like nothing has changed on that horizon for centuries.'

'The field patterns have altered, that's all. And there's probably fewer trees, otherwise it's the same.'

'You know a lot about it.'

'Sure. It's one of the most beautiful baronial homes in England.'

'Is that you or the guide book?'

She shrugged. 'Both. You must have felt it. Meldon is special. It's not one of those monstrous public places like Blenheim. It wasn't built to be worshipped. It was always a family home.'

So many words with so little anger or cynicism. So she was not untouchable after all. 'How big was the family?'

She ignored the sarcasm. 'It wasn't designed like some imperial statement. It began small and grew gradually. Every generation from the eleventh to the seventeenth century added something. Layer by layer.'

'Like Tescos and Marks & Spencers, you mean?'

She frowned this time. 'Listen, do you want to fight, or do you want to hear about Meldon? It's all the same to me.'

He raised a hand in submission. 'Sorry. Old habits die hard. What happened after the seventeenth century?'

'Why did they stop adding things? The family married into another larger estate and they moved homes. Meldon was just left, uninhabited from 1770 onwards. That's what makes it so different from all the others. It missed out on all the ravages of eighteenth-century reconstruction and Victorian ponce. By the time Victoria came to the throne it was already a museum piece, albeit a rather crumbling one.'

'When was it lived in again?'

'Not until the early years of this century. It was bought by an American millionaire with a passion for English history. He ploughed his entire cosmetics fortune into restoring Meldon to exactly how it must have looked the day it was deserted.'

'He did a good job.'

'Yeah . . . There's even a story that when the work was finished, some time in the early thirties I think it was, he left a little box embedded in the main beam of the baronial hall, detailing what was original and what was replaced. Don't you think that's great?'

'You're very tender about the place.'

She cocked her head at him. 'Romantic is the word you're reaching for. Yes, I am. I think it's an incredible house. Does that shock you?'

'I don't know. I think I find it rather touching.'

'Patronizing bastard. Drink your coffee and I'll give you the full guided tour.'

She was right. It was impossible to resist. Maybe in the winter it would have been easier, when the windows leaked rain and wind and there was nowhere you could go to keep warm. But summer was a pushover. The afternoon sun streamed in through the diamond panes, coating everything with molten gold, and the silences shimmered with still heat. William did not put up a fight.

Through a corridor leading off the main hall they came into the Tudor dining room, now a misnomer because there was no table. It was a long, panelled room with a semi-circular alcove at one end looking out over the gardens, and at the other a large window by an oak settle giving out onto the courtyard. Above the deep, dark fire-place an elaborate coat of arms was engraved in the wood, and arranged round it were two soft armchairs with footstools and a card table: just the ingredients for winter evenings by the fire. On the table was a small vase of wild flowers. They caused William almost as much wonder as the room itself.

'Yours?' he asked, with evident disbelief.

She inspected the display, poking back an errant snapdragon which had keeled over. 'Well, I do think it makes a house look like a home, don't you?'

He watched the light filter in through the window. It was as if his elbows were being jostled by invisible figures, others who had stood there before him. It was a powerful, almost tangible sensation, and for him, usually immune to such tricks of time, it was an act of conversion. She had not exaggerated. The house was special. Not only did it have beauty, it also had a sense of itself. The feeling was not entirely comfortable.

'How much did Rob pay for it?' he broke the atmosphere deliberately.

She made a face. 'I'm not sure. Three quarters of a million, I think. It was going cheap, I seem to remember. It was a bad year for stately homes, there'd been something of a glut, and they were determined not to let it fall into the hands of a developer. That was one of the conditions of sale – that it would go to someone prepared to keep it in the manner to which it had grown accustomed.'

'Rock stars come in that category, do they?'

'Sure. Why not?'

'Well, they don't exactly have great reputations as conservationists. So I understand from the managers of certain hotels I've stayed at. Most people's idea of them would involve champagne corks through the Rembrandts and vomit in the priest's hole.'

'Yeah, well I expect they recognized a cultured rock star when they saw one. Anyway, you're a child of the sixties. It's not all Mars bars and amphetamines, you know.'

'So what is it? I can't quite imagine you two sniffing glue together. How did you pass the time? Reading each other alternate chapters of Engels?'

'Sure. A fat lot of good it did him,' she said, gesturing round the room.

'Yes, well, it is something of a political disaster in your terms, I would think.'

She shrugged. 'We always did disagree about some things. I should have expected it really. For instance, we never quite saw eye to eye on the small print of redistribution of wealth. Actually you'd probably have got on famously together. Pragmatic politics he was into – in other words, if you can't change 'em, screw 'em for all they've got. Use them for your own ends. You could say he's stuck firmly to his principles. Me, I blame it on student poverty. He was broke for too long. I always knew the money would go to his head.'

'Is that why you split up?'

She scuffed the stone floor next to the fireplace. A little storm of dust rose into the air. 'That, and other reasons.'

'And you never came back. After he'd bought it?'

'Nope. But by then we weren't seeing each other – I think that's the phrase.'

'He didn't invite you, just for old times' sake?'

The dust settled. 'He did actually, to his house-warming party – a grand affair, I later heard. But . . . I didn't fancy it, seeing Meldon as a film set for the anybodies of the eighties. I figure it would have been a bit of an insult to the previous inhabitants.'

'You're a puritan, you know.'

'Oh, don't tell me you've only just noticed.'

She moved to the window. Cupping her hand round her eyes to filter out the sun, she peered into the courtyard. Then she turned back to him. 'I told you. I'm in my element. I love it here. It's a fantasy.'

'Though a politically reprehensible one, wouldn't you say?'

'So? That's what fantasies are all about, didn't you know? They wouldn't be any fun otherwise. They're the unacceptable face of ideology, the underbelly of your psyche. Even puritans have them. God knows what yours are. Come on, I'll show you Meldon's pride and glory – the chapel.'

Chapter Twenty-one

The House of God proved less of a success in William's eyes. Objectively it was a beautiful little building, with cool stone arches, faded wall paintings and exquisite stained-glass windows filtering light onto the flagstones below. A family chapel, marking the rites of passage: births, marriages and deaths through the generations. The place felt cold to him. There was no sense of welcome, and the silence oppressed him. He had been brought up an atheist – that and socialism were the twin pillars of his father's philosophy of life – and the worship of God had always seemed to him an unnatural act. Churches always gave him the same feeling of not belonging. Josie, however, was in her element, darting hither and thither, finding a stream of history in each window and altar carving. The one that struck most ice into William's soul was her favourite. She beckoned him behind one of the arches and pointed to a brass plaque. In a crouching position and in the half-light it was hard to read the inscription.

'Who is it?' He was impatient to finish the history lesson and get back into the sunlight.

'Lady Caroline Childenhurst, daughter of the third Duke. She died of typhoid when she was only ten, in 1645, the third year of the civil war. Look at the words here.'

He peered in further and read, 'Virtue not rolling suns the mind matures.' It took him a moment to work it out. Cold comfort. 'Poor kid,' he muttered.

'Yes, but it was a useful death. Watch this. Move out of the way.'

She ran her hands over the plaque. At the bottom right hand corner she located a small brass ring embedded in the wall. She hooked her first two fingers round it and turned it sharply to the right. Nothing happened. She tried again. The third time he heard a small click. There was a soft, scraping sound and the right side of the plaque began to fall inwards into the darkness. A musty, damp smell rushed out to greet them. William bent forward but could see nothing but blackness.

'A priest's hole!' he exclaimed. 'In a chapel? Seems a pretty stupid place to put it.'

She pushed the plaque further open, and fresh and stale air

mingled around them. 'It's not a priest's hole. That's the point. It's a king's hole.'

'What do you mean?'

'I told you. She died in 1645, the second of April. It was the month that Cromwell's forces closed in on the King's court at Oxford. Time was running out. Old Duke Childenhurst was a royalist – the blue blood of privilege and loyalty ran in his veins. The unthinkable was about to happen. His Majesty, ruler by Divine Right, was about to be deserted by the Almighty. When that happened he would need a place to escape to. And he would obviously want to flee to friends. So Childenhurst built this. It was both his daughter's memorial and his sovereign's sanctuary. The idea was utterly unrealistic, of course. In the end the King surrendered, and Childenhurst and the rest of them watched in horror while he talked himself onto the scaffold. Nevertheless, it was a gesture.'

William stared into the hole. 'Where does it lead?'

She shrugged. 'I don't know. I've never been down there. Originally, apparently, it burrowed right under the outer wall and came out in the middle of the forest outside. But there is no record of anyone ever using it. In fact, apart from one entry in the local records, no one knew about it at all. Classified information. The cosmetics millionaire restored some of it, I gather, but when we first came here the guide said no one had been down there for a couple of decades. He thought it might have caved in halfway down. He was loth to show it to us at all. It was only because I'd heard about it and insisted that we got to see it. I wonder if Rob's been down there.'

'I doubt it,' William muttered, turning away from the dank smell. 'If it was built for royalty, I don't think commoners should push their luck.'

'You mean you'd prefer to leave it for another day?'

'Something like that.'

She smiled, turning the brass ring the other way. The plaque clicked back into place. She gave it a little push. It didn't move.

'What happens if you're on the other side and you want to get out again?'

'Dunno,' she said. 'I never asked. Presumably there's a catch. Or maybe a bell like they used to have in coffins in case people were buried alive. See, there are worse fates than being on the run from the police. You remember that when you can't sleep at night.'

'Thanks. Now, can we get out of here?'

Out in the courtyard the shadows were long and gentle. The land of the living. It soothed William's goosepimples.

'You all right?' she asked playfully.

'I'm fine. I just don't like churches. They're cold places.'

'But don't you feel the sense of age in them?'

'I don't feel age. I feel death. I would have expected you to feel the same. You're supposed to be a materialist. What about all the opiate of the people stuff? Surely you ought to see churches as symbols of people accepting their fate as God's will, instead of going out and trying to change things.'

'I'm not saying I agree with how they lived their lives, I'm just saying the place feels alive with all the energy that went into it. I get a buzz off the imprint left behind, that's all.'

'If I'd said that, you'd accuse me of romantic mysticism. You'd never be so tolerant of other forms of comfort today, like people who go and see Billy Graham. You'd condemn that as reactionary. Remember it was the Church that kept the status quo intact for the best part of two thousand years.'

She grinned at him. 'Very good. We'll have you renouncing the SDP yet. Listen, I'm not disagreeing. I'm just adding that I have other reactions as well as anger. Anyway, I can't do anything to change the past. I reserve my energies for the present and the future. Talking of which, how about dinner? You do remember, don't you, that you agreed to cook?'

It was suddenly like real life again. Just a couple of friends on a never-ending holiday in someone else's stately home.

'Very well. Shall we say meat and two veg at eight p.m. in the baronial hall?'

'Formal or informal?'

'It depends if I can get my suit pressed in time.'

'Informal then.' She strode off across the courtyard to the stairs which led up to the gallery and library. He called after her:

'What will you do?'

'Guide myself round the rest of the house. Then institute a search. If this really is Rob's house, then somewhere, no doubt hidden away with cunning architectural taste, there has to be a music system. I'll take it upon myself to find you music while you work.'

Later, as he stood in front of the great slab of a chopping board, with a hunk of defrosted steak lying as a sacrifice to their hunger, he was forced to admit that Rob kept a good larder. And a good cellar. It was strange, forming your impressions of someone's old lover on the strength of their frozen foods and vintages. Clearly though, from his taste in the latter, success had gone to Rob's palate. William picked modestly, but even so it would be wise not to mention to Josie just how much money they were drinking. No wonder they had split up. And I'm the one with the northern puritan background, he thought. Where had she picked up hers? Maybe he could ask her that tonight over dinner. It no longer seemed such a struggle having real conversations. Coming here had definitely changed her. That knot of resentment had been dissolved. She was more accommodating, less defensive.

From somewhere a soft wave of choral music began to seep in through the walls. He stopped in mid-cut, knife poised. Monteverdi's Vespers. But from where? Evidently Josie had found the music system. He put down his knife and stood in the middle of the room, like a dog after a scent. Eventually he tracked it down. It came from two miniature speakers concealed behind the ends of a cross beam. Of wires he found no trace. Very impressive - one up to Rob. Presumably this meant there was music in every room in the house. What would the old Duke Childenhead, or whatever his name was, have made of that?

At that moment Josie burst in. He glanced at her, then back at the steak, then back at her again. If he didn't know better he would have said she had made an effort with her appearance. Her hair was washed and possibly even brushed. She was wearing another T-shirt, bright pink with Special Branch Far East Tour 81 stencilled on the front and something incomprehensible in Japanese on the back. And could she have put mascara on? No, surely not Josie.

'Pretty amazing, eh?'

'Well, different anyway. Is this your definition of informal?'

'What? No, not me, crudface. The music. You won't believe the system he's got. Behind a library shelf, of course. I should have guessed he'd go in for an architectural cliché. It connects to the whole house, every single room - excluding the chapel, that is, but then Rob always was a conservative underneath. It's everywhere, at the flick of a switch.'

'It's devilish what these little nippons can get up to now.'

'Oh piss off,' she replied affectionately. 'What do you think of my choice of music? Especially for you, a little high church boogie.

Beautiful, don't you think? It was either that or the Eagles. Would that have made you feel more at home?'

'You mean Rob has both?'

'Rob has everything. Eclectic, I believe the word is. But good taste, no dross. Classical, jazz, blues, rock 'n roll, reggae, punk. It's a veritable sound archive up there. Tomorrow if we're still talking I'll DJ you through an instant nostalgia trip. "California Dreamin" on "The Eve of Destruction." '

'For someone who professes to despise the sixties so much, you know an awful lot about its music.'

'Yeah, well you'd be surprised how quickly your generation got hold of the air waves and started dictating nostalgia fashions.'

'Tell me, what exactly have you got against the sixties? I would have thought from where you stand that generation was a damned sight more political than the ones that came both before and after.'

'That,' she said, hitting the word with relish, 'is exactly what I'd expect from a man who probably first fucked to the sound of the Loving Spoonful.'

'The Doors, actually. Get your facts right. And answer the question.'

She moved across the room and hoisted herself onto one of the chestnut worktops, where she sat cross-legged. He caught a faint whiff, a smell that was not Josie but something more rich and strange. He opened his mouth to comment, but she was off out of the starting block before him.

'The Doors, the Loving Spoonful . . . it makes no difference. The thing about all you sixties children is this sanctimonious belief you share that yours was the only generation that did it right. You think you had a monopoly on political consciousness, and the one blueprint for peaceful revolution. Make love not war.' She wrinkled her nose. 'Jesus, it sounds like such a Utopian museum piece now.'

'Does that mean you feel the same contempt for CND? Are they naive too?'

'No, of course not. But they dropped the bit about love, didn't they? Anyway, that's not the point. The point is that you were an impossible act to follow. You really thought you could change everything. "Could do what's never been done." You felt you were the first and last *real* generation. It was all bullshit. Wisdom on a dot of blotting paper. The most original thing about you lot is how completely you allowed yourself to be manipulated by the media.

And what happened to all your precious ideals? What's left of them? A few bozos living off alfalfa sprouts in some Colorado paradise? Or selling mung beans and stripped pine dressers in underdeveloped bits of Wales? The rest sold out and bought in long ago – using your good self as an example. You not only betrayed your ideals, you played straight into their hands. The right swept back in on a ticket of supplanting permissiveness with authority, and as a result the next generation – mine – have no jobs. I tell you, as far as I'm concerned the sixties were the last *un*real generation. "I can see for miles and miles" – crap. You never made it over your own back fence.'

Something she said touched a chord, but maybe it was the emotion rather than the logic. William was never a hippie, he had no reason to feel threatened. But it was his youth – its values, tone, atmosphere – she was knocking. He said, 'Are you sure you're not jealous?'

'Jealous? Sure I'm jealous. I'm jealous that when you were growing up it was a time of plenty and boundless opportunity, whereas kids today have fuck all to look forward to. You could afford to drop out – we have to fight to get in. Ten, fifteen years ago the power was there to be taken, but you just frittered it away in style.'

'Come on, Josie. Don't be naive. Power is always unattainable almost by definition. And everything is about style at some level. Safety pins and Bostik are style. Marijuana versus glue, what's the difference?'

'Glue's cheaper. It's a question of economics.'

'Exactly. So punk is no more political than hippies were.'

'You're wrong. In essence it is more political. Because it's about not having enough, rather than having too much. That's a much more powerful protest. It's the establishment that labels it as style, flatters it, encourages it, to try and divert people from its content. It's a deliberate way of defusing the danger.'

'That's just theory. You think kids today are political? What do you know about working-class kids?'

'I could ask you the same question.'

'But I have an answer. I work with them, don't I? Skinheads, dreadlocks, punks, they all pass through my office, and some of them, one or two, come out with a job. I can see what being on the dole means, I can see it on their faces. But if you think that's made them political, then you're deluding yourself. They still read the

Sun, just like everyone else. And anyway, what's it got to do with you? Your trouble is you don't belong to either the sixties or the eighties. You don't have the confidence of my generation, but nor have you experienced the poverty of this one. There really isn't anything for you to be personally angry about. You have all this energy and you don't know what to do with it, so you invent a myth that you belong to the class of underprivileged youth. You're not underprivileged - you're not even young. You're twenty-eight, Josie, not eighteen.'

'Just the age to stop fretting about the exploited and change sides, right? How old were you when you made the leap? Unemployment isn't a law of nature, you know. We could be doing things differently.'

'Yes, but whether you like it or not, this government has a mandate. It was a democratic decision. And it wasn't only the upper and middle classes who voted them in.'

'Yeah well, stupidity always was a working-class characteristic,' she said mockingly.

'I didn't say that.'

'No, but you implied it. And if you're not going to start frying the onions I suggest you take the pan off the heat.'

Hard to concentrate on two things at once. The pan on the Aga was spitting. He used the crisis as an excuse to stop the conversation. She picked up a ragged end of it.

'Maybe when all this is over I'll get a job writing jingles for crazy hair colour. Get into the swing a bit. Put on a little style.'

'I don't know. You're not looking too bad,' he said, his attention deliberately fixed on the frying pan. 'Something of a transformation, I would say.'

'I had a bath,' she growled a warning.

'And I suppose the bottle of Chanel No. 12 just toppled in of its own accord.' Might as well be hung for a sheep as a lamb. He waited to see how she would react.

To his surprise, or perhaps relief, she found it very funny, expressing her amusement with a great hoot of laughter. He hadn't seen her laugh like that before. 'I know. I slapped on a bit of Rob's aftershave, but I fancied I'd overdone it. I just couldn't resist it. You should see the cupboard up there. It's crammed with the stuff. Real poncy chunky-man selection.'

'Maybe Meldon is where he brings his young virgins to seduce them?'

She snorted, disentangling her legs and jumping off the table. 'Virgins! I can't imagine there are many of those in the music business. Anyway, it's not Rob's style. He's more the "Hey babe, let's be honest about this, do you want to fuck" type. Or at least he was.'

'Was he? Is that how you and—'

'That's how he tried it on first, yes.'

'What did you say?'

'I told him to get stuffed. He's not really like that anyway. It's just his way of covering up his insecurity.'

Ah, the subtle ways in which women destroy their menfolk, he thought. 'Well, I'm sure you did a lot for his confidence.'

'Actually . . .' she dug into the cutlery drawer. 'You're right, I did. In all kinds of ways. He was very unsure of himself when he met me.'

'In which case you no doubt see yourself responsible for his success today. Behind every great man . . . etc., etc.'

'Yeah, and let me tell you it won't be long before we're crawling all over you.' She brandished a handful of knives at him. 'When's dinner?'

'Half an hour.'

'Fine. I'll lay the table. Then I'm going to read a book. Ring the gong when it's ready.'

'Very well, memsahib. Me cook, you eat. Very politically pure relationship.'

They ate after sunset in the film set of the baronial hall, inside a circle of candlelight with darkness lapping all around. But the atmosphere proved too strong, and after a few failed attempts at conversation they lapsed into silence. The sounds of cutlery and glass echoed up into the great roof. He remembered other silences between them, when her anger or fear had clogged up the airwaves. It was not like that now. Nothing in their situation had changed much. They were still fugitives, still outlawed and pursued, but she had quietened and he had relaxed. It was that simple. He did not risk questioning it. After dinner she went to bed. It seemed the stillness had released an exhaustion in her. He let her go. He stayed for a while in the hall, staring into the black half of the room, his mind imagining celebrations of centuries past. Then he cleared away the plates and took a brandy up to the study with its cunningly concealed stereo system.

He sat in an armchair by the light of a standard lamp and

pretended to read a book. It was there, for the first time that day, that he thought about home. And it was there, for the first time since this whole crazy roller coaster began, that the thought did not disturb him. Images of normality came to him: alone in the flat reading the electronics and computer magazines he kept up with not just because of work but as a hobby; with friends, eating, drinking, talking; at work, interviewing, at meetings, hustling. There they were, pictures of him that he recognized, but all of them caught behind glass, as if they now belonged to someone else. He could see but he couldn't touch. Eleven days, that was all. Eleven days since that thud of her body against the frame of the car. Could one's reality prove so fragile? Surely no one adapts that fast to chaos. The questions seemed academic. He was here and, like a traveller stepping off the plane after a long journey, the place he had come from had, in some ways, already ceased to exist. The William Stevens of two weeks ago was a different person.

Even the thought of Penny was blurred. He concentrated on recreating her face as he had seen it two days before. It swam in and out of vision. So be it. He brought himself back to the present, and soon he stopped worrying about the fact that he was not worrying, and went to bed. This time he did not lie awake registering the night moves of the house. And so ended the first day.

Chapter Twenty-two

There were times later when William would cross-examine himself about the days spent at Meldon. They seemed to blur into one another, as if glued together by the heat. He would be able to pinpoint certain specific hours spent exploring the gardens and the wings of the house, or playing games of snooker with himself; he would recall a certain conversation that took place in a certain room at a certain time of day, but the exact chronology was to defeat him.

Until, that is, the night when panic brought back an enforced structure and a new awareness of time. But that was the beginning of the end, and from there it moved faster than sense itself. Before that, it was all a haze, coloured by a feeling of quiet waiting, and without the perpetual headache that the tensions and sudden reversals of the week before had given him.

She too responded to the magic, but in a different way. For a while she was preoccupied, taking time off on her own, exhibiting what to him seemed an uncharacteristic talent for silence. It did not last long, maybe a day or so. He assumed the house had awoken ghosts, and she was exorcising them. He left her alone.

She would have put it differently. She would have told of bad dreams that, for the first nights, plucked her from sleep and made her early rising involuntary. Not, as she might have expected, nightmares of pursuit and danger, but insistent, chaotic images of frustration and failure. In one of these she was on board ship with Rob, heading for port. Just before disembarking, they lost each other in the crush. She searched for him everywhere, growing more and more frantic, until at the very last moment she ran across the gangplank to the shore, leaving one of her bags behind. As the boat pulled away again, she spotted him on deck, arms leaning on the rail, watching her solemnly as the water grew wide between them. When she awoke she was disgusted by the flagrant symbolism of the dream, its absurd over-simplification. She tried to fall asleep again, and when that failed she crept downstairs to drink coffee and stare out over a lawn covered in dew. And there, amid a chorus of birdsong, the pictures faded. But the feelings remained: the sense of business unfinished, of circumstance directing outcome, luggage left behind in the rush. She was not helped by the occasional shadows of Rob that leapt out at her from odd corners of the house. In the end it seemed easier to confront them, to regurgitate the half-digested emotions and aggressions of four years ago. And finally, exposed to the open air and the sunlight, it proved not so traumatic an experience. What she found was a little sad, a little raw in parts, but not, as she had always feared, some gaping, unhealed wound. There was the feeling that they could have done it better, been a little more honest, a little less rough, but then, who couldn't? Afterwards (she used the word defiantly, as if it were only a matter of time), she decided, she would get in touch with him again, if only to shake hands and agree to part friends. That night she slept without dreaming.

William and Josie travelled towards each other in ever-decreasing circles. At first neither of them noticed, assuming the distance between them had become fixed and reliable. On the third afternoon they found themselves together in the rose garden. He was trying to read a book. She was sitting cross-legged, like an apprentice yogi, absorbed in the delicate process of picking bits of peeling skin off her back.

'There are two sorts of people,' he said. It might have been disapproving. 'Those who pick, and those who leave well alone. You look like a Peking duck.'

She carefully lifted off a long line clean from her neck to the edge of her shoulder and brandished it triumphantly. It hung like wet rice paper from her hand. 'It's a bit like over-stretched bubble gum, don't you think?'

'No, I don't think. Did your analyst ever tell you there's still an unhealthy element of the rebellious child within you?'

'And did yours diagnose a surfeit of the over-protective parent? I wonder which is worse.'

She flicked the piece of skin his way. He dodged. The sun got hotter by the minute. A summer for the record books. It would make repetitive conversations for years to come. Certainly too hot to read. He pulled off his shirt and lay back in the grass. The stalks pricked his bare skin. He closed his eyes. The afternoon stretched into infinity.

He wondered what Joshua was doing. It was a question they had learned not to ask each other. If either of them was worried by his silence, they did not show it. For William the fact of his absence prowled on the perimeter of their sense of security but somehow never penetrated it. After all, what seemed a lifetime of them was still only a few working days in the real world. When Joshua had news, he'd call, not before. It became harder and harder to imagine what he would say.

'Do you think about what will happen next?' he asked, his eyes closed.

'Not really. Not any more. Do you?'

'Occasionally. But it's hard to get the picture to stay in focus. I can't conceive how it would be if this doesn't get sorted out. But then I can't imagine going back to the real world when it is. That's the strangest thing of all - and I can't seem to worry about it. Do you think everyone in danger has this same reaction - to disconnect?'

'I don't know. Maybe it's Meldon?'

'What do you mean?'

'Just that it's as unreal as we are. Maybe more so. That's why we fit in so well.'

He looked up. She had desisted from flaying herself and was playing with a piece of grass, running it along her bare leg. She looked different. Maybe it was the light. Her cheeks were flushed with sunshine and her hair a jet black halo against the glare and the blue sky. I like you when you're easy, he thought, when you're self-contained and still. He wondered whether he found her attractive. He said:

'So, would you like to have lived here?'

Her glance moved up the façade of the house, with its windows glinting and the trails of ivy patterning the red brickwork. A fantasy building. 'I don't think I would have been able to live up to it. That's the point. You can't be unreal all the time. It would have gone sour.'

'Even with a lover?'

'Especially with a lover. Rob and I would have torn each other's throats out. It would have been a bloodbath.'

'So you were never tempted?'

'By what?'

'I don't know. The prospect of another kind of life. The freedom to do anything you wanted to do.'

'You mean the money? No, I think my fear was always bigger than my appetite. I remember coming back from abroad, when he was flavour of the month and his face used to stare out at me from every teen magazine on every bookstall, then - sometimes - I used to wonder what it would have been like if we were still together. I was a bit lost then, and he seemed so definite. It's funny. You're not usually presented with such a clear distinction between the path you've taken and the one you haven't. But it wouldn't have lasted. I know that much. He knew it too. He knew I would have freaked out because it was his life and his money, with no role for me in it apart from being "Rob's lover". I would have caused untold damage getting free from that definition.' She shrugged. 'Anyway, we always wanted different things. We just got on well for a while, that's all.'

He had never heard her make a speech so long off her soapbox. He recalled the spitting, bullying tornado who had hurled insults at police officers and caused caravans to rock with her suppressed fury. Maybe he was that different also. The idea disturbed him slightly, like being caught in public with the wrong clothes on. Possibly the idea had occurred to her too. She had turned her attention back to her shoulder, the tip of her tongue poking through the side of her mouth in precise concentration. The way was open for more conversation. But he felt a little more exposed.

He got up and collected his shirt. She registered the move but did not look at him.

'Getting too hot for you?' she said brightly.

He chose to take the remark innocently. 'It's my turn to cook again. I've got things to prepare.'

On his way back he thought, for an instant, that he detected the sound of a telephone ringing, muffled by closed doors and summer distance, but the house was its usual soft, silent self. He put it down to his imagination, but later, after an evening walk and then dinner, when they were having coffee and brandy in the Tudor room, he mentioned it to her.

She nodded slowly. 'If it was him, he'll call again,' was all she said.

'I sometimes wonder, you know, even if he does get the story, will his editor print it?'

Her answer was a shrug.

'Assuming that there is a final explanation. I have the impression sometimes that the truth behind this is impenetrable – like some gigantic tapeworm, all entwined around itself.'

'What a great image. Truth as a leviathan,' she said, staring into the empty fireplace. She seemed to be thinking of something else. Her sense of ease was almost tangible.

'You know, I'm amazed at your apparent optimism, and your sanguineness. I would have expected you to be running round in mental circles by now.'

She smiled, stretching herself slightly, tucking her legs further under her as she sat curled up on the floor. 'No doubt it's all the practice I got doing sixteen-hour bus rides through the middle of nowhere when I was travelling. Nothing to do but let your mind wander. It breeds a kind of unholy patience.'

He took another sip of brandy. It tasted good. Outside, the night pressed harder on the window panes. They could be the last two people left in the world. Funny, he thought, to be in such close contact with a woman who is not a lover. Hard to know the rules. He caught her eye and smiled. She did not respond. He felt a pinprick of tension dance between them. It was too late to duck. The blow was already on its way.

'I'm not intending to go to bed with you, you know.'

The words marched over to his seat and poked him hard in the chest. He flinched, but did not give ground. She retreated just a fraction. He nodded slowly. Josie was Josie. He should have known.

'I see. And do you always refuse before being asked?'

'I just felt it was in the air. Or would be soon. I wanted to avoid any confusion.'

'Well, you certainly have done that. Thanks a million.'

Silence. This time she looked for him. 'Did I offend you?'

'No.' It could be forgiven as a white lie. 'Although I admit I've had more sensitive interchanges.'

'I just thought it would be more honest to say what I felt.'

'Josie, not saying what you feel is certainly something you could never be accused of, believe me.'

'It's not that I'm not attracted to you.'

Another body blow. But this time he had his muscles already tightened. 'Wait a minute. Let me get this straight. It's not that you're not attracted to me?'

'No.'

'I see.'

'No, you don't see. It's got nothing to do with that. It's just that I think it would be dangerous. What we're beginning to feel now is the kind of attraction that's about circumstance. We didn't fancy each other when we met. And in real life we'd never be the type to go to bed together. It's just that we've been flung into each other's company, and —'

'Now sex has reared its ugly head. Is that what you're trying to say?'

'Something like that. Don't laugh. I'm serious.'

'I'm not laughing. You think it would be dangerous?'

'Yes, in fact I think it would be a disaster.'

'You know for certain, do you?'

'Yes.'

'And you're always right? I mean, every time you don't do something, you can be absolutely sure what the outcome would have been if you had?'

'You *are* offended!'

'No. No, I'm not. I'm intrigued.'

'But you were thinking about it, weren't you?'

'About what?'

'About us sleeping together.'

'It had crossed my mind. But I can't say I was getting obsessive about it. And I had no intention of pushing it. If it was going to happen it would happen, if not –'

'Well, isn't it better that we've got it out into the open?'

'No. Not really.'

'You just don't like me taking the initiative.'

He allowed himself a little obvious sigh. 'Josie, you've been taking practically all the initiative for the past two weeks. Do you think I'm going to start complaining now?'

'You are laughing at me.'

'No, I'm not. Well, maybe just a fraction.'

'What does that mean?'

He thought about it. This wasn't the time to misjudge. 'I think you're reacting rather oddly. Here we are, for the first time possibly since we met, getting on really quite well together. I mean, even the arguments feel all right. So here we are feeling good, and you have to come along and stomp all over it. You say it's plain speaking. I say it's just the opposite.'

A pause, which she didn't fill. Small steps now, William, and watch out for snipers. 'You see,' he continued. 'It might, just might, you understand, have been O.K. to sleep together. I agree that the attraction is one that's been made rather than born, but sometimes it's like that. I'll go further. Not only might it have been O.K., it might even have been rather nice. And – God forbid that I should suggest it – we, that is, you as well as me, might have enjoyed it. And it could have been entirely without consequences. Sleeping with someone doesn't cause instant destruction, or at least, not in my limited experience.'

'It would have complicated things.'

'And they are, of course, not complicated at all now.'

'In some ways they're still simple. I want to keep them that way.'

'You're frightened of letting go.'

'That's bullshit.'

'And that reaction is a giveaway. What kind of men do you usually sleep with? Since Rob?'

'Will it make you feel any better to have a vicarious conversation about sex?'

'Josie, I'm knocking at the door, that's all. I'm not forcing it open, or breaking any windows. It doesn't give anything away to just let go of the catch and open up. You can keep the chain on. I've just come to chat, that's all.'

'Personnel Management. I don't need any today, thanks.' But she didn't move. She seemed smaller than she had been, as if she had withdrawn herself physically as well as emotionally.

'I'm sorry,' he said. 'I didn't mean to intrude.'

'You didn't.' The answer came hard on his words, too fast to be considered. 'I just don't particularly want to talk about it.'

He left a pause. 'Do you want another drink?'

She nodded and put out her glass. He had the bottle next to him. He was glad of that. To move would be to break the spell. He leaned over and poured the brandy. It was up to her now. He let the time pass. Somewhere in the house a plank of wood stretched. Despite the conversation he still felt good.

'It's hardly of major importance,' she said quietly, addressing her brandy glass with great concentration. 'There was a time when I slept with a lot of people. As a matter of principle really. I didn't even fancy all of them. I just did it. And it felt O.K. But it takes a lot of energy, that kind of thing. Having to be the person you want them to think you are. So I stopped. I didn't miss it. Occasionally now I might find someone for a night or two, but usually I don't. It's fine. My decision. Does that answer your question?'

'Why?'

'Why what?'

'Why was *that* your decision?'

'I told you. I get fed up with—'

'Maybe you were picking the wrong men.'

'Maybe I just prefer being on my own.'

'I find that hard to believe. Few people really do prefer it. What's so inspiring about being alone?'

'You answer the question. You broke up with Penny because you wanted to be free again.'

'No. I broke up with Penny because I didn't think I wanted to commit myself to her, and that was what she wanted. It's not the same thing.'

'The result's the same. You're alone.'

'Yes, and I missed her.'

'Did you?'

'Yes, although I don't think I realized it until a few days ago. Until I saw her again.'

'True love born out of crisis?' But her tone was gentle. 'So, when all this is over, you'll go back and propose to her?'

'I don't know. Missing someone is not the same as wanting to live with them for the rest of your life.'

'You could always live together for a while.'

'I don't think that option is open to us now. Ten years ago, perhaps, but not now.'

'Well, I shouldn't worry about it too much. It may never come to that. There's many a slip betwixt here and normality. And anyway, would Penny want to shack up with a wanted man? It doesn't exactly enhance your respectability rating.'

'Thanks for reminding me.'

'Oh, you'll be O.K. I'd even go so far as to say you're improving. I think being an outlaw suits you.'

'Refreshes the parts that other experiences can't reach, you mean?'

'Something like that.'

'Well, maybe it's mutual. How does it feel not needing to be angry all the time?'

'Fuck off.'

'Aaah, thank God for that. I was beginning to think I'd lost you altogether. It would never do for you to turn sentimental on me at this stage.'

'Don't disturb yourself. You don't have a thing to worry about.'

'Good.' He got up and stood for a second looking at her. 'It's late. I think I'm going to bed.'

There was a pause. She nodded. 'Sleep well.'

The exchanged look continued. 'I will,' he said softly. He took a step towards the door. 'I enjoyed the evening, Josie. Maybe we could do it again sometime.'

'Yeah,' she nodded. 'I'll look in my diary. Good night.'

'Good night.' At the door he turned. 'By the way, you do understand that the real reason you won't sleep with me is that you're beginning to like me, don't you? I can't decide whether to be flattered or alarmed.'

He moved out of the room swiftly, before she could find a missile to hurl at him.

She poured herself another drink and sat for a long time gazing at the fireplace. She thought of the first time she had slept with Rob; of that potent cocktail of fear and desire that propels you to take the leap in the dark, and the glory that comes from losing yourself, for however short a time, in sex without thinking. It seemed, when she looked back on it, that she had spent years thinking. It was hard to know if the magic could ever work for her again. Listen to her! Here they were, outlawed, pursued, their very lives in danger, and all they could think about was the mating ritual. What was that old newspaperman's cliché? That in every war zone you'll come across journalists getting their end away while bullets scorch overhead. When it came down to it, maybe the adrenalin of fear was not so far removed from the adrenalin of sexual attraction. They were both about loss of control.

The thought took her back to Joshua. She wondered if he felt the excitement, or just the burden of their lives in his hands. She wondered also how far he had got. Did his silence mean that he was still tugging at the ends of William's great tapeworm, or had he, perhaps, managed to find the centre? In which case, why hadn't he called? She fell asleep debating the answers.

At a point somewhere in the black of the night the telephone rang.

Chapter Twenty-three

It should have been Joshua. In a world of just deserts it ought to have been him. Even at the very moment when Josie was conjuring up thoughts of him in the Meldon darkness, he was hunched over his typewriter in the office hammering out the final draft of the story which would surely make him famous. In only a matter of time he would pick up the phone, dial long distance, and say to the sleepy voice that greeted him, 'You're safe. I've done it. I've got the story.'

It should have been. It ought to have been. There were many reasons why it wasn't. But if one could draw a line through the mixture of fate and chance that makes up people's lives, then, in Joshua's case, that line would run directly through Chief Superintendent Daniels's room in Highgate police station that Friday afternoon when William, in the midst of perjury, let slip a half truth about Josie: 'She said something about contacting a journalist.'

When Josie repeated that remark to Joshua from the call box at the caravan site on the Saturday morning, it disturbed him more than he cared to admit. Of course there were dozens of journalists covering the Royal Highgate story. And he wasn't even one of them – officially, as far as his news editor was concerned. Nevertheless he was relieved he had not left a name when he had called De Villiers' home and office two days before. From now on, he resolved, he would tread very carefully.

Except that William's visit to the police made everything more urgent. William's subsequent flight meant the attempted wedge between him and Josie had not succeeded. The frame-up would now have to include both of them. In police eyes William might still get away with being the duped accomplice. But for the conspirators he had crossed the line from being a nuisance to a threat. They would be out for another electric kettle solution. It was up to Joshua to get to them before they got to William and Josie.

But how? Where did it start? What did he have to go on? A BOSS agent with a watertight alibi, friends in high places and a death squad at his fingertips. A conspiracy that set out to smear the left, organized by the South African right, endorsed by the police, and involving a hospital security guard with a murky political past. A leftwing accomplice in a rightwing plot? And someone who apparently knew so much that he had to be eliminated in the blast. The only witness. But to what? Now it seemed the loose ends led back to O'Grady.

Sitting at his desk that Saturday morning after he had put down the phone to Josie, he thought back again to Mrs O'Grady's living room, and their polite, pointless interview. The room had been tidy, precise, just like the woman herself. He remembered that self-possession, the way her contained grief had kept him at arm's length. A woman guarding her home, guarding her children – guarding also her husband? She had given the impression of strength, of being the kind of woman a husband might talk to if he had something on his mind. The house had felt as if there was love in it. If O'Grady had been in trouble, surely she was the one he would have gone to for advice? Yes, Helen O'Grady had to know more than she'd told.

He dialled her number. No answer. He took a shower, dressed, had coffee and tried again. The phone was still bleating in an empty house. But it was Saturday morning. There were two kids, a house to run, and probably a gauntlet of neighbours, well-wishers and plain busybodies to get through every time she went out. She could be anywhere. Supermarket, laundrette, cemetery even. Or maybe she simply still wasn't answering the phone. In which case it would just have to be a doorstep vigil.

The satisfaction of a decision achieved lasted with him all the way to work. Entering the building he encountered Bert Williams, one of the photographers, on his way out. 'Hi,' said Joshua. 'Know who else is doing a shift today?'

Bert gave him an odd, what's-it-to-you? look, muttered 'Tony Morris, I think,' and sped out.

Tony Morris. The day was improving. He'd once given Morris a lift to the pound the day the fuzz had towed away his car for covering a double yellow line near Blackfriars. The bizarre demarcations of Fleet Street made a favour returned Joshua's best chance of having the job done. Upstairs in the large, open-plan newsroom, Joshua found Tony at the picture desk squinting at a sheet of contact prints. Joshua didn't interrupt. When Tony finished marking them he made his pitch. Tony's memory seemed to have got shorter.

'Oh come on, Joshua. If I'd wanted a vocation printing other people's holiday snaps, I'd have joined Kodak.'

'Tony, I told you, it's work. And it'll only take ten minutes.'

'Yeah, and my son's annual school cricket match begins at two thirty. Now that won't mean anything to you, because you don't have a family, but believe me, neither will I if I get home a minute after two.'

'I wouldn't ask if it wasn't important.'

'I know. That's what I'm worried about. What've you been doing taking pictures? Not moonlighting, I hope. Come on, hand 'em over. Let's have a look.'

'Thanks, Tony. I'll buy you a drink.'

'Yeah, every day next year.' He pulled the prints out of the envelope, then the negs. Against the light box his face creased up in professional disgust. 'On second thoughts, maybe you should stop drinking altogether. What did you do, forget to read the instructions?'

'Something like that. Can you do anything with them? I need to get a better look at the faces.'

'You gotta be joking,' he shrugged. 'Who are these geezers anyway?'

Joshua shook his head.

'Oops. Pardon me. I'm not after your story. Looks to me like a couple of Gulf oil ministers carving up OPEC in a London cemetery. I just hope it's not for the colour supplement.'

'Tony –'

'All right, all right. But I leave here at one thirty-five on the dot. If you're not here to collect them . . .'

'You'll leave them on my desk upstairs. Good idea.'

'You sure you don't want me to write the story for you?'

'Oh, and Tony?'

'Yeah?'

'In a brown envelope – O.K?'

'You cheeky sod. Don't be so paranoid. Who'd touch this story with a barge pole? And you watch your step. You know what happens to people who write the wrong stories about the Gulf states.'

From the door Joshua grinned back. 'Listen, I'll do you a deal. If your son scores a century, I'll take the pictures and you can write the story for the sports page.'

His answer was unprintable.

At his desk, Joshua took out his address book. Rob Taggart, superstar, proprietor of superior hotel accommodation for old lovers fleeing from justice. He had better be in. He imagined the phone ringing near an elegant bed in a gold lamé apartment littered with the debris of pleasure. Eleven thirty. The morning after the night before. Rob took a long time to answer. But he woke fast when he heard what the call was about.

'We've got an old friend who needs a place to stay.'

He understood immediately, asked no questions, just gave the details required and made it clear there were other kinds of help he could give if and when needed. It was as if he'd been waiting for the call. 'Josh, presumably this conversation is best forgotten about.'

'What conversation?' Joshua replied as he put down the phone.

All he needed now was for a widow to talk.

On a second visit the Dartmouth Park Hill council estate still looked better than most. The red and gold bricks, the rust-coloured railings and the unexpected arrangement of space and light reflected an imagination not usually consistent with a local authority budget. But then Camden was not a usual local borough. 'Well, we qualify for a rent rebate, so it doesn't affect us.' Mrs O'Grady had been almost tempted into conversation on the topic of new council housing. 'But I daresay you'd hear a different story from the private house owners round here. But they've got the money haven't they?'

Outside her front door the window boxes looked tired and brown. Maybe she had felt the need to watch other things die in memory of him. It didn't feel like her though. There had been too much of the practical about her. Through the letterbox he saw a bare hall and closed doors. No newspapers, not even any circulars. The plastic milk crate had its needle pointed to No Milk. It wasn't promising. He released the doorbell and stood thinking. Down the street across the road a man in fawn trousers was sitting on a bench reading a newspaper. Joshua did an automatic check on the masthead. Not his. His stomach rumbled, reminding him he'd had no breakfast. One p.m. Maybe she was picking up her daughter from ballet lessons. Unlikely. He had a memory of Saturday lunch always being late as they awaited the return of his sister Sarah, a carthorse with pretensions to grace. For some the powers of auto-suggestion are not enough. Maybe there was a pub nearby where he could sink a pint and a sandwich.

After lunch he took a walk round the block. A few hundred yards up the road Dartmouth Park Hill narrowed as it rose towards Highgate. On the right, houses gave way to the railings of the hospital compound. It was somewhere up here that Josie and William had seen the car. Joshua hadn't realized it was quite so near. O'Grady had lived close to the job. He would have been able to stroll to work. That Friday night she would have heard the blast that tore her husband apart. Had she been woken from sleep? Or was she perhaps sitting up waiting? How long was it before she knew? Back at the front door he put his finger on the doorbell and left it there. A woman's face apeared at a window in the flat above. She was not pleased.

'Bloody scum. Which one are you from?'

'I'm sorry. I'm looking for Helen O'Grady.' He gave her the benefit of his *Times* impersonation. It did not impress.

'Well, she's not here. She's away.'

'Do you know where I might find her?'

'No, I don't. She didn't say where she was going, and she didn't say when she'd be back. But even if she had, you'd be the last to know. Why can't you leave her alone? You and your bloody newspapers. You've got no respect for human misery, you lot. How would you like it if some bastard had blown up your wife and you had to answer the door twelve times a day to scumbags from the papers, wanting to know what she ate for breakfast? I told you, she's not here, and you're causing a disturbance. If you don't get off her doorstep I'm going to call the police.'

The window slammed. Joshua stood for a moment wondering what course of action other members of his profession might take. A few blue bank notes pressed in the back of a hand? He thought better of it. Clearly Mrs O'Grady and her neighbours had had enough of the fourth estate. He didn't blame them. But he did blame himself. He should have come back sooner. Or got her talking the first time. Wherever she was now, probably the only people who knew were the police. And they weren't likely to tell. That left him with no story at all. And a couple of wasted hours. He checked his watch. Josie and William might be pulling into a service station at any time now. He had to get back to his phone fast. The photos could wait.

Eighteen floors up across the river, there was a message from Culverwell on the answering machine. He was about to return the call when the phone rang and Josie's voice jumped over the pips.

'Where are you?'

'In the middle of nowhere still. We hit roadworks. What did he say?'

He told her briefly.

'Great. I'll call you tonight, when we arrive. After that, it's up to you. Call when you have something to tell us. How you doing?'

'Fine,' he lied. 'Good luck.'

Next he called Culverwell.

'Ah yes, Mr Barnes. I've had a little news I thought you might like to know. Your Mr De Villiers left the country this afternoon. On a South African Airways flight to Jo'burg. A rather sudden departure. His mother, I gather, has been taken unexpectedly ill.'

'I see,' he said, for want of anything better. With so many characters leaving the action, soon there would be no plot at all. 'Did he give any idea when he would be back?'

'No. One often finds, though, that in such cases people are so consumed with filial duty they never return at all. The call of the mother's country, we call it. It can be very powerful.'

'I see what you mean. Do you know if he went alone?'

'There I can't help you. Anyway, I didn't mean to interrupt your weekend. I thought you might like to know.'

'Thank you. Mr Culverwell, when we met you mentioned that you have certain associates who might know more about De Villiers - or his friends.'

'Yes, I did.'

'Well, I'd be very interested in meeting them.'

'Very well. I'll try and contact them for you. But not over the weekend. That would be difficult. Perhaps some time on Monday. You could call round to the office. Let's say eleven thirty unless you hear to the contrary. I think I can arrange something by then.'

'Thank you. Thank you very much indeed.'

So De Villiers had left the country. Virtually an admission of guilt. With two witnesses loose someone had decided on damage-limitation steps. But him and who else? Where, for instance, was egghead? Drinking champagne on a first-class flight to the sun, or holed up in some west London bedsit? And, more important than where, who? It was time to collect the pictures.

In the office things were revving up for the Sunday edition. Tony had been as good as his word. There was a large brown envelope with a string tie, his name in capital letters on the front and within brackets, 'Highly Confidential. Joshua's Scoop'.

'You're very dedicated.' From across the room Carole, the news desk secretary, looked up from her typing and fixed him with a bright blue stare that someone had told him came from coloured contact lenses. They had been out to dinner once, but he'd never summoned up the chutzpah, or motivation, to ask. It had been a nice evening, but a little tense around the edges. She was the kind of girl who tended to invite men into her life to walk all over her. Joshua had liked her, but he had been looking for a contest not a massacre. She'd held a candle for him ever since.

'Hi, Carole. Just picking up some mail.'

'Mmmm, I know. You're a popular man today. But how come you're in here at the weekend? Don't you have anything better to do?'

He made a face. 'You wouldn't believe it. My mother's in town. I think she's here to discuss my future.'

Carole's eyes twinkled. 'Well, I wouldn't show her the photos if I were you.'

He looked down at the envelope. 'Why not?' he said sharply.

Her eyebrows flashed conspiratorially. 'Oooh, just something Tony Morris said, about spending his weekends developing your blue films.'

Joshua smiled weakly. 'Listen, the nearest Tony ever gets to blue films is when someone drops crème de menthe on his negatives.'

'Well,' she giggled, 'they certainly didn't want them in the darkroom. Have a nice weekend,' she added a little wistfully.

'Not a chance. Don't work too hard. See you Monday.'

Safe in the car he unhooked the envelope. A clutch of large, stiff prints cascaded out. He flicked through them. Tony had done a set of the two faces together, then a couple of each separately. The pictures of De Villiers weren't bad; the features were sharp and kept some of their shape even in the coarsened blow-up. But egghead was still hopeless, an abstract of light and dark expanded grain. At arm's length a face of sorts was discernible, with big forehead, slightly bloated cheeks over a square jawline, but Tony was right. On balance the prints were still useless. The pictures editor would certainly think so. Attached to one by a paperclip was Tony's final judgement: 'I warned you. Next time focus the bloody camera and wait till it stops raining. Mine's a triple Glenfiddich.'

He sat back in the car, placing the photos on the seat next to him. He noted with surprise that his hands were sweating slightly. He must be more nervous than he'd realized. His eyes strayed into the wing mirror. Without thinking, he focused on the figure of a man standing in a doorway some way down the road. He was reading a newspaper. Not his. Not his. His memory fed in the picture and came back with another. A man sitting on a bench outside Mrs O'Grady's house. He looked again. He couldn't see the face, but the trousers were a fawn colour. He whipped round in his seat to get a better look out of the rear window. The man left his position in the shop window and strolled away in the opposite direction. Joshua was halfway out of the car when he disappeared down a subway. He got back into the driver's seat slowly, aware of his faster heartbeat. *She said something about contacting a journalist.* Impossible. How could they have found him so quickly? Surely there just happened to be two men reading newspapers wearing fawn trousers in London this Saturday. He hadn't even seen the face. It was his paranoia. Nothing else. He put the key in the ignition. He looked round carefully. There was nothing unusual in sight. He should know better than to breed shadows in his own mind. He drove home slowly, stopping to buy food. No one seemed to be following.

Back home he put the Chinese take-away into the oven to warm up, and took the photos out again. He studied them one by one, hoping for a miracle, then scooped them up to put them back. The envelope felt slightly bulky, as if something else was inside. He put his hand in, expecting to locate the batch of negatives at the bottom, but halfway down his fingers closed on more photographic paper. He pulled, and came out with two more photos of the bomber. But these were different.

The head was turned slightly to the left, as in the others. The grain was a little coarse. But the focus was sharp and clear and the light was perfect. The man staring out of the picture could have been recognized by anyone. His hand shaking, Joshua brought the two photos next to the others. There was no mistake. It was the same man.

But it was not the same film. Even the photographic paper was different: thinner, less shiny, and half the size. Tony had not developed these photos, and what was more Josie had not taken them. He went back to the envelope, searching for the negatives. Josie's originals were there, but nothing more. He picked up the photos again, as if frightened they would disappear unless he held them in his hands. He thought back carefully over every minute of the day. The only time they had been left unattended was on his desk. If seeing was believing, then the only possible explanation for the extra prints was that someone, at some point between one thirty and four thirty had opened the envelope and slipped the new prints inside. But why? And who?

One question at a time. The switchboard took an age to answer, the kind of delay that was the despair of foreign correspondents. Eventually he got through to the news desk. 'Let me speak to Carole.'

A pause, then an extension raised, her voice.

'Carole, hi . . . this is Josh. Josh Barnes.'

'Oh, hi Josh.' Undisguised pleasure. 'Don't tell me your mother stood you up?'

'. . . Er, no. No. Carole, I need to pick your brains for a moment. Is that O.K? Are you busy?'

'Oh,' she said, instead of a speech of disappointment. 'What do you want to know?'

He explained.

'Yes,' she replied. 'I thought I told you. Someone came up, oooh probably about two o'clock, not long after Tony. Said they found a couple of prints in the wash bowl and they thought they might belong to you. So I said it was most likely Tony's lot, and they put them in your envelope.'

'Who were they?'

'Joshua, how should I know? Some guy working on the Sunday, I suppose. You know what they're like down there. It might have been a cleaner.'

'What did he look like?'

'What's up? Did he steal the best ones?'

'Carole, what did he look—'

'Listen, I saw the guy for maybe thirty seconds. He was . . . I don't know . . . ordinary. Thirty, maybe older, fair hair – oh no, it could have been dark. What can I tell you, Josh? I didn't take any notice.'

'Was he wearing fawn trousers?'

'How should I know? I've told you, I was busy. He just came and went. Have you lost something?'

'No, it's O.K.'

'Well, it don't sound O.K.'

'Sorry, I didn't mean to disturb you.'

'S'all right.' A little sullen. 'I was just leaving anyway. Is that all you wanted to know?'

'Yes. Thanks a lot, Carole. And really, don't worry about it. It wasn't important.'

'Yeah, if you say so.'

'Listen, why don't you and I have a drink sometime next week? Are you free?'

There was a pause. 'You don't have to ask me out just 'cos you're feeling guilty, you know. You weren't that rude. I'm not offended.'

Good old Carole. 'No, I mean it. Let's fix a day on Monday. And do me a favour. Next time you see this guy around, just point him out to me, yes?'

'Yeah, all right. Have a nice evening, Joshua. I'll see you next week. Bye.'

At his desk Joshua wrote the whole thing out from beginning to end, hoping the words would find a logic on the page. Someone, it seemed, wanted him to find out more about the bomber. That someone knew who he was, where he worked, where, presumably, he lived. And he knew he had the photos. That must mean he knew he was in contact with Josie. But how —

From the kitchen came the smell of charred chop suey. Halfway through the culinary rescue operation the phone rang. He left the silver foil tray steaming on the table and headed for the receiver. It was after ten. It had to be Josie. The thought stopped him in his tracks, the words he'd just been typing running round his brain - they knew who he was, where he worked, where he lived. The next step wasn't paranoia, it was pure logic. They would be bugging his phone, how could he be sure they weren't? His mind raced. What would they have learned? That depended on when they began. The caravan? But so what? They weren't there any more. Since then they had been careful. Josie had always had a healthy fear of phones. She had used no names for places or people. There would have been snippets of information about Meldon, but nothing concrete. Joshua hadn't talked to Rob from here, only from the office. Phone calls from call boxes all over England, voices in the wilderness. Anyway, it might have only just begun. They might only have traced him today. They might still be setting up the wires. But if the plugs were in and he picked up the phone now . . . Then they would have Meldon.

He forced himself to walk to the other side of the room and sit in an armchair. The phone rang and rang. Pinned up on the cork notice board, the bomber surveyed the room. It didn't make sense. Was he being helped or trapped? The noise stopped abruptly in the middle of a ring. From now on he would have to call them.

It was then that he remembered the reason for the phone call. Josie was going to give him the Meldon number.

Chapter Twenty-four

He was up at seven and went out for a run to get his brain started. He took his usual route, across the Highway, down Wapping Lane to the docks. The streets were deserted. On a derelict plot by the river he spotted a prostrate body half covered in newspaper. There was something in the way it was lying. He approached apprehensively. The man grunted and heaved over in sleep, the smell of stale booze wafting upwards. Joshua retreated. A tramp. Just paranoia again.

Back home he showered and resolved to take the day by the jugular. On his answering machine he recorded the words: 'Hello, 480 2348. Call me at the *Daily Post*, 353 1121, news desk. This machine is not taking messages.' It was deliberately abrupt. Josie and William would pick up the subtext. Anyone else needing to talk to him would just have to do as they were told.

On the way in to Fleet Street he detoured via the Dartmouth Park council estate and a crescent in Notting Hill Gate. Without success. Mrs O'Grady and Rob remained unavailable. He told the news room to refer all calls to the library, and set to work.

First Malcolm O'Grady. But whatever his alleged misdemeanour of six years ago, it hadn't rated a mention in the nationals. Perhaps the locals? Where did the O'Gradys come from? He re-read all the reports of the case, but no journalist had seen fit to mention this. He thought about Mrs O'Grady's accent. Midlands, or north wasn't it? He tried the few regional papers the *Post* library kept – the *Northern Echo*, the *Birmingham Post* – and again drew a blank.

Joshua then turned to De Villiers. He trawled the index and came up with nothing new. BOSS and National Intelligence Service was a different story. He took out a small mountain of cuttings, skimmed through them, then started on back numbers of the *Economist* and the *New Statesman*. At the end of four hours his head was reeling. He collected his notes and went out for a walk.

In a way it helped, refreshing his memory of South Africa's recent history, but in another it didn't, it only compounded the mystery. The treaties with Angola and Mozambique, and the new constitution, giving limited franchise to coloureds and Asians, were meant to isolate black nationalism. But it didn't work. At home, the fires of Soweto were fanned into life again, the flames hotter than before. Abroad, Botha took a trip to Europe, trying to present the acceptable face of apartheid. To party leaders, heads of state, even the Pope. And in London he had lunch with his British counterpart. Public friendship. Public friendship, private favours? Who knows what secret deals were made over the smoked salmon and roast venison? The press had speculated about this. What did Britain want? A settlement of the Namibia problem. And what had she to offer? Arms technology? Economic favours? And a little help with the opposition . . . In South Africa the struggle was with guns and bombs and street battles, but outside the weapon was propaganda. Exile groups, like the ANC, all had offices in London that produced material damaging to Pretoria; had Botha asked for them to be squeezed? Was that why Joshua had found Culverwell so nervous?

Joshua's walk took him along the Strand into Trafalgar Square. He sat down on the steps against a stone lion, and gazed up at the ugly, imperial façade of South Africa House. He imagined De Villiers slipping in here for his regular meetings with his controller – or would it have been somewhere else, somewhere more clandestine? One of the cuttings he'd read that day related the extraordinary story of Craig Williamson, a dissident student leader in the early seventies, who fell foul of the South African authorities and fled to Europe. He joined the ANC, met African politicians like Mugabe and Nkomo and became friend and confidant to dozens of fellow exiles. He was a dynamic figure in the opposition, channelling money and information to liberation groups back home. Then in January 1980 he suddenly disappeared. A few months later he turned up again, revealing himself as a major in the National Intelligence Service. For almost ten years he had fooled everyone.

Joshua tried to envisage De Villiers as another Williamson. The two images failed to coalesce. There was nothing in the Williamson story to suggest he was implicated in sabotage. To do so would have compromised his effectiveness as a two-faced bureaucrat. So why De Villiers? Business and politics was his sphere. And why bomb a hospital? What possible relevance could it have to South African interests? Joshua felt moved to question everything he thought he knew about the case. The South African connection might be nothing more than an inflated red herring.

He wandered slowly back to the office. There were no messages. Mrs O'Grady was still out. He thought of ringing the ninety-six O'Gradys in the London phone book on the off-chance she was staying with in-laws. The prospect appalled him. And what about her own relatives? Wonder what her maiden name is, he thought gloomily. Probably Smith. He tried her number one last time. And Rob, who now officially joined her on the missing persons list. He was beginning to feel distinctly hard done by. And tired.

'Not again. Josh Barnes, don't you have a home to go to?'

He looked up. Blue eyes, clear and shining. Carole. Surely not contact lenses. They looked too real.

'Did you hear me? You look like a zombie. How long have you been here?'

'Hi. What are you doing in on a Sunday?'

'I asked you first. Have you been in all day?'

He nodded, momentarily too weary to open his mouth.

'God – and you've forgotten to eat by the look of you. Honestly, you've been watching too much Lou Grant, that's your trouble. What's the story? Will it make the first edition?'

He smiled. 'No. It isn't even written yet.' She looked lovely, all fresh and untroubled. She was right, he was pushing himself too much. 'Why are you here?' he asked again.

'Finishing this.' She brandished a folder heavy with manuscript. 'Alex Croydon's masterpiece on chequebook journalism. He asked me to do the typing. I think I must be cheaper than an agency. I've got tomorrow off, but he needs the first chapters to show some publisher he's having lunch with. So –'

'You've been at it all day?'

She nodded. 'Didn't have anything else to do. And I've only got a lousy portable at home. It looks better on the electric, so I come in and use the one in Ken's office. No one's there over the weekend.'

People's private lives. They're never what you expect. He had always assumed Carole was the kind of girl with her weekends booked months in advance. Funny how you never think of other people as lonely. He looked towards his evening, sitting with a packet of fish and chips, staring at a television he wasn't watching, waiting for a phone call he couldn't answer. She was wearing baggy dungarees over a white T-shirt. He was aware of the outline of her body through the clothes. Just a couple of hours listening to her chatter. A little company, a little food, a little sunshine, a glass or two of wine. He owed her a drink. 'Everybody needs somebody sometime.' After all, what else was he going to achieve tonight?

'Hey, Carole. Since we're both here – what about that drink?'

It was dark, it was not his flat, his head hurt and he was fully clothed. He registered these four facts simultaneously. It was understandable that he missed the fifth, which was that the sofa was too narrow for any rapid movement.

On the floor he woke fully, picked himself up gingerly and fumbled for a light. He looked first at his watch, then at the room. Three twenty-five. A small but attractively decorated living room. The makeshift bed had a pillow and a patchwork quilt. On the table two brandy glasses, one a quarter full. On the chair his jacket neatly folded. On the floor his shoes. Otherwise he was intact. Carole had been a real gentleman.

Memory was returning. After the drink had come the meal, and after the meal the lift home and the invitation to coffee. It had gone through his mind that they might end up in bed together; presumably it had gone through hers too. He remembered the coffee and the first brandy. He was on the sofa, she was on a chair. They had talked of work, and the difficulty of holding together the professional and the personal. They had got on well. Then had come the second brandy. After that he remembered nothing, except feeling tired and pleasantly comfortable. Altogether too comfortable, if appearances were now to be believed. He opened the door gently and tiptoed into the hall. Her bedroom door was open a fraction. He pushed it further. Across the room he made out the gentle contours of her sleeping body. In the living room he used a sheet of kitchen towelling to write her a note.

Carole. I think I passed out, and I think you put me to bed. Thank you. I'm sorry. It was a great evening. Perhaps another dinner will cover the bill. See you at work. Thanks, Josh.

Driving slowly home, he gave himself a hard time for whatever it was he had or hadn't done. But the castigation was half-hearted. They had enjoyed each other's company. Against all the odds she had made him feel good, lifted the burden a little. Maybe it wasn't such a disaster after all.

By the time he'd parked and taken the lift to his estate in the sky he was feeling almost human. He stepped into his flat, thinking longingly of bed. As he did so his foot crushed something on the doormat. He looked down. It was a plain white envelope. He picked it up and opened it.

Inside was a newspaper clipping. The *Twickenham Gazette*, dated April 3rd. Above the caption, 'Mayor salutes fund raiser at gala evening', was a photograph. It showed a mayor in full regalia shaking hands with a woman in a white, possibly satin dress. On either side of them were spectators. And the face of one of these, a man standing next to the woman, had been marked by a careful circle in red.

Joshua stared at the face. It was that of a complete stranger. Someone he'd never seen before in his life. Another billet doux from Joshua's anonymous donor. But who the hell was the man, and where did he fit into anything? The questions ruined his sleep.

Monday morning. He breakfasted in the office. The *Twickenham Gazette* didn't believe in early starts. Finally at ten they answered. The photographer in question had left two months before to run a restaurant in Wales. The story would probably have been covered by Bill Catley, but he was out on a job. Did he want to leave a message? No, said Joshua, he would call back.

In Camden he was early for his appointment with Culverwell. He waited in the outer office, clutching his briefcase of photos like a model on an assignment for a top job. Just after eleven thirty Culverwell came out to meet him. He was accompanied by two men, one black, one white. They shook hands and went to the nearest pub. Joshua handed out the four pints and they carried them to a table in the corner. There he carefully laid out the photos, a selection of Tony's blow ups and the two free gifts.

He waited.

'De Villiers.' Culverwell tapped his finger on the thin-faced man in Josie's picture. 'Definitely Joe De Villiers.'

'What about the other guy?'

Culverwell shook his head. Joshua looked to the others. The black man picked up a photo and studied it. 'I've seen this man before,' he said. 'But not here. Not in Britain. Back home somewhere.' He handed the print to his friend.

'Do you know who he is?' Joshua prompted.

He shook his head. 'No, but he's not one of us.'

'How do you know?'

The man shrugged. His white companion smiled. 'Litmus paper. Thomas has strips of it behind his eyes. It's what comes of having so many friendly chats with secret policemen. Black man's magic.' He grinned at Thomas. 'But whoever he is, he's not one of their regulars, that's for sure. Unless he's very new.'

'Could he have been brought over for just one job?'

'Sure. What else have they got to spend the taxpayers' money on? He was probably on a first-class weekend return. When was he last seen?'

'Tuesday. Four days after the job.'

'In that case he must be local,' Culverwell said. 'He would never have stayed around that long.'

'But we know De Villiers has gone. I'd say you'd be lucky to find his friend staying after him.'

Of course he had gone. Why keep him? Especially with the smell of trouble. Across the table Joshua noticed Harry Culverwell watching him closely.

'Cape Town,' said the black man quietly.

'What?'

'Cape Town. That's where I've seen him. I knew it. He had a respectable front . . . some kind of business. I don't remember what. But on the side he did strong arm stuff for BOSS. Very good at helping to organize spontaneous demonstrations – perfect excuse for the police to come in and crack skulls. Where'd you get this?'

Joshua swallowed. 'A friend.'

The man nodded. 'O.K.'

'But you can't give me a name?' Joshua pushed. 'It's very important.'

The black man looked to Culverwell. A message passed between them, but it was too quick for Joshua to read. 'Can you leave one of these prints with me?'

'Yes.'

'Good, then I'll show it around. There are some folk with more recent memories than me. Does Harry have a contact number for you?'

'Yes, but my office, not my home.'

He felt the question in Culverwell's look.

'Just to be on the safe side,' he explained.

Harry nodded slowly. 'Mr Barnes, you will tell me that it is none of my business, but you should know that these people you are dealing with, they may sometimes be stupid but they are never charitable. If you find yourself in a position to expose them then you should be absolutely certain that they are ignorant of that fact . . .'

'I understand.'

'And if you have something on these people then, as I'm sure you realize, it would be of the greatest interest to us.'

Maybe I should tell him, Joshua thought. The prospect of sharing the anxiety seemed suddenly so comforting. But it was not his story to share. The more people who knew the more dangerous it became. And anyway, there were still too many pieces missing.

'I promise you'll be the first to know. One more favour, if I may.' Joshua took out the newspaper clipping. 'I wonder if by any chance this man means anything to you.'

The cutting did the rounds. It met three blank faces. Culverwell handed it back. 'Sorry. This one we don't know.'

Joshua thanked them and stood up to take his leave. He shook hands with each of them. The parting had an element of ceremony to it. Culverwell's grasp lingered longer than was necessary. 'Goodbye, Mr Barnes. And be careful.'

Back at the office Bill Catley had arrived at the *Twickenham Gazette.* He had a little trouble remembering that particular gala evening out of so many, but when he had recovered the article from the files he got there.

'The guy on the right? Yes, it's Mrs Gough's husband. Mrs Gough is the one shaking hands with the mayor. She's the leading light of the Twickenham Women's Institute. Very good at raising the pennies. This little celebraton was over £25,000 to help build a new swimming pool for physiotherapy at the local hospital. But I've taken this photo before, except the cheque is going to a different charity. Mind you, he's not usually in the picture. A retiring sort of chap. Doesn't like being centre stage.'

'Gough, you say. First name?'

'Nigel. Sheila and Nigel Gough.'

'And what does he do?' Joshua closed his eyes and prayed.

'Oh, I don't know. Something pinstriped. The city maybe. Civil service. I'm not sure.'

'I see.' Joshua's voice trailed off in disappointment.

'What's the interest? Mind if I ask. There might be a local angle.'

Joshua hesitated.

'Perhaps I can help . . .' the reporter said carefully.

He made up his mind. 'I can't reveal what the story is at this point. But I'll tell you what – I'll tip you off before it goes into print, so you can do a follow-up.'

'Done. I'll make a few phone calls and be back to you in half an hour.'

'Thanks. Oh – and er, be discreet, will you?'

'Naturally.'

Catley was as good as his word. 'Defence Ministry,' he said briskly when he called back twenty minutes later. 'He's an undersecretary dealing with naval estimates.'

'Great.'

'No problem.'

'I don't suppose you have a phone number for him, do you?'

'I do. Thought you might be wanting it.' He gave the number. 'Only home though. Work you can probably get through the switchboard.'

'Thanks a million.'

'Look forward to hearing from you. Bye.'

898 9375. It rang three times. Sheila Gough's voice was twinset and cut glass.

'Mrs Gough? Barclaycard accounts here. May we speak to your husband?'

'I'm afraid he's at work.'

'You see, we've received notice of a rather large payment put through on his card. We need to check if there has been some mistake, or if the card has perhaps been misappropriated. We've looked at our records, but we don't seem to have a work phone number for him. Can you help?'

'Certainly. Just give me your name and number and I'll get him to call you back.'

Not the reply Joshua was looking for. He put the phone down.

He leaned back in his chair and thought. Joe De Villiers, BOSS agent. Nigel Gough, civil servant? Surely not. Looking round the newsroom for inspiration, Joshua's glance fell on Stephen Turner, the defence correspondent, in conversation with the pictures editor. When he was free Joshua approached him.

'Steve, can I ask you a favour? What do I do if I've got the name of a civil servant and I want to find out if he's for real?'

Steve didn't look up. 'Ask him.'

'Any other suggestions?'

'Why ask me?'

'You have the best contacts in the business.'

'Huh. And?'

'He's supposed to work in defence.'

From across the room the news editor launched a small hand grenade. 'Joshua, I would appreciate that Islington rates capping story *before* we go to press, if that's convenient with you. We do find it easier to get it into the paper that way.'

'Come into my office when you're free,' Stephen said, 'I might be able to help you.'

Joshua spent the next hour earning his living. Just before five he found time to knock on the defence correspondent's door.

'I won't ask what on earth this story's about,' the defence correspondent said, taking out a black loose-leaf book from his desk. 'Know what this is?'

'No.'

' "Distribution of Business". It's a directory of all staff at defence and what they do.'

Joshua made out the words Ministry of Defence, and Not to be removed. Admiration was called for. He gave it. 'Brilliant. How'd you get it?'

Stephen shrugged. 'What's the man's name?'

'Gough.'

Stephen flicked through the book. 'No Gough.'

'Could he be in MI5?'

'Could be. Like me to ring someone and check?'

'Please.'

'O.K. I'll come back to you tomorrow.'

'Great. Thanks a million.'

Tuesday a.m. The heavens broke. Joshua was in early and halfway through breakfast at his desk when the telephone rang. 'Yep. Joshua Barnes,' he managed to say, while trying to masticate a currant bun.

'Mr Barnes.' A man's voice, no accent, quiet. 'Have you got a pen ready?'

Joshua swallowed fast. 'Yes. Yes, who am I talking to?'

The man answered briefly, then the line went dead. Joshua grabbed his briefcase and was out of the office in ten seconds flat.

Chapter Twenty-five

121 Galveston Crescent was a plain semi-detached in the suburbs of St Albans. The downstairs curtains were still drawn, perhaps against the sun, and at first he thought no one was in. He was about to ring a second time when he detected a movement behind the newly painted green door. The door opened a fraction. A woman in her late forties, thin with a pinched mouth, glared at him.

'Good morning. I'd like to speak to Mrs Helen O'Grady.' He put on what he hoped was a disarming smile.

It failed. 'Who are you?' she replied in a freezing tone.

'Joshua Barnes. I talked to her last week.'

'Who told you to come here? Go away. She isn't here.'

She began to withdraw. For the first and only time in his newspaper career Joshua put his foot in the door. 'I'm sorry, but I know she is. Would you tell her that I have found out something of great importance, not just to me but to her also. And that it is vital that she sees me.'

The woman's expression did not alter and the door stayed on the chain, but it did not close. From inside he heard a whispered conversation. When the bolt was slipped back and the door released it was Helen O'Grady herself.

'You'd better come in.'

The sitting room had a rose-patterned carpet with wallpaper to match, and smelled of furniture polish and aerosol. There was a modern gas fire and above it an elaborate display of horse brasses. The sofa against the wall was covered by a neat line of scatter cushions. It seemed a pity to spoil the arrangement. He chose the armchair.

She sat opposite. A woman perhaps just turned forty, still attractive but with worry lines around her mouth, she wore a slightly dated floral dress and sandals. Her hair was not as neat as he remembered, but she looked less drawn, as if there had been a few nights' sleep at last. Around her neck was a small gold crucifix. She sat quite still, hands in her lap, her only movement an occasional touch of her thumb on her wedding ring. She gave off the same sense of self-containment, waiting for him to make the first move. Once again he liked her. This time she also had to like him.

'I'm sorry to disturb you. I promise you I wouldn't have come if it hadn't been important.'

'How did you know I was here?'

'A tip-off.'

'What do you mean, a tip-off?'

'Someone rang me at the *Daily Post* this morning. He said, "Helen O'Grady is at 121 Galveston Crescent, St Albans." Then he put the phone down.'

The expression on her face said it all.

'Who knows you're here, Mrs O'Grady?'

'Apart from the police, no one. Not even the neighbours.'

'And the children?'

'They're with me.'

Joshua's attention wandered from the woman's face to a coffee table near the fireplace. There was a collection of free-standing photographs. One showed the O'Gradys – father, mother and two children – the same snap he'd noticed in her flat in London. Another was of Helen with her arm round the woman who had opened the door. They were both smiling. Of course, he should have guessed.

'She's your sister?'

'Yes.'

'You don't look alike.'

'Mr Barnes, who do you think rang you?'

'I don't know. I was hoping you might.'

She said nothing. He waited but still she didn't speak. Whatever she knew she wasn't saying. In her lap the hands clenched a little.

'Mrs O'Grady.' He leaned towards her. 'I have to speak frankly. I came to see you last week. You gave me an interview. My paper has printed nothing of this interview, even though there were things you said that we could have used. At the same time other newspapers have reported a lot of remarks, very personal ones, that I'm sure – I can tell from your style – you never said.'

In her eyes he thought he detected anger. 'So?'

'So I want to assure you that, if I may put it bluntly, I'm not interested in exploiting your grief, but in finding out the truth.'

'The truth doesn't sell newspapers.' It sounded like a phrase she had used before.

'Oh, but it can, Mrs O'Grady, believe me it can.'

She sat back on the sofa, even relaxing a bit. 'All right, I accept you're not here to exploit me. Now what do you have to say? Myra said there was something you wanted to tell me.'

'I know the police have questioned you.'

'Is that surprising?'

'No, but I can also guess what they said.'

'Can you? Tell me.'

'They suggested your husband was not simply an innocent victim of the hospital bomb. Their investigations showed that he was a man with a somewhat unhappy past. He might have been able to tell them how the bomber gained admission to the building. I expect they also put it to you that it would only be fair to his memory to do all you could to help bring his murderers to justice.'

He paused for a moment. Her face was impenetrable.

'That would be how the police would see it,' he went on. 'But there is another way of looking at it. Your husband's past contains a secret. A secret he wouldn't have wanted to share with his employers. Because if they had known, he would have lost his job. So, what if someone comes along who knows this secret? That person would have a lot of power over your husband. He could, perhaps, use this power to make your husband do something against his will. That is another possible reading, wouldn't you say?'

She hesitated, then nodded slowly.

'Mrs O'Grady, would you mind telling me what happened to your husband in Peterborough six years ago?'

She answered carefully. 'And if I tell you, what's to stop you printing it?'

'Nothing. Except that I'm not interested in what your husband did then. Only in what he was made to do six years later because of it. But to understand one I have to know about the other. I don't believe your husband was involved in the way the police say he was. That's what I'm trying to prove. But to do that I need details.'

'How do you know all this?'

'Mrs O'Grady, I can't tell you that. But I can tell you that people's lives are in danger. And what you know may help them.'

There was a sharp knock on the door and Myra entered. 'Are you all right, Helen?' she asked, ignoring Joshua.

Helen smiled. 'Yes, Myra. Everything's fine. I think Mr Barnes will be staying for a bit.'

'Well, you mustn't get yourself upset. You know what the doctor said.'

'I won't. Don't worry. Perhaps next time you put the kettle on . . . I think we'd both like a cup of tea. Mr Barnes?'

Joshua nodded vigorously. 'Yes, thank you, that would be very nice, Mrs . . .'

'Very well. As long as you're not getting tired.' She marched out, snapping the door closed behind her.

'You're very different,' Joshua ventured in gratitude for her protection.

'We're in different social classes, Mr Barnes, if that's what you mean. But she's been very good to me and the children. Even though she never really approved of my marriage. She thought I could have done better.' She said it matter of factly, as if she was talking about shopping.

He waited.

'I don't know you from Adam, Mr Barnes, and I've never had much of a good word to say for your people, press men and the like. But I don't think you're lying to me, and even if you were it will all come out eventually, I know that now. Maybe it would be better to make a clean breast of it before the police do it for me.' She paused. 'Don't you want to take notes?'

He scrambled in his case for notebook and pencil. Something told him this was not a job for the recorder.

'Six years ago, Jack – that's what he called himself then – was an engineer for British Telecom. You know, one of those men who come round in a van to mend your phone. It was a bad time for us then. We couldn't get into a council house, and the place we were living in wasn't cheap. Our youngest, Sally, she was just turned seven, we found out she was dyslexic, and Jack was very keen for her to have special tuition, you know, to catch up on what she'd missed in school. What with that and other things we had a lot of expenses.

'So . . . Jack started to pick up a little extra on the job. It wasn't difficult, everyone was doing it. He'd have been holding out. You know the kind of thing. They're out in the road digging up the lines, and some bloke comes along and offers them a tenner, his phone's on the blink and he's bottom of the queue. Or someone wants an extra extension, twenty-five under the table, no questions asked, nothing goes on the form . . . that kind of stuff. Except that Buzby didn't like it. The odd backhander – well, I think they knew everyone went in for that. Quite honestly, that's how they kept the business running, but this other racket involved equipment. A phone goes from the store – that's theft. The bloke who wants it is receiving stolen goods. That's criminal too, but then they're middle-class householders. They get off scot free.'

Joshua was beginning to hear the kind of conversations that might have gone on in the O'Grady household. He wondered if she had used such language to the police. He doubted it.

'So anyway. One day he gets done. Just like that. They've had a couple of detectives on his tail. He goes in for work one morning and the manager pulls him in. He gets the push and ends up in court. Three months inside.'

'That's a bit stiff for a first offence.'

'Of course. An example to others, as the judge put it. Except there weren't others.'

'What do you mean?'

'They were all in on the fiddle, three-quarters of the depot. But Jack was the only one to get done.'

'Because of his politics?'

'Because of his politics. He'd always been a union man. And a good one. He'd been a shop steward for years. The lads had a lot to thank him for. But not management. So when this came up, they saw their chance. Get rid of the troublemaker, disgrace the union. I'm not saying what he did was right. There was a lot of words between us because of it. But two wrongs don't make a right. He was a good man. He didn't deserve it.'

'So he had a record.'

'Yes.'

'How did he get the job as a security guard?'

'It was just luck. The first we'd had in years. After he got out we came to London, to get away from it all. He changed his name, started calling himself by his middle name – Malcolm. He got taken on to be a hospital porter. Me and the kids stayed with Myra till he found somewhere to live. He needed references of course, but he had a mate in a building firm in Peterborough who covered for him. Then while he was working at the hospital he got to know some of the security people, and later they asked him if he'd like to move over. It was more money and it's a better job, hospital security. So he said yes. No one checked.'

'How long for?'
'Over a year.'
'What about politics?'
'He joined the union, of course, but he kept out of the limelight. He wasn't ever quite the same again. He pretended to be, but he wasn't.'
'What did the police say when they talked to you?'
'You were right. They cared less about his record than about his politics. I told them the truth. He was a member of the Labour Party. We both were. It went way back. They asked me if he was Militant. I said why didn't they ask Special Branch . . . Oh yes, Mr Barnes, it's not just journalists who know what's going on. Anyway, they said they had, and they knew he was in Militant. There wasn't much else I could say to change their minds.'
'Was he?'
'He had been. But they missed the point.'
'How do you mean?'
'They wanted to show that he might have been involved, right? But if he was in Militant he certainly wouldn't have been involved. Not a bombing. It's not their style. Leftwing adventurism they'd have called it. Party discipline would never have allowed it.'
'Anyway by then, you say, he wasn't involved with politics?'
'That's right.'
He paused and looked up from his notes. 'But he was involved in the bombing.'
'Look, my husband didn't hold with terrorism. And neither do I. He supported HNW, and he was as mad as anyone else about the leasing out of the unit. But blowing the place up wouldn't help. He was never that kind of man.'
'I know. But he was involved.'
Her face showed a mixture of anger and anguish. 'I don't know. But one thing's for sure. He didn't help anyone plant any bomb. If they did kill him it was because he was trying to stop them.'
'Who were "they", Mrs O'Grady?'
The door opened and Myra came in burdened by a tray full of matching cups and saucers and little plates. Joshua got up to help her. Helen O'Grady stayed where she was.
'I brought some biscuits for you,' Myra said loudly. 'You know what the doctor said about eating properly. And I don't think you should stay talking too long. You look tired.'
'I'm all right, Myra. We'll be finished in a little while.'

Myra shot a murderous look at Joshua and left the room.

He poured the tea, handing her a cup with the plate of biscuits. She took the tea but refused the food. He continued the ritual. When he was back in his seat she said:

'I'll tell you what I know. Three months ago Jack was in the pub one evening when he got in with some bloke at the bar. Eric, he called himself. They got onto politics and, according to Jack, Eric came on really strong, you know, the disgrace of running down the National Health Service, squandering money on cruise missiles, the fascism of unemployment, and so on. Naturally Jack didn't disagree. Who would? At the end of the night the bloke stood him a drink and said how much he had enjoyed meeting him, hope to see you again and all that. All well and good. Next week he's there again. This time they get into some real drinking. Eric's paying and my Jack's not one to refuse a pint. It turns out this chap's an electrician, contract labour, just moved to London from the west country and a bit lonely. No mention of a family. No matter. It takes all kinds. Jack likes him. He's got a sense of humour, not stupid, and he knows what's going on in the world. They start talking about work, the kidney unit. Eric makes some comment about how he'd like to see the whole lot go up in flames, so no private bastards could get onto it. Jack tells him that wouldn't change anything, it'd just play into the bastards' hands. And they have a bit of a barney about that. But Eric goes on buying and they both end up a bit plastered.'

'Jack told you all this?'

She nodded. 'Yes, we talked a lot. We always did. He said he couldn't stand wives who didn't have a head on their shoulders. Oh yes, we talked. Trouble was he didn't always listen. Stupid bugger.' She sipped her tea, bringing up the cup to hide her face. He let her take her time. 'Anyway, a couple of weeks later Eric's in there again, and they're talking about jobs and how nowadays you have to stick with the one you've got, what with mass unemployment and so on, when Eric makes this comment, just drops it in, about how things might be tricky at work if they were to find out about Jack's past. "But don't worry, mate," he adds, "Your secret's safe with me." Well, it puts the wind right up Jack, and he asks him what he meant. But Eric just repeats how it'll be all right, and that maybe, in gratitude, Jack might be interested in doing something for the cause. "Like what?" says Jack. Eric just shrugs and says, "And there'll be a few bob in it for you too." Then one of Jack's mates comes up and Eric slides off.'

'What did you say when he told you?'

'I told him to steer clear of it. To keep out the pub, avoid seeing the bloke. "How can I?" he says. "He can find me any time he wants. And what's to stop him walking into the personnel office and just telling them?" I said, if that's what you're worried about, then you should come clean first. You've done a good job, there's been no trouble. If they're going to find out, better it comes from you. "Don't be so bloody stupid," he says. "That's the one thing they never forgive. Faking your references. They'll take one look at my record and I'll be back pushing wheelies down corridors – if I'm lucky and I'm not out on the street. I've been done over once. I'm not going to be done over again." You could see his point really.'

'So what did he do?'

'Nothing for a bit. Just kept out of the boozer. But now I think about it, you know, there was something fishy about it, right from the start. I remember Jack saying, early on, how this Eric seemed a good bloke, but he couldn't figure him. He was very vague about his past. Union stuff, politics, all that. Course, so was Jack, but not in the same way. This bloke seemed to know a lot. It just didn't always fit in with what he'd done. Anyway, about three weeks ago Jack was working a late shift. He was on his way home, around ten o'clock, when Eric stopped him in the street and said he wanted a word. The way Jack described it later it sounded more like a threat. So they went to the pub. Jack called me to say he was going to be late. And then Eric told him about the deal.

'On a certain night Jack was to let a certain man into the kidney unit. Inside, this man would do a little sabotage on the lithotripter. He explained it all, had a fancy phrase for it – "mangling the microprocessor". Nothing obvious. Not so anyone would notice immediately. Only when they came to use it, they'd plug it in and the machine wouldn't work. Extensive damage. £250,000 to replace. Teach the bastards a lesson, that was his line. "What about me?" Jack said. "They'll know it was me." "No problem," Eric said, "they won't discover it for a couple of months, maybe longer. By that time it could have been anyone. The last thing we want is for you to get done, comrade. You're one of us." Those were his exact words. Then when Jack didn't reply, he said, "You can always look on it as a business deal. £500 down. £500 to follow. Only you have to keep quiet about it. Not a word to anyone, even the missus.'

'Presumably he didn't follow instructions.'

'He told me, if that's what you mean.'

'And you said?'

'That he'd be a fool to have anything to do with it. And that if they pushed him he should tell the authorities.'

'But he didn't listen?'

'Oh, he listened. He agreed with me –'

'But finally he did it anyway.'

She nodded.

'You're sure?'

'We needed the money.' Her voice was quiet and she wouldn't look at him. 'The flat was lovely but moving cost a lot. We were getting behind with the H.P. Then the kids were still at school – Jack wanted them to stay on. And his brother got ill, lost his job. I'm not making excuses for him. I told him being short of money made no difference. It was money that got us into trouble in the first place. We'd get the money, but not this way. I told him.'

'So why are you so sure that he didn't listen to you?'

'Because he stopped talking. Got very silent. Bad tempered with the kids. He always did that when he had something to hide. And I found the money. £500. The electric clock stopped. I looked inside, there it was, in new twenties. He'd pulled a wire out hiding it.'

He said nothing.

She shook her head fiercely. 'They did it. They were going to kill him all along.'

'We've no proof of that. Maybe he got nosey. When he found out what they were really doing, maybe he tried to stop them. We'll never know.'

'I know. And I know that whatever happened in there it had nothing to do with the left. Eric was no left winger, he just knew the jargon. If he had been, he'd never have tried to bribe Jack with money. And they'd never have killed him. All that talk about the cause – it was rubbish. They were going to get Jack to unlock that door by hook or by crook. Politics had nothing to do with it.'

'What did you do with the money?'

'I burnt it. I found it the day after he died. I'd been at his bedside since Friday night. Hadn't slept since then. I got back in the early hours of Friday morning. The kids were in bed. A neighbour was looking after them. I wanted to know what time it was . . the clock was stopped. I knew the police would be round. I knew it was only a matter of time before it all came out – about him being in prison and all that. But they couldn't prove anything. I was the only one he'd told. I knew that. If there was no money, there was no proof. I put it in the sink and set fire to it. That way, if anyone asked, I could tell them truthfully I didn't have it.'

'And did they? Did anyone else come round?'

'No. Not yet.'

'And Eric? Jack never gave you any idea where he lived, or where he could be contacted?'

She shook her head. 'But I'll tell you one thing. I'd know him if ever I saw him again.'

'What?' Joshua's pen stopped midway to the page.

'He doesn't know I saw him. No one knew. Not even Jack. That last night when Jack called me from the pub. He didn't say anything about Eric. But I knew he was with him. I could always tell when he was lying. So I got my neighbour to keep an eye on the kids and I went down there. I suppose I had some half-cracked notion that I'd get in there, go up to him and give him a piece of my mind. Take my husband home with me. I must have lost my courage on the way to the pub. Anyway, I got in the door. It was a Friday night, packed. I pushed my way in a bit and then I saw them. They were in one of those cubby holes. Jack had his back to me. But I could see Eric's face, bright and shining.'

'Did he see you?'

'No. They were too busy talking.'

'Can you describe him?'

'Tall, not so young, maybe late forties or fifty. His hair a kind of mousy colour. Not long. I couldn't see the style because he had a cap on, but I saw his face all right. Bastard.'

'Mrs O'Grady,' Joshua's voice was shaking slightly. He reached for his briefcase. 'I have a picture here, a cutting from a newspaper. I want you to tell me if you recognize anyone in the picture, all right?'

He unfolded the clipping. She took it from his hand and examined it. 'That's him. The man on the right. He's smarter, and there's no cap. But that's him. I told you I remembered his face.'

Joshua's lips parted in a smile of triumph. He felt like going over and hugging the woman. She was smiling too, but grimly. 'Who is he?'

'I don't know. But he's certainly nothing to do with HNW. You'd testify in court?'

'They killed my husband.'

He stood up, returning the tea cup to the tray.

'What are you going to do?' she asked.

'I'm going to write my story. And the day after tomorrow you're going to read it, every word of it.'

'What about Jack?'

'I'll tell the truth, Mrs O'Grady. He won't be a hero, but you won't be ashamed of him either.'

She nodded. 'All right, Mr Barnes. That'll do.'

She saw him out. At the front door they shook hands. Halfway down the path he turned. 'Well, at least we know someone else who'll be looking forward to reading the first edition.'

'Who's that?'

'The man who rang to give me your address.'

'And you don't know who he was?'

'No, I have absolutely no idea.'

He got back to the newspaper just after seven. On his desk there was a mosaic of messages all in Carole's handwriting. They read, in chronological order:

11.46 Ed wants to see you IMMEDIATELY you get in.
12.03 Rob Taggart called. He's in all day. Call him.
12.23 Harry Culverwell. Ring him at the office.
1.05 Ed wants to see you NOW.
1.17 Steve says your man's intelligence is confirmed. (?)
2.50 Harry Culverwell again. Same message.
4.40 Ed has gone home. He says you no longer work here.
6.04 I have gone home. You need a fulltime secretary.

Joshua rang Culverwell first. He was, thank God, still at his office.

'Piet Conradie. That's your man's name. By profession a locksmith, born Cape Town 1942, resident in Britain six months, employed by MacDonald & Co, Mile End Road. He is known to be an experienced handler of explosives. Identified by two different sources. Thomas was right.'

'Thanks Harry. Thanks a lot.'

'You sound pleased.'

'I am. Listen, can I ask you one more question?'

'Go ahead.'

'What's the relation between BOSS and British Intelligence?'

'Ambiguous. In general they're much nicer to BOSS than to us.

They speak the same language. They share prejudices as well as politics. But it's not as straightforward as you might think.'

'How do you mean?'

'Well, however they might feel, they have to be realists, they have to end up on the winning side. Four million whites can't suppress twenty million blacks for ever. If they can't prevent revolution, they will support it, in order to have influence with the next government, a government which gets closer every day.'

'Cover their bet by backing both sides?'

'Yes. And we mustn't assume they all agree with one another. Intelligence agencies have factions, like every organization. Not left and right exactly, but let's say some people are smarter than others.'

'What about in Britain? Harold Wilson used to talk about the pro South African faction in MI5.'

'He did. And there must be. Over the years we've suffered hundreds of break-ins, small acts of sabotage, even a bombing once, of the ANC offices in Penton Street. But was anyone ever prosecuted?'

'No.'

'Well then, Joshua, draw your own conclusions.'

'That's a hell of a favour BOSS gets, to operate with such impunity. If the KGB did that, there'd be fifty diplomats on the next Aeroflot flight back to Moscow.'

'You said it.'

'What's the price? What does MI5 get out of it?'

'I imagine they keep each others' files up to date.'

'Is that all?'

'What do you have in mind?'

'Contract labour. Operational muscle. The job executed and no questions asked. The favour returned. Ever heard of MI5 using BOSS in that way?'

'Not to my knowledge.'

'But it is possible?'

'Yes, it is possible. Why, have you evidence of that?'

'I think so.'

'And will they publish it?'

It was a doubt he hadn't before dared contemplate. He did so now. 'They have to.'

'One favour for me, Joshua Barnes.'

'Yes.'

'Make a copy of it. Make lots of copies of it. And send them to your friends. Just in case.'

'You'll have it by the end of the week. But you'll already have seen it in the paper by then.'

'I look forward to it. Good luck.'

It was time to write the story. He laid out notes, tape recorder, a stack of paper and two packs of cigarettes. Done with a sense of ritual. He pulled the typewriter towards him and rolled in the first sheet. He typed out a headline:

BOSS/MI5 LINK IN HOSPITAL BOMBING

He tried another one:

HIGHGATE BOMB SUSPECTS FRAMED

Then finally:

BOMB VICTIM BLACKMAILED

Shit. The biggest story of his life and he didn't know where to begin, which handle to use. He knew he should have talked to Ed. He'd go mad when he found out. And that wasn't the only problem. Ed knew his job, but he also knew his limitations. He'd call the editor, who'd panic and call the publisher, then the lawyers would start combing through it. There'd be questions about the Official Secrets Act, libel, the possibility of a D notice - the whole lumbering paraphernalia of state censorship.

Worse than that, they might take it away from him. Not on professional grounds, he could fight them there. No one else had his sources. And they were confidential. That much was hallowed ground. But they might try it on in the name of objectivity. 'You're too close, Joshua. The girl's an old friend. You could be accused of bias. We'd better have someone else write it.' No, he wasn't going to take that risk. If he wrote it first and presented it to them as a fait accompli, then they'd have to publish it.

Or not. Suppose they spiked it? Cowardice, the vice of British journalism. What would he do then? Come on, Josh, he told himself. Don't think about that now. Write the damn thing.

He plotted out three versions of the story, getting all the information into each of them. Then he wrote. It took him the best part of the night. He was ready for the final draft when the telephone rang.

'Hey, Josh, do you know what time it is?'

Rob, home from a night on the town, eager for news, high as a kite. Joshua extracted the Meldon number and promised more information tomorrow. 'I can't talk now, Rob. I'm doing the story.'

He ploughed back before the line of thought was broken. An hour later he pushed his typewriter aside and read. They were good. The BOSS/MI5 version was the most dangerous, and he had left his editor with the softer option of leading in on the Mrs O'Grady. Of course it was no longer heresy to do a story that accused MI5 of dirty dealings. In recent years revelations of phone taps, buggings, break-ins had become commonplace. The pattern was always the same – the press growling about civil liberties, questions in the House, reassurances given and disbelieved, then things would go on exactly as before. Britain was still the only Anglo-Saxon country not to have had an inquiry into the illegal activities of its security services in the last ten years. Maybe his editor would bite. He'd run enough editorials deploring official secrecy. Let's see if he had the courage of his convictions.

Joshua considered mentioning the secret postman, but as quickly rejected it. It was unethical to reveal a source – even though he had made no promise, and anyway had little to reveal – but his main reason was less high-flown. The tip-offs were a story in themselves, there might be more material, and if any journalist was going to build a career out of this he wanted it to be Joshua Barnes.

Under the papers on his desk he scrambled to find the Meldon number. He lifted the phone to ring them. Then he caught sight of the office clock. Five past three. A call echoing through the house in the middle of the night. It would scare the shit out of them. It was only a few hours till morning. Nothing was going to change between now and then. Why not give them the good news with a little sunshine. He tucked the scrap of paper away in his wallet.

He ran off three copies. One was put in an envelope addressed to Culverwell and dropped in the mail box. The second he locked in his bottom drawer with the original. The third he put in the news editor's in-tray with a covering note. He would be back anyway by the time he read it.

Outside the building, London was ghostly, the streets alive with vans and delivery people getting out the last edition. He drove in a trance through Ludgate Circus by St Paul's into the City. In Cheapside he shared the road with a mechanical road cleaner, a huge, lumbering vehicle spurting jets of water around it and dragging spinning brushes over the tarmac. He followed it slowly, between futuristic office blocks and classical façades. At Bank he overtook the monster and hurried on to the Tower and thence to Cable Street, that dividing line between those who have and those who still have not. He felt light-headed, like someone released from a long fast. When he had first dreamed of being a journalist it had been a teenage ambition, suffused with the glow of moral righteousness, a vision of glory – alone in a corrupt world, exposing the ruthless, protecting the weak. Bullshit. The reality had been the normal, slightly murky compromise. But he, like every other contender, had been secretly waiting for that one story . . . And now? Now he could feel nothing but candyfloss in his brain and a growing desire for sleep.

The flats were in darkness. Someone had bust the bulb in the lift. He counted the floors as he travelled upwards, passing the time by fantasizing about the future. He imagined sitting in a restaurant and a well-dressed man approaching, extending a hand and saying quietly, 'We're very grateful to you, Mr Barnes. Very grateful indeed.' The lift creaked to a halt. Maybe it would be less ostentatious – a man in a boiler suit in a crowded tube. Deep throat in the underground.

He was still in never-never-land when he turned the key in his lock and pushed the door open. At that point of exhaustion where the senses are still acute but the brain no longer able to translate signs into warnings he noticed something strange, a smell that wasn't his, an alien quality to the air, but nothing he could tie down. He let it pass. Probably the outcome would have been the same, whatever he had done. In the living room, by the dull glow of the London street lamps eighteen floors below, he dropped his briefcase and reached for the light switch.

'Not the main light, Mr Barnes, if you please. It will hurt my eyes after the darkness.'

The voice hit him like an electric shock. Through the gloom he made out the bulk of a figure in the armchair by the balcony. A table lamp next to him snapped on, and Joshua stared at a strongly-built man with red hair, ruddy complexion, thick neck, an air of rude health about him – a long way from Joshua's effete fantasy of educated subversion. The man extended a hand, not in greeting but to reveal the black, squat-nosed gun pointed firmly at his host.

'Working so late, Mr Barnes? I'm sure it must be a good story. Please, shall we move over to the table. You and I have business to attend to. Business and pleasure.'

He did as he was told. Before him on the table was a small mirror glass, on which lay two long lines of white powder, a razor blade and a short black straw. Cocaine? Yet again, just when he thought the mist had lifted, nothing made sense. The man joined him, his gun a third member of the intimate party.

'For you.' He motioned to the mirror. 'Perfect and pure. Please. It'll help us both think more clearly.'

Their eyes met, and in the moment before he obeyed Joshua understood the power of the litmus paper behind Thomas's eyes. Who's going to write this story? he thought. Whatever it will be . . .

Later, when the man had gone through Joshua's wallet, he settled himself in the chair and dialled a number.

Chapter Twenty-six

At a point somewhere in the black of the night a telephone rang. In a corner of her dream Josie heard the rhythm but failed to locate its source. Tring tring. She woke with a start, yanking herself out of sleep. The telephone. Joshua. News. She had no watch. Outside, it was pitch dark. She stumbled to her feet. As she opened the door the ring got louder. Upstairs she registered movement.

Tring tring. William must have woken. He would be making for the extension in the study. Bare feet on stone-flagged floors, Josie reached the kitchen first.

Her hand was halfway to the receiver when she froze. What guarantee had she that the caller was Joshua? What about their agreed signal? Ten rings, a pause of sixty seconds, then call again. The phone might have been going for half an hour – or just nine rings – it was impossible to tell. And this might be not the first but the second call, the one she was supposed to answer. She stared at the phone. It would be at least as dangerous not to pick it up. To do so would give nothing away.

She lifted the receiver and held it to her ear. Nothing. Just the hollow silence of a connection without a voice. Not even any breathing. She waited. Someone was there, she was sure of it. A small click, pause, the single word, 'Josie?' It was a question, sleepy and close. Too close. The sound of it faded into the air waves, still alive with an undisclosed presence.

She slammed down the receiver and ran out of the kitchen to the foot of the stairs. 'William,' her voice boomed up into the darkness. 'Put the phone down. Put it down.'

Fifteen seconds later his figure appeared at the top of the stairs, dishevelled, wearing just a pair of trousers.

'Who was it?' The sharpness in his voice gave him away.

'How the hell should I know? Why did you speak?'

'Because I wasn't sure if you'd picked it up, or if it had just stopped ringing.' Not the whole truth. In fact it had been more reflex than judgement. And he had known it was a mistake the second he had done it. But by then it was too late. 'I'm sorry. I thought it was Joshua.'

'If it was Joshua he would have said so,' she snapped.

'Maybe he wasn't sure. Maybe we should wait. If it was him, he'll call again.'

'Maybe.' She tried to calm herself.

They stood rooted to the spot, the great, grand staircase between them. She counted slowly to herself. When she got to fifty, she knew that Meldon's force field had been penetrated.

'What's the time?' she asked.

'Just before four.'

She nodded glumly. He came downstairs and put his hand on her shoulder. She looked rumpled with sleep. 'Josie,' he said gently. 'Listen . . . it could have been anyone. A wrong number, some fan trying to speak to their idol, one of Rob's friends from abroad getting the time difference wrong, a high-class burglar checking the premises. There are any number of innocent explanations.'

She shook her head stubbornly. 'You said my name. Whoever it was heard you. What if it was them?'

Them. Back again. He had got used to life without them. Yet with just the word here they were again, coming out of the darkness, faceless, capable of anything. He had come to believe that Meldon could withstand them. How naive to suppose this mediaeval relic could keep out the forces of modern evil. Beside him she shivered slightly. She didn't want to give up the faith either.

'Josie, it's the middle of the night. We're still both half asleep. No wonder it feels there are demons all round. Let's go back to bed and talk about it in the morning.'

She shook his hand off her shoulder. 'You sleep if you want. I'm going to get ready.'

'Ready for what?'

'For leaving.'

Leaving? The thought appalled. 'Leaving for where, for Christ's sake?'

'Anywhere. Just out. Away from here.'

And then what? Start roaming the countryside like a couple of desperate fugitives, and all because of a phone call that might mean anything. It made no sense.

'And what if Joshua really does try to get in touch and we're not here? I say we stay. We can be careful. Stay out of sight, keep watch on the gardens. I'm not going to be flushed out into the open just on the strength of a telephone ringing in the night. That's crazy.'

She stared at him. 'And what if you're wrong? What if they come for us here?'

He thought about it and swallowed. 'Then they come. If it was them, and they know we're here, then they'll find us anyway, even if we go. I don't fancy being run to ground in the middle of the great outdoors. At least here we know where we are. Meldon has been our salvation. If they are going to get us, maybe it would be better for it to happen here.'

He hadn't intended it to be a speech. But now it was out he felt like owning it. They stared at each other across silence. Just like old times. Energy wasted on the clash of wills. He was tired of being the one who lost. To his surprise she gave in.

'O.K. We stay. But we take precautions. Clear the place up so as it looks like we've left. Keep in one room out of sight. Have somewhere to hide. And when the morning comes we call Joshua.'

It was not so far away. Already the darkness was beginning to recede. Soon it would be dawn. There was no question of sleep now. They were both too alert. Upstairs he packed, stuffing their meagre belongings into the bag, smoothing down sheets, straightening coverlets. In the kitchen she cleared up last night's meal and made coffee. They sat huddled round the table watching the light grow outside. At seven twenty they called Joshua. His machine replied:

'Hello. 480 2348. Call me at the *Daily Post* 353 1121, news desk. This machine is not taking messages.'

They did so. He was not in. He had worked late. He was not expected in before midday. 'Maybe he's sleeping, and the machine is on so no one will disturb him,' Josie said. William nodded. What else were they to think?

The sun helped to chase away a little of the night fears. How could there be malice planned under such bright skies? They settled themselves in the Tudor room because its windows overlooked two sides of the house. The room where just a few hours ago they had dallied and flirted now became charged with another kind of tension. How would they come? How many would there be? They passed the time constructing deliberately elaborate fantasies of forthcoming SAS invasions. Images of an army of police marksmen zipping down country lanes on Harley Davidsons, rifles strapped to their backs. Soon the jokes wore thin. At midday they tried Joshua again, at home and at work. The office asked for a name. She hung up immediately. This time they did not speculate on his whereabouts.

Morning turned into afternoon. Time passed grindingly slowly. They sat at opposite ends of the room studying the outside. They did nothing else. There was nothing to do. They stopped talking. He began to understand the horror that must come with imprisonment. The boredom and the waste. The room became unbearably hot. He longed to go outside, to experience yesterday's freedom and yesterday's faith. He had thought Meldon strong enough. He had been wrong. Suspicion had poisoned it. They should have left after all. Anything would be better than this enforced vigil.

In the mid-afternoon she slept. He marvelled at the ease of it. She just laid herself down on the settle cushions by the window, curled up and slipped away. He watched her from the other side of the room. It was the way she had slept in the caravan, the same position, like a child. He suppressed the desire to wake her, to have her share his anxiety. He turned back to the outside, squinting into the sunlight, searching the golden horizon for malevolent stick men. Finally he too grew drowsy in the heat and the stillness. But he dared not rest. What if they came while he was unconscious? He began to see the Garden of Gethsemane from Peter's point of view. He blinked himself awake.

After a while he made tea and brought it to her. She woke suddenly , as if startled by his shadow. She sat up, body hunched, her face closed and troubled. She looked lost and helpless. He sat by her and put his arms around her. Briefly she relaxed against him, then gently extracted herself from his grasp. He let her go. 'Did you have a bad dream?'

She shook her head. 'I don't know. I can't remember. Something woke me. I felt bad. What time is it?'

'Twenty past five. You've been asleep for hours.'

'Sorry.'

'That's all right. You haven't missed anything.'

They sat together for a time. The late afternoon sun sent long rivulets of light along the dark wood floor. On the table the wild flowers were drooping in their vase. Despite themselves it was beautiful. The light softened everything. If this had been a vigil of choice, now would have been the most perfect part of the day. A long sunset began. The sun blazed pink, then crimson, finally a luminous grey. Time passed faster now. The gardens grew hazy in the fading light. If it should end tonight, he thought, this sunset will stay with me. Beside him Josie had a more prosaic reaction.

'I'm hungry,' she said. 'I need to eat.'

There was no use staying here anyway. It would soon be too dark to notice stalkers in the grass.

With the kitchen shutters drawn and a multitude of candles stationed in saucers round the room, casting small circles of light into the greater gloom, things did not feel much better. Over the stove she prepared a basic meal of tinned meat and frozen vegetables. They sat fiddling with the food, distracted by the flickering darkness, failing to make conversation. It's got us, he thought. The fear has us by the throat. Opposite him he felt Josie about to explode.

'Damn it!' she exclaimed, pushing her chair back with a deliberate screech. 'This is ridiculous. We might as well drive straight into town and give ourselves up. We'll surrender to our own shadows at this rate. No one came. There's been time enough. I was wrong. You were right. I say we're safe now. I'm going to turn on the light. Then I'm going to get a bottle of wine out of the cellar. And I'm going to put on some music and listen to the news. Fuck the risk. I want to know what's happening.'

She growled down at him, defying him to object. He smiled. The day he left school his headmaster had delivered his usual preparation-for-life homily. It contained the motto, you have nothing to fear but fear itself. It had taken twenty years for this cliché to acquire meaning. Thank God for her defiance. A little of the old Josie went a long way.

'Absolutely,' he declared. 'But just one thing – let me pick the wine. At the risk of enraging you, I do have a better eye for a good vintage.'

'Done.'

He moved through the pantry down the steps to the back cellar where Rob kept his wine. He turned on the switch by the heavy oak door, and the place exploded into light. He felt more human already. He was in the process of debating between a claret and a burgundy when he heard her voice, caught halfway in her throat, harsh and very frightened.

'William!'

He was back up the stairs into the kitchen in seconds. As he smashed into the room he registered the scene in fragments. Her standing with her back against the table, staring across the room where, framed in the open doorway, stood the large figure of a man, in anorak and jeans, hair unkempt, a half smile on his face. They acknowledged each other's presence with a sharp look. In the instant their eyes met William felt he detected a change. The man's face stiffened slightly as he stepped, or rather shambled, into the room, deftly pushing the door closed behind him with his foot.

'Hey, I'm sorry. I didn't mean to scare you. I didn't see any lights on. I just tried the door and it was open.' He sounded slightly nasal, an impression of a cold that never cleared up, the accent a little rough around the edges.

'Who are you?' It was William's voice. He was as surprised as anyone to hear it. But it sounded firm, thank God.

'Kevin,' the man replied, as if that would explain everything. He turned to Josie. 'Don't tell me you're Sandy, Rob's—'

'No, I'm not.'

'Ooops, sorry. Put my foot in it again.' He was further into the room now, although William could not remember having seen him move. 'I just assumed . . . But you're friends of his, right?'

'How do you know Rob?' Josie's hands were clenched in tight fists by her side. William could see the whites of her knuckles.

'Rob? Oh, he and I are old mates. Met in Amsterdam.' Kevin sniffed loudly and wiped the back of his hand across his nose. If it was meant as a gesture of street credibility it failed. His fingers were long and well manicured. 'That's why I'm here,' he continued good-naturedly. 'Rob invited me. "Any time you're around," he said, "just show up. There'll always be a place to stay." I did phone, but I couldn't get any reply so –'

'When did you call?'

'Phew – I dunno. Some time yesterday afternoon. You were out. Don't blame you in this weather. Hey, why all the questions?'

'Where did you leave the car? We didn't hear you drive up?' Josie this time.

'Car?' He pulled a face. 'I don't have a car. I got a lift. Some farmer let me out just down the road. Listen, if I'm disturbing something, then I'm sorry. I wasn't to know. Rob did say any time.' He paused. Neither of them responded. 'Anyway, you don't mind if I just sit down and get my breath back?'

He was in the chair already. He smiled up at Josie, who remained rooted to the spot. 'Pretty amazing place, eh? I couldn't believe it when I saw it from the road. Rob said it was big, but I never imagined . . .' He frowned and looked round at the candles, as if he'd only just noticed them. 'Hey, what's the problem? We got a power failure?'

'No, *we* haven't,' said William, hitting the word hard, and at the same time snapping on the light. The man blinked. By the wonder of electricity he was older than his style of dress and haircut. Late thirties, early forties even. The stubble was a recent addition.

He held William's gaze and gave him an obvious corny wink. 'Oh, I see. A little romantic lighting. Shit, I really did disturb something. Sorry . . . but, as Rob—'

'You can't stay here.' Josie's voice was like piano wire.

William came up behind her, placed a tender hand on her shoulder, and said in her ear, 'Oh, I don't know, love. We can hardly turn him out into the night, can we? I mean, any friend of Rob's . . .'

She whipped round, her eyes screaming. He smiled back. Better to have him inside the tent pissing out . . . She read enough of the message to hold her tongue.

'Well, I appreciate that. I really do.' Kevin beamed at them. 'Thanks a lot. I must admit it would have been pretty hard trying to get a lift at this time of night. But I don't want to disturb you. If you show me a bed I can . . .'

'No.' Josie's smile took the edge off the exploded word. 'No, you must be hungry. If you like I can open a can of something.'

He grinned. 'Great. Thanks a lot. I wouldn't mind a spot of something, if it's not too much trouble.'

'And a glass of something too,' William chipped in. 'I was just on my way down to the cellar when you came in. Won't be a minute.'

As soon as he got downstairs he called, 'Have you got the key, darling? The cellar door is locked.'

She scrambled in the drawer for a set of keys and joined him quickly. He pulled her into the shadows behind the door.

'Who the hell is he?' he hissed.

'I don't know. If he was going to harm us, then why sit down and chat first? I suppose he might just be for real. It's the kind of thing Rob used to do – give out some casual invitation one night when he's drunk and have some fucker take him up on it. This guy scares the shit out of me, but so would John Wayne in the circumstances.'

He jangled the keys so the sound covered the words. Under his breath he said quickly, 'Real or not, I don't feel prepared to risk it.'

'So what do we do?'

'Get him down here.'

She glanced at the heavy oak door. 'O.K.,' she nodded.

Back in the kitchen Kevin was gone. Josie felt sick. The door through to the main house was open. She fled into the passage. No sign. She called tentatively, 'Kevin?' No answer. Running lightly up the carpeted stairs, she noticed from the landing that one of the bedroom doors was ajar. She peeped in.

He was standing flat against the shutter, looking obliquely out of the window. From the outside no one would have seen him. She took a step forward. He spun round.

'Oh hello.' The grin returned, just as irrelevant. 'I was trying to find the john.'

'You missed it.' She managed to keep her voice steady. 'It's the last on the left, at the end of the corridor. I'll show you.'

'It's all right. I'll find it.'

She waited while he went in. She went over to the hall window and looked out. The back lawn shone ghostly under the moon. Trees lining the garden shivered in the breeze. What else? Nothing.

The toilet chain was pulled and Kevin emerged, doing up his flies. She followed him downstairs. She poured both of them large glasses of wine and heated up some soup, before sitting down opposite him.

'Thanks a lot,' he said, mouth full. She watched him eat. Either he was a good actor or it was the first meal he'd had in a while.

'When did you say you met Rob?' she asked, with what she hoped sounded like friendly curiosity.

'Oh, about a year ago. He was in Amsterdam recording some stuff. We got to know each other a bit.'

'What do you do?'

'Oh, this and that. You know Amsterdam.' He shot her a conspiratorial grin. Sex and drugs and rock 'n roll. Take your pick. 'And you? How do you know him?'

'We were at university together.'

'Oh, that far back? Were you . . . er . . ?'

She let him flounder. 'Friends,' she said. 'Just good friends.'

'Yeah,' he leered. 'That sounds like Rob.'

'So, you've followed his music a long time, then?'

He pushed aside his plate and grabbed the wine bottle. 'You don't mind, do you?' He poured himself another drink.

William appeared at the doorway and joined them at the table. Josie brought him a glass. The bottle was almost empty. They exchanged glances.

'I said, are you a big fan of Rob's music?'

Kevin shrugged. 'I don't know much of the early stuff. Well, you get a bit out of touch in Amsterdam. But I know the big hits – "Thunder in the City" and "Tramlines".'

Even I've heard of those, thought William. You don't need to be an expert. Josie was watching Kevin intently, a puzzled look on her face. He took a couple of swigs of wine and reached for the bottle. Josie didn't take her eyes off him. After pouring the dregs into his glass he set the bottle back on the table with a clatter. William took this as a hint. He got to his feet, rubbing his hands.

Josie joined him. 'You can show Kevin to bed, can't you love? I'll put on some sheets. Don't drink Rob's cellar dry now, will you?'

'We'll leave a little,' William said.

'Good night, Kevin,' she said, brightly waving a hand. 'We must pick up on some gossip tomorrow morning.'

'Sure.'

Leaving the door ajar, she made a meal out of climbing the stairs and slamming an upstairs door, then crept downstairs again and stationed herself in the shadows near the kitchen. She heard a mumble of voices, then the scraping of chairs and their footsteps leaving the room. She followed silently.

Down the cellar steps with Kevin in front, William was babbling trivia. 'I tell you, I've never seen such a selection. He's got brands of whisky I've never heard of. It's a real Aladdin's cave.' The cellar door was open. 'Go right ahead. Take your pick.'

It was never going to be that easy. He should have known. When they reached the threshold, and William motioned him forward into what was meant to be his prison, Kevin hesitated. William was seized by doubt, about whether he had the means, the strength, the will to carry it off. It looked as though guile was failing. That left force. But William was two stones lighter, and his sport was squash not weight training. If it came to a grapple, he'd lose. He glanced round wildly for inspiration.

And next to the wall was a wine rack. William reached out behind himself and his hand clutched at the dusty neck of a Vosnes Romanee 63. He brought it up, tightened his grasp and started to swing. Then Kevin turned.

'Hey, you know –'

It glanced off Kevin's head and cracked him on the shoulder. He didn't yell, he didn't crumple, but nor did he react. He stopped in mid-sentence and stared at his assailant, stunned, it seemed, as much by the effrontery as by the blow itself. William was already moving, and he kept moving, bringing his body up against Kevin in a great shoulder-charge that bundled both of them to the floor inside the wine cellar.

William scrambled to his feet and cleared out. Josie was by his side. They banged the door closed and he swung the heavy key in the lock.

'Hey, what is this? Open the door! What are you doing?'

The man must have the constitution of an ox, to have recovered his wits so quickly. There came an almighty thud against the door, a shoulder on wood. Then the voice again:

'Listen, Josie, William. It isn't what you think. Let me out and we'll talk about it.'

This time he didn't sound at all like Kevin. They took one look at each other and fled.

Chapter twenty-seven

It was too fast now for thought. At the top of the stairs they heard another crash from below. There was no time for strategy, no time even for talk. There was only the panic of flight. They flung themselves out of the house, smashing open the night silence with an orgy of feet on gravel.

He grabbed her by the hand and pulled her after him. The way down through the gardens was across the lawn to where a gap in the shrubbery marked the stairs down. But instead he headed left to where the path met the border hedgerow. Instinct told him they should keep cover. The wide expanse of moonlit grass was a death trap. Once free – and he would get free, that was clear – all Kevin need do was open one of the dozen windows looking out on the lawn and take aim.

They ran crouched, under the shadow covering the hedge, following the circumference of the grass until they reached the gap and the steps down to the next level of garden. It was narrow and exposed. He glanced back at the silhouette of the house. Nothing. He squeezed her hand hard, then let go. 'Me first,' he whispered. She nodded. He moved forward.

He took the steps carefully, that was the idea. But he was half in panic, one was out of line, the moon chose that moment to go behind a cloud. It was the kind of thing that could have happened to anyone. A simple mistake of judgement. It saved his life. As he missed his footing on the fourth step and plunged forward into the darkness, a shot rang out.

He felt it as a burning whizz of light just over his head. He tumbled down the remaining steps onto the grass at the bottom. He lay still, heart thumping, a stab in his right ankle telling him he was still alive. Above him he felt Josie's fear. 'I'm O.K.,' he hissed, but his voice sounded huge and he could risk no further communication. It would, anyway, bring little comfort. The bullet had destroyed all sense of security, and had brought with it a doubling of the fear. Because the shot had come not from the house but from another direction entirely, from below, somewhere in the dark, wild garden. Kevin had an accomplice. The moon broke free again, giving the gunman a perfect view of the stone steps; steps with William at the bottom and Josie at the top. Their joint flight was over. In their separate huddles they both understood that. For a while neither moved, then he heard above him the slight swish of a body against leaves. It gradually grew fainter. He stepped inside Josie's brain, and saw what she saw. There was no following him. Nor could she stay there and wait for Kevin to come up from behind. She had no alternative but to retreat. The sound was of Josie worming back through the border. But from there? Surely not back to the house?

That was her business now. He had his own life to preserve. Still flat on the ground, he reached down to his ankle, feeling around for the centre of pain. He moved the foot a little, working it in a careful semicircle. It did as it was told. Not broken. Not even sprained. The pain lessened. Two miracles: alive and well. He bent his hips up slightly to put weight on the ankle. It held. Now what? Down through the garden? Over the fields? Back towards the house? One thing at a time. First the next few feet.

He squirmed forwards, pulling himself along on his elbows with his abdomen close to the ground, a technique plucked from random movie memory. On celluloid it looked good, man and earth intermingled. In real life, in the silver-grey of the night grass, he felt about as unobtrusive as a black adder on tinfoil. Will I hear the shot that kills me? he thought. For some reason the question seemed to matter. He remembered reading an account by a survivor of falling from an eighth storey window. A page and a half to describe six seconds. He should be so lucky. The thought helped him lose the fear. Face it. Either you survived or you didn't. It was as simple as that.

He survived, at least as far as the hedgerow. There he stopped and took stock. Down through the gardens to the stream there was a more or less unbroken line of shrubbery and hedges. If he crawled this way he might, with luck, make it as far as the fields, and thence over the back roads to the village. It was the safest and most logical route. Too logical. Its benefits were ambiguous. He didn't doubt that the assassin had been around long enough to have reached the same conclusions himself.

So what else? A considered retreat. A lateral movement to the stables and barns at the side of the house. Following these would bring him out near the main drive, and from there it was a mere hundred yards of open path to the main road. Of course it might be blocked by a firing squad. But one could only deal with one thing at a time. At least that way he might find Josie. If he went on without her, he might have to wake every morning for the rest of his life knowing he had left her to her fate. There could be no sweetness in such an escape. He felt his way to the bank of earth and scrambled up through the shrubbery.

He bargained without the noise. It was deafening. With each foot he climbed, twigs and dry leaves crackled like bonfire sparks. The gunman must be locating his position as clearly as if he were shouting at the top of his lungs. If only it would rain, or thunder, anything to cover up the damn silence . . .

Then, with a timing that smacked of divine intervention, Meldon erupted into sound. From the belly of the house it came first, waves of it, pouring sobbing guitar chords out through the windows and into the night. He froze, paralyzed, while from every room in the house now Rob's sensational music system pounded out the opening bars of "Hotel California". Josephine Ridley, he thought, I love you.

'On a dark desert highway, cool wind in my hair . . .'

She was halfway down the back stairs when the voice hit. She was amazed by its volume. In her panic she had flipped all the knobs as far as they would go, unable in the darkness to tell one from another. She had wanted it loud to cover her progress. Well, loud she had it. At the bottom she entered the courtyard and, taking courage from the flamboyance of her protection, took the first steps into the open. The vocal wrapped itself around her, warning:

'I was thinking to myself, this could be heaven, or this could be hell.'

Fair enough, she thought – and ran.

It had not all been so confident or so colourful. After the shot she had wormed her way back to the house, cowed and shaking. She too had thought longingly of the freedom to be found on the main road, flagging down cars, seeking sanctuary in village cottages. But it wasn't on. Between here and there was a long strip of open stage lit by moonlight. Instead, she had crept round the side of the house and slipped in the kitchen door.

The house was silent, the room, eerily lit by a few candles spluttering in their wax, empty. She hesitated. But not for long. From the cellar came a final splintering sound and the clatter of boots on stone. She catapulted herself across the room, her thigh making sudden painful contact with the edge of a table. It hurt but she hardly noticed. She took the stairs two at a time, then sprinted along the landing. Somewhere en route a cell in her brain clicked and submitted a plan. She didn't stop to consider, but obeyed it instantly. It revolved around the study.

Inside she locked the door. The study was the only room in the house with two doors leading to different levels, one from the landing, the other down the back stairs into the courtyard. It also had a phone. The receiver purred in her ear. Finger on the buttons, she hesitated. Where was he? She imagined him prowling below, checking the rooms one by one. Had he got to the stairs? It was a question of the devil and the deep blue sea. She punched the three numbers.

'Emergency. Which service do you require?'

'Police.'

'I'm sorry. Can you speak up?'

'No. Police.'

An indeterminate noise from below. A footstep? A creak on the stairs? In her ear came a click, then a voice.

'Police? What number are you calling from?'

In the darkness it was hard to read. 'Meldon Hall, near Bakewell. Come quickly.'

'Just a moment, madam. Can I have your name and the number you're calling from?'

No doubt now. It was the even tread of a man's footsteps on the stairs. She squinted desperately at the number.

'Oh . . . Bakewell 78967. They're trying to kill us. Meldon Hall. Just get here. Please . . .'

He was in the corridor. She couldn't risk more speech. She put her finger on the connecting button and lowered the phone gently. It pinged softly. She glanced at the door. The lock was paltry. It would give with the first smash of a shoulder. She should just get the hell out, no time for the rest of the plan. Instinct shouted to cut her losses and run. This time she resisted it, distrusting the bias of fear. At the wall she pulled back the upper bookcase to reveal the flash console. She felt her way round the board, switched it on and plucked a tape at random from the long line above. The steps got closer. It was a matter of seconds. The tape in place, she let her finger hover over the buttons and, with a direct appeal to the deity she didn't believe in, pressed. Silence. The world stood still. Under his breath a musician in a studio nine years ago mentally counted out the intro. One, two, three, four . . . From what might have been the master bedroom the first chord twanged out. She didn't wait for the second. In a final gesture of defiance she pushed every button in sight and made for the back stairs. She was inside the chapel by the end of the second verse. She was heading for Royal Sanctuary.

Out in the open the music stopped as suddenly as it had come, leaving William stranded on gravel, his back flattened against a barn wall. His first concern was his breathing. He had sprinted the last fifty yards in the noisy darkness, and now it felt as if a throat mike were broadcasting his rasping clutches for air. He closed his eyes and forced himself to take longer, deeper mouthfuls.

But his real problem was not sound but space. He was on a road between a run of open stables and a long, half derelict barn. Ahead of him was a darkness that would eventually lead him to the front drive and freedom. Behind him a marksman was stalking his prey. But not directly on his tail, of that he was sure. Gravel was gravel, and even experts had to register some footfall. William could hear nothing. He should move, to retain his advantage. He continued, hugging the wall, feeling a spurious safety in its shadow. The end of the corridor between the buildings grew nearer, his fear subsided slightly. He passed a clump of ivy, its thick, full roots bulging out from the stonework. It was then that he saw the gunman. And he was not behind him but ahead.

In the dim light he was more a presence than a person, large, looming and silent. William wriggled in among the ivy. His heart hit amplification again. Surely it couldn't be the pursuer? How could he have covered the distance in so short a time? Or was it Kevin out in search of his second victim? He cautiously took a step back. Then stopped. If it was Kevin, that left the other one somewhere behind him. He couldn't go forward, he couldn't go back. He contemplated the stables opposite, but it was a run across moonlight and once inside he would be cornered. In desperation he looked upwards.

The ivy beckoned. Back through the years into childhood the call came. The plant was sturdy and well established, its roots strong and its hold on the masonry confident. And there was a lot of it, a mass of leaves rising up the wall and spreading over the roof and along the ridge of the barn. It was a stairway with perfect cover. They would not expect to have to look there and, more important, there was nowhere else for him to go. This was the place he had been led to. Here he would make his stand. He probed among the leaves with his foot, seeking the first hold. Then he reached up and found solid veins of branch stapled to the wall. He began to climb.

After the first six or seven feet he hardly needed to think about it. His hands and feet were moving of their own accord. Two decades since he last shinned a wall but the knowledge came flowing back. I have been waiting for this moment the whole of my adult life, he thought, and for an instant all the fear and horror faded away leaving the pure pleasure of achievement. Only for an instant. When he reached the top of the wall, where the roof began its graduated rise, he found the going much more treacherous. Parts of the roof were rotten, tiles were broken and wooden beams revealed. The climbing was easy, but he could not be sure the structure would support him. He held tight, and risked a look down.

What he saw made his fingers grip harder. A man – which one he couldn't tell – was standing thirty yards away, arms locked in front of him pointing an object whose nature William didn't need to guess. He froze. That is, he tried to. But he had been too long in one spot and the plant would not stand his concentrated weight. He felt the root giving slightly and let go immediately to find another hold. Too late.

He saved himself but dislodged a tile. It plunged down inside the barn onto the stone floor. The noise was appalling. William stared helplessly at his adversary. The man whipped his body flat on the ground and his arm jerked up to find the target.

William closed his eyes and waited to die. A pulse began thumping inside his head. Now, he thought. His life refused to flash before him. Now.

Nothing happened. From the barn beneath him came a scuffling sound. Still he kept his eyes shut. And still he was not dead. When he could bear it no longer he looked down. He raised his head and looked long and carefully all around him. There was no one there. But the man must have seen him. He had been impossible to miss. Then he heard a series of sounds. In time to come he would never be able to make sense of them, or even be sure which were real and which were imagined. But two of these stood out. There was a rustle, like the scurry of giant rats across straw. Then there was the scream. A long, dark, dreadful cry that told of agony and the losing of life. William clung to the roof, hands aching with the force of the grasp. The cry died away and he heard nothing more.

He waited and waited. When he felt he could wait no more, he buried his face in the smooth mass of leaves, smelt the mix of rotten timber and sprouting ivy shoots, and decided that whatever threatened him below, now was the time to meet it.

He retraced his steps gingerly, testing each hold first, concerned more with safety than speed or silence. Someone was dead, apparently, and it wasn't him. This encouraged him and gave him an exaggerated sense of his immortality. He began to believe he had got away with it and started to plan what to do next. So preoccupied was he with these thoughts and with the task of descent that what happened next took him completely by surprise.

A beam of torchlight flashed up and hit him. With it came a voice, ringing out into the night.

'Here he is!'

William lost all sense of security and self-preservation. His feet slipped their hold. He hung suspended by his arms for a second until the ivy came away from the wall. He fell eight feet through the air, bang, and landed in an undignified heap on the ground.

Josie was close to the ground too, much closer than she would have liked. People had been built smaller in the seventeenth century. It must have been the milk. She had tried standing, shoulders hunched and head down, but it affected her balance, and the touch of stone on bare arms when she swayed was like ice fingers in the darkness. In the end she resorted to squatting, which brought her in proximity to the dank earth, but at least it gave her a sense of space. And all the time she took care to hold the door open against the spring. Just a fraction. Incarceration versus the bullet? No contest.

How long had she been here? One hour? Two? It had been so easy. Once inside the chapel she edged her way round the wall until she came to the cold brass plaque and the ring. She felt only the slightest flicker of apprehension when the door slid back and a wave of bad air rushed towards her. She resisted it and stepped inside. She had made it. She was safe. They could search and search and they would never find. All she had to do was wait. King Charles had hidden in an oak tree after the Battle of Worcester. Fat lot of good it had done him. He would have been safer here. The ruler of England in a stone hole. He might have coped better with the stench.

After a while it began to get to her, the smell of damp and decay. It was as if something had died in there, trapped and starved in the darkness. The thought tugged her away from her stubborn pursuit of the rational, and little madnesses began to trickle in. She faced the door, crouching with her back to the expanse of tunnel behind her. She was becoming aware of this, and feeling its possibilities of horror. She remembered a film she had once seen about two young Guatemalans making an illegal crossing into America by crawling through miles of unused sewer pipes that ran underneath the city of Tijuana. Halfway along they were attacked by an army of rats. She shivered and a rash of goosepimples ran over her flesh. She swallowed and thought hard about sunshine and the pleasure of early morning in hot countries. My favourite things: what horrors had Julie Andrews ever had to dispel? In her head she began guiding a tour of Americans down the river to the Tower. As a fantasy it aborted all too soon when they reached the dungeons and the torture chambers.

Then something ran over her foot. She started violently and let out a cry, her hands shooting up instinctively to protect her face. The door swung to, and closed softly with a small click.

No! Her brain refused the message. She took the handle and pulled it confidently towards her. It didn't move. She pulled again. And again, this time without illusion. From the pit of her stomach she felt a wave of panic building, and she knew that once it hit her there would be no more coherent thought. Come on, Josie, hold it together. Think. There has to be a way out. They would not have left a king to suffer such a gothic death. Her hands flew over the stone, searching for the magic spot that would release the catch. They could search and search and they would never find. What had been the comfort now became the terror.

She felt the door. It was a tight, close fit. She hammered on it with closed fists. Dull little thuds rebounded. She shouted. Her cries echoed deafeningly in the enclosed space, with barely a whisper to be heard outside. Apart from William, who knew about the passage? Probably only the old caretaker, retired to Eastbourne. Apart from William, who knew she would have chosen to hide there? No one. Apart from William . . . And where was William? Splayed out in a flower bed with a small river of blood running from a hole in his head.

She would never be found. A small skeleton two generations later, oh how interesting. She turned from the door and faced the tunnel. Childenhurst had built it to save life. There must be a way out: where else did the air come from? She thought of soft moonlight sliding through branches onto mossy earth. She got down on hands and knees and started to crawl. She had gone only eighty or ninety yards when she collided with a solid bank of earth. She put her hands round her ears, she opened her mouth, and she started to scream.

Behind her the stone slid open, and a voice called her name. When they got her out she was still shaking.

She sat quiet in the sitting room, a tartan blanket wrapped round her, cradling a mug of tea generously laced with brandy. With bare feet and rumpled hair she looked like a child who had had bad dreams and been brought down to sit by the fire with its parents. William was next to her, a concerned look on his face.

'I'm O.K.,' she said stubbornly. 'Really. I'm better now. Tell me what happened.'

He was dubious. 'How about some sleep first? Talk about it in the morning.'

'I told you, I'm all right,' she said. 'Don't fuss.'

The room was small and cosy and very ordinary. It had a sofa and two chairs, a few ornaments, a television. They had been brought here because it was the closest place. The village constable's wife welcomed them at the door. She was a big woman, all warm flesh and efficiency, by profession a comforter, a provider of pots of tea and seventy-proof medicine. One look at Josie and she took control, shooing away the men and ushering her into the house proper. 'You can save your questions for ten minutes. Let her alone with me.' Even William obeyed. Josie went like a child. Now, though, it was time to return to adulthood.

'Tell me.'

'The man in the garden is dead. He followed me up to the barns and in the darkness walked into a pitchfork in the hay. The police found the body after they got me down from the roof.'

'And Kevin?'

'No sign. They've searched the house and the grounds and they've got men out on the roads, but he seems to have disappeared into thin air. The police think he might have been for real, and that we just frightened him off.'

She frowned, as if the information made no sense. 'How did they find us? Was it the phone call?'

He looked at her steadily. 'Partly.'

'It was Joshua?'

'Yes. It was Joshua.' He didn't take his eyes off her. 'He published his story.'

She pulled off the blanket. 'I knew it. I knew it had to be him. Where is he? Is he here?'

He didn't answer. She looked at his face, at the set of his jaw with teeth clenched together. And she knew.

'What happened?'

This time he answered. He picked up the newspaper lying on the floor beside him and handed it to her.

A policeman entered the room. He stayed in the doorway, waiting, awkward. Outside it was beginning to get light. Josie's eyes rested on the front page, unseeing. She made herself focus. The banner headline read:

MI5 BLAMED FOR HIGHGATE BOMBING

She started to read, but her eye was pulled downwards to a box at the bottom of the page, framing a picture. Above it were the words:

JOSHUA BARNES POST REPORTER FOUND DEAD

She read the ten lines or so silently. Then she looked up at William.

'No one knows,' he said. 'He was found dead next to a mirror with the remains of a line of cocaine on it. They reckon the stuff was cut with poison – maybe Ajax, or something like that. When he didn't come into work yesterday, they sent someone . . .'

She put her head down. He placed his hand over hers and held it there. She sat like that for a long time. When she at last lifted her head, the police officer had been joined by a tall man in plain clothes. His face was familiar. She frowned. Then remembered.

'Miss Ridley. You remember me. Detective Inspector Gill, Highgate Police. I'm sorry to disturb you at such a moment. But there are a few questions I'm afraid I must ask you. Do you feel well enough to answer?'

She stared at him for a long time. The room waited. The silence was not comfortable. Finally she stood up and, holding the newspaper close to her chest, she walked straight past the two policemen and out of the room. William watched her go. The detective turned to him expectantly. He got up and followed her out.

Chapter Twenty-eight

Saturday morning, June 19th. Overcast and dull. This one was an ordinary summer. William stood in the middle of what once had been his living room, surveying the debris of packing cases. Three days to go. On the floor was a carved teak chess set, his leaving present from Actonics – that and a sledgehammer in the back of his head from the party the night before. June 19th. A year to the day from the Archway roundabout. In less than a hundred hours Archway would be in another country. So many things still to be done. He turned his attention to the bottom drawer of his filing cabinet. From a brown envelope a newspaper clipping fluttered to the floor. More haste, less speed. He bent to retrieve it. The headline caught his eye. A souvenir of times past. He had always intended to mount them in a scrapbook, but when it came to it, he had been too intent on getting back to normality. Now, four months later, it was already past history.

Daily Post February 18th

TEN YEARS FOR MI5 TERRORIST

Nigel Gough, the MI5 agent who masterminded the bombing of the Royal Highgate Hospital, was jailed yesterday at the Old Bailey for a term of ten years. The explosion last June destroyed the hospital's kidney unit and killed a security guard, Malcolm O'Grady. Gough admitted conspiring, but denied responsibility for O'Grady's death and the death of *Post* reporter Joshua Barnes, whose investigations led directly to Gough's arrest. It is believed that Gough's guilty plea saved him from having to face more serious charges.

Absent from the court was Joe De Villiers, 43, whom Gough accused of being his accomplice to the terror act. In the witness box Gough alleged that De Villiers was an agent of the South African National Intelligence Service (formerly BOSS) who had proposed and carried out the bombing, in order to ingratiate himself with MI5. De Villiers, born in Johannesburg but a naturalized British subject, left his London flat on June 27th, and has not been seen since, despite the efforts of police in three continents. The South African government has categorically denied any connection with them.

During the trial Gough was described by the defence as an 'over-zealous intelligence officer who believed he had been given the nod to rid the government of a meddlesome pressure group'. He claimed to have acted without the knowledge or consent of MI5 or any of his colleagues, and was content to accept the prosecution depiction of him as 'a dangerous maverick'.

Gough, who is 56, will be eligible for parole in five years . . .

'Five years!' William smiled, recalling Josie's explosive scorn as they sat together in the pub after the trial, the last time he had seen her. 'Just enough time for him to spew out his memoirs, then when he gets out, a sly helping hand into a sleeping directorship somewhere. Justice!'

William hadn't been so sure. In his experience the establishment wasn't necessarily so loyal to those members who disgraced themselves. He couldn't quite shift the image of a prison cell and the humiliation of obeying rules when you were used to making them. Throughout the trial Gough's expression had been impenetrable, but at the moment of sentencing William thought he detected a slight change in body language, as if the years were a physical weight lowered onto his shoulders. He seemed to stoop as he was led away. The end of the story. Even then, not quite.

'So, what are you going to do now, Josie?'

'I dunno. I've been offered some criminally large sum from a well known leftie publisher to write it all down for the faithful to read.'

'Will you take it?'

She shrugged. 'I sort of feel I owe it to Joshua. He should have been the one to write it. It would have made his name. I might do it in co-authorship. In memoriam. "The Whole Story".'

'But what else is there to tell? My God, Josie, what more do you want? MI5 in disarray, with a flurry of resignations and the promise of a judicial inquiry. The South African government disgraced and under threat. A bullying health minister replaced by a peacemaker, and the privatization issue dropped. I would have thought you'd just got everything you ever wanted in a Christmas stocking.'

'Hmmm. Maybe,' she replied darkly. 'And maybe not.'

'Well, if you want my advice I think you should let it rest. It's time to redirect your energies. You're famous now. You can get any job you want. Get on with your life. Don't rake over the past.'

She punched him affectionately on the arm. 'Aaah William, if I'd got into the habit of listening to your advice, Gough would still be dining at his club tonight, and the NHS waiting lists would be even longer.'

And Joshua would still be filing copy, he thought, but not aloud. 'Well, do what you want. You will anyway. But just remember – the next major conspiracy you uncover, I'm not answering the phone.'

'Going back to the real world, eh?'

'Yep. Diners' card, mortgage, pension. The lot. And plugging in the electric kettle each morning with a serene sense of security.'

'It won't be the same. You'll be bored.'

'We'll see.'

Standing there surrounded by packing cases, William pondered that she had been right. It hadn't been the same. It was hard to work out whether it was he that had changed, or people's attitudes towards him.Certainly no one was quite normal with him any more. They had employed a personnel manager. They didn't know what to do with a public celebrity. No wonder Clark Kent always chose empty phone boxes. The more they 'behaved' towards him, the more isolated he became. And the less he enjoyed the work. When he saw the ILO job advertised in *Personnel Management*, it had felt as if fate were tossing him a lifeline. Working at the UN would take him out of the minefield of British industry, where the blood was still flowing, and out of England, the country where his face had been on the front page of every newspaper. And it would bring him into another reality. International Labour. He didn't know enough, but he would learn. Josie would be astonished. It really would be a shame if he didn't get the chance to tell her. He was surprised she hadn't answered his note. Maybe she was away. He picked up the chess set and debated which case to put it into, the going or the staying. He was still deciding when the phone rang. The voice said:

'William, what are you doing this afternoon? I've got a conspiracy I'd like to discuss with you.'

'Are you sure this is a good idea?' he said, lowering himself gingerly into the boat. 'It's not part of my working-class heritage, messing about in boats.'

She was busy fixing the oars in place with all the expertise of a committed landlubber. 'It will be if you sit down. I told you, I've done it before. It'll only take us ten minutes to row to the island. It'll be lovely there, so long as it doesn't rain. Anyway, I promised you a river trip, remember?'

'You promised me a guided tour. Not an outward bound course.'

She grinned. 'You'll get the tour. Starts now. Not far from this very spot, 1878. The worst inland waterway disaster in the history of maritime Britain. The *Princess Alice*, a passenger ship, was returning down river in the twilight when a collier, the *Bywater Castle*, ran straight into her and cut her in two. Six hundred people died, most of them from asphyxiation and poisoning as they bobbed up and down in the water – or rather in the sewage which then passed for the Thames. The lightermen were bringing up bodies for weeks. A shilling a corpse. Some of them made a tidy fortune.'

'Wonderful. How come you always know the most gruesome stories?'

She shrugged. 'They're always the ones that go down the best. Sit still. I can't row properly if you keep shifting around.'

He watched her, the small frame heaving on the oars. She was looking good. Her hair was cut shorter, cropped close to her head, and she was brown from something stronger than an English sun. He remembered the moments of attraction, and smiled at the memory. After all this time there was still no one quite like her. Thank God.

By the time they reached the island she was sweating slightly. They pulled the boat up together and left it by a fallen tree trunk. It was a scrubby piece of land, with just a few trees and some undergrowth, the river banks clearly visible on both sides. They were the only visitors. Above them the sky gave a warning rumble. He followed her to a half-broken bench by the edge and sat looking out over the fast flowing river. He imagined it swarming with bodies. Maybe there were worse fates than the gauntlet of an ivy staircase in a firing range. He still had nightmares. Perhaps she did too.

She settled herself on the ground, leaning against a tree trunk, and rummaged in her bag. Two paper cups were followed by a cheap bottle of champagne. It popped in a wide arch of spray. She slopped some into one of the cups and handed it to him.

'Here's to you and your new future. Congratulations.'

'How did you know?'

'William, you can't have failed to notice, we're still minor public property. Your appointment made three lines on page two of the *Guardian*. You're sure, I suppose, that you got the job on merit?'

Good old Josie. Age cannot wither her, nor time withdraw her sting.

'I leave on Tuesday. I didn't think you'd be in touch.'

'I've been away for a while. I had some things to sort out. So, tell me about this new William Stevens image. Could it really be that our little escapade did change your life?'

'No, I just got bored with the colour of my wallpaper. Fancied a change.' He smiled. 'Work it out for yourself.'

'Where do you start?'

'New York for a two month training course. Then maybe Africa or Indonesia.'

'You going alone?'

He nodded.

'What happened to Penny?'

'She married an auctioneer from Sotheby's. They met while we were in Meldon. She kept it quiet for a while, when she thought I needed support.'

'Jolly sporting of her. How did you feel about it?'

'A bit bruised. I suppose I wanted to be the one to decide it wasn't going to work. But she did the right thing. They're very happy. No doubt I'll be a godfather before long. Anyway, I don't think she would have flourished in Africa.'

'And will you?'

'I'll get on with it. I might even enjoy it. I never did my compulsory year travelling. I was always too anxious to get on. I'm just growing young late in life.'

'Well, you'd better get yourself a memsahib on the way. I hear the sherry parties can be pretty dull for UN bachelors.'

'You offering?'

She grinned. 'Over my dead body.'

'That's what I thought. I shouldn't worry about me, Josie. After all we've been through I think I'm quite good at looking after myself. What about you?'

She kept her face in her cup. 'What about me?'

'I heard a lot of rumours about you and Rob.'

'Yeah, I heard them too. Funny that. I kept reading about places we'd been and things we'd done together, when I was somewhere else entirely. Par for the course, I suppose. "Superstar fucks framed heroine". If we didn't exist they'd have to make it up.'

'I kept expecting to see you up on a charge of assaulting photographers.'

'You know what it's like - hit one, and four sprout up in their place. I tell you, you would have been proud of me. I finally learned the lesson about discretion being the better part of valour.'

'And no Rob?'

'No Rob. We saw each other a couple of times, nothing more. He should worry. He owes me. We did wonders for his political credibility. Any PR agent would have cost him a fortune to get that kind of coverage. He even made money. They re-released the "Josie" track, you know.'

'I know. I bought it.'

'Did you?' she laughed. 'Sentimentalist.'

He took a sip of champagne. It could have been colder but the bubbles worked the same. 'What about the book? Is it finished?'

'No,' she said, looking away. 'I decided not to write it after all.'

He waited, but she volunteered nothing more. 'Just like that?' he prompted.

She gazed out over the water. 'Just like that.'

He balanced his paper cup on the ground and studied her profile. 'You know, there never was any point in you lying to me. I always knew when you were doing it.'

She frowned and shook her head. 'William, the very last thing you said to me the day the trial finished was that whatever else happened, you didn't want to hear about it. I'm just obeying orders.'

'In which case it'll be the first time in your life you ever did. Let's try again. Why did you stop writing the book, Josie?'

She looked straight at him. 'Because I found out something I couldn't print, that's why.'

'And you didn't tell me.'

'I thought about it. Honestly. I just didn't think you'd want that responsibility.'

The old flame of frustration fanned into life again. 'Listen to me. I'm leaving the country on Tuesday. I've spent the best part of a year being pestered by oddballs who think that because your name's been in the paper you're public property. I never wanted to get into this in the first place, if you remember, and the last thing I want is to go through it again. But what we did, we did together. And if you've found out something, then I have the right to know what it is, O.K?'

'O.K.,' she said, in a voice that was only partly convinced. 'I would have told you eventually. I thought of writing you a letter once you'd got abroad. But now is as good a time as any.'

She sat silent for a moment, then turned herself round to look at him. Her face was grave.

'But one thing before we start, right? What I'm going to tell you is not just some crazy piece of Josie-fantasy. It's the truth, the whole truth this time – and you're going to be hard pushed to believe it.'

He said nothing. How many times had she surprised him before? Now, just before his departure, it was right there should be one last cracker to be pulled.

'Let's begin at the end. Remember something you said to me the day before the trial. It stayed with me. Your exact words were, "You know, Josie, for a high-class conspiracy, this really had some stupid mistakes in it." I agree. Gough, De Villiers, these guys were intelligence experts. So how come they were so bad at their job? Take the car, for instance. Who in their right mind would use a car that could be traced back to them for an act of terrorism? That always stank.'

'Sure. But that was explained at the trial, remember? The car they were going to use, hired with the false ID, got smashed up just an hour before. No time to hire another and too dodgy to steal one. De Villiers' car was sitting on a parking meter outside a Mayfair restaurant. Just so long as he stayed inside until the early hours, he didn't have to report it stolen till after the bombing. It was that or call the whole thing off. In the circumstances it must have seemed like a risk worth taking.'

'Maybe. But a bit unlucky, wouldn't you say, to have a hit-and-run driver wipe out your car at such a crucial moment? O.K., let's move on. To that fateful day when I sat in Canning Square, watching De Villiers' house. Now, he knew I'd been snooping, he told the police as much. Yet not only does he drive up in broad daylight and fail to notice me, but two minutes later he's out of the house and letting me trail him halfway across London to a rendezvous with the bomber. At the time even you thought that was a bit strange. And you were right. Christ, William, I'm an amateur. I've never tailed anyone in my life. De Villiers is supposedly a top BOSS agent. He's probably thrown off more pursuers than I've had hot dinners. So how comes he still didn't spot me?'

'Clearly he's not such a top agent after all.'

'Or the mistakes are deliberate.'

'What?'

'Look at it another way. What if I were to tell you that up till now we've been getting the whole thing wrong? That this is not a cock-up that we stumbled on, but a conspiracy that was always intended to fail, that contained its own time-bomb. In other words, what has happened is exactly what was meant to happen. Now, if that's the case, who are the people who've gained from this?'

William shrugged. 'Health Not Wealth? The left? You're not seriously suggesting –' She shook her head, waiting for him to work it out. He thought again. South Africa. 'O.K.,' he said. 'BOSS's enemies. The ANC and others. They've had a field day over it.'

'Exactly. So much so that it could hardly have gone better if they'd planned it.'

'And did they? Did the ANC plan it?'

'Yes. Through De Villiers. De Villiers is a spy, right? With BOSS, the South African secret service. What's the aim of a secret service? They try to penetrate the other side. Men and women trusted for years turn out to have been traitors all along. Over the years BOSS has been spectacularly successful at infiltrating the opposition. But if BOSS can do that to the ANC, then why not the other way round?'

'You're telling me De Villiers was a double agent?'

'That's right. De Villiers was really working for the ANC. His role in the conspiracy was to organize the actual bombing, and then subtly, by a series of "accidents", to fuck it up. First, the hit-and-run smash. He got someone to do that. Then the substitute car – his own – is traced. And finally there's me. He led me to the meeting with the bomber.'

'Yes, but that wasn't planned. How could he possibly have known you were going to be there?'

'He didn't. That was pure improvisation. He saw me and set up the meeting. It was also a way of getting Gough more involved. Though I have to hand it to him, Gough was good at his job too. He nearly took us out with a little home pyrotechnics, and when that didn't work, he doctored my file, fed in some political dynamite, planted some bomb equipment in my flat, and bingo, I'm the suspect. Two birds with one stone. Discredit an inconvenient witness and convict a Health Not Wealth sympathizer at the same time. Brilliant.'

'So what's De Villiers doing all this time? If his job was to muck things up, then he damn nearly failed. If Joshua hadn't been such a good newsman, Gough would have got away with it.'

She smiled at him. The cat who got the cream. What else did she 'know'?

'Aaah no, William, that's just the point. Joshua wasn't that good. You remember how far his inquiries got him? Sweet nowhere. Gough's secret number? Dead end. Mrs O'Grady? Wouldn't talk. Police leaks? Gummed up. Yet two days later he's showing Culverwell a print of the bomber and Mrs O'Grady a press photo of Gough. Didn't you ever wonder where he got it from?'

'Tell me.'

'De Villiers had an accomplice. A partner. Someone who would make sure "the truth" came out. It could have been any journalist. It just happened that Joshua was the one asking the right questions.

He selected himself. He was helped.'

'And then he was killed.'

'Yes, but not by them. Gough's men did that. They traced him back as an old buddy of mine from that remark you made in the police station. They just didn't realize they were too late.'

The champagne had gone flat in his paper cup. But he needed something to wet his throat. The pain that was Joshua's death had not healed with time. More so because he understood the fear that must have accompanied it. He remembered his own terror, clinging by aching arms to ivy roots while he stared down the barrel of a gun in the shadows beneath him. He remembered also that long scream of pain. Gough's man skewered on a rusty pitchfork. An own goal in the last seconds of the match. Of 'Kevin' nothing more was heard. No one claimed him, least of all, despite police appeals, himself. He remained a loose end that everybody – the police, the lawyers, finally even the press – seemed content to forget. William too. Until now. Now he knew. Those last moments of terror made sense. At last.

'The pitchfork in the barn. It was no accident. We had help too. It was Kevin. Kevin killed Gough's man.'

She smiled a sad smile. 'Yes.'

'Kevin was sent to save us.'

'Yes.'

'But who was he? Did he come from the ANC?'

'No. He came from MI5.'

William stared at her. 'Wait a minute. This is not making sense. Why should he want to destroy the organization he worked for?'

She looked pleased with his consternation. 'Aaah well. Now you have it, William. Not destroy. Transform. MI5's still there. It'll always be there. It'll just have different guys in charge, that's all. You see, there's one final layer of the onion to unpeel. Then you reach the real conspiracy. De Villiers and his partners in MI5. The men who sent Kevin. Joshua did a lot of work on this. He knew there was a faction in MI5 that was pro South Africa and reckoned anyone left of centre was a subversive. He also knew there was another faction with a different view of intelligence. They're not radicals, these people, they just don't automatically believe that playing dirty tricks on trade unionists is what national security should be all about. But what could they do? Their views aren't getting through, their careers likewise, they're stuck. At least they were. Things are different now.'

'I don't get it.'

'Neither did Joshua. The one thing he never understood was that the people helping us weren't just passing on information, but were using him, and us, to bring down the conspiracy they themselves had set up.'

'Sounds a rather convoluted kind of power struggle to me.'

'Aaah, but this is intelligence. It's their job to be devious. That's their currency, what they're trained to do. And it had to be something pretty dramatic to make such a clean sweep. Take this guy. Joshua's MI5 mole. He's known as a dissident, so he appears to reform, to change camps. It takes time, but then that's what intelligence is all about. He gets to be trusted. He looks around for a candidate. A man who's a bit fascist and easily led. Gough. He wins Gough's confidence, and then he suggests this brilliant plan . . . A chance to bring all the friends into the fold. Gough bites, and the mouthful includes De Villiers.

'The plan works fine at first. Then things start to go wrong. Gough tries to reconstruct the defences. But at each stage someone within is quietly undermining them. The breach widens. Our man jumps clear just as it breaks. The government gets soaked, Gough and BOSS go under. And it all looks so innocent. Two passers-by who just happened along and took the first brick out of the dyke. The rest is inevitable. Perfect. Blame it all on fate.'

She stopped, her eyes shining, and picked up her cup to take a sip. William stared at her, his brain hurting from the amount of information it had to assimilate. Yes, it was perfect. Yes, it did answer all the questions. Save one.

Two passers-by who just happened along . . .

'But what if we hadn't . . ? How were they to know we'd be there?'

She smiled, waiting to see if he'd get it. He didn't. 'Then it would have been someone else instead,' she said. 'Don't you remember? The man we saw in the compound before the bombing. The man who never came forward. He'd been in casualty before us. He was going to be the witness. We were just a bonus. A bonus that meant they didn't have to use their own man. We fell into their laps.'

Brilliant. So brilliant that Josie could never have penetrated it alone. Surely? 'How do you know all this? Who told you?'

'The man in the compound,' she said simply.

'What? How did you find him?'

'I didn't. He found me. Presumably he heard I was digging

around and thought it was safer to tell me the truth. I was having a drink in my local, and this guy comes over and asks if he can sit at my table. After a moment he leans over and smiles and says he's been waiting to meet me for a long time, and he just wants to say how much he admires me. I thought, oh God, not another one, I bet he's just about to ask me for my autograph. So I got up to leave and then he said quietly, "Please don't go, Josie. I've come to talk to you, and I think you'll want to hear what I have to say." And there was something in his voice that made me sit down again. So I did. Then he told me exactly what I've just told you. By the end of the story I knew I'd seen him before, so when I asked the same question as you did now – about how we might not have come alone that night – he told me how he had just "happened" to hit his finger with a hammer that night, badly enough to warrant a visit to casualty.'

'Who was he?'

She shook her head. 'He wouldn't have answered, and I wasn't meant to ask. Presumably he had ANC connections. You would have liked him. He had a kind of quietness to him. He probably would have made a more reliable witness than either of us.'

William smiled. 'Although nowhere near as adventurous. And you think what he told you was the truth?'

'Yes, I do. It all fits.'

'So why did he tell you? Wasn't he afraid you might publish it?'

'He told me in order to stop me publishing. If it came out, the propaganda point would backfire.'

'You mean neither Gough nor BOSS really know what happened.'

'Not all of it. Gough must know some. He must suspect that he was set up by his own men, though presumably they worked out a way of defending themselves against that accusation. And he may have suspicions about De Villiers. If he has, there's precious little he can do about it.'

'Because De Villiers has disappeared. But has he really disappeared?'

'Well, yes and no. This man told me a lot about De Villiers. He's obviously an amazing guy. He comes from an old Afrikaaner family. Very well connected. The last person they would have suspected. I don't know when he started feeding stuff to the ANC. A long time ago. It was him that made the MI5 contacts. First he found a partner, then together they chose Gough as the fall guy. He knew it would have to be his last operation, because the only way he'd be able to explain his mistakes was to say his nerves were shot and resign. So he did that. He went back for his debriefing. It went O.K. It seemed he'd got away with it.'

'And then?' William asked.

'He staged a drowning. At sea. And left South Africa. Not for ever, but for the time being. A new passport, a new country. He's earned his retirement. He succeeded. Look at South Africa now. Apartheid can't survive. But it won't help anyone if we reveal his secret.'

William said nothing. For a while he watched an ant unsuccessfully trying to crawl its way out of his cup. There were so many things to think about. He became aware of her eyes resting anxiously on his. He kept his face serious as he met her gaze.

'So, in the cause of ultimate justice we subvert the truth. One law for the right, one for the left. Is that it, Josie?'

'William,' she said fiercely. 'We can't say anything. It's not our battle. People's lives would depend on it.'

He allowed himself a smile. 'You see, you never could tell when I was teasing. Don't worry. My lips are sealed. I never heard a word of what you just told me, and even if I did, I doubt very much whether I could remember it. I'm the one who believes in a quiet life. You know that.'

She blew out a breath between her cheeks. 'God, William, you gave me one hell of a fright.'

'And you didn't give me the benefit of the doubt. I kept telling you, Josie. We weren't that far apart. You just never listened.'

She made a face. 'Yeah, I know. Blame it on my childhood. Sorry.'

He picked up the bottle and emptied the last of the champagne into their paper cups. Then with a certain ceremony he raised his arm to meet hers. 'Well, here's to "them". To new intelligence and old protest. May our silence buy progress.'

They drank, and for a moment neither of them spoke. His words hung in the air and drifted slowly down river to the sea. 'So,' he said at last. 'No book. What are you going to do instead?'

She grinned. 'You wouldn't believe me if I told you.'

'Try me.'

'In September I'm starting the first part of a law degree.'

'What?'

'See, I told you. I decided if you can't beat the fuckers, then the least you can do is learn how to bend the rules. Seriously, why not? I was made for the bar. I've got a photographic memory, a good head for dates, I like talking and I look great in a wig. I have to do something. I think it was you who told me I couldn't go on guiding for the rest of my life.'

He laughed. 'Well, all I can say is God help any judge you come up against. I think it's a great idea. Will you stick it?'

'Who knows? Ask me again in two years' time. When you get back on home leave.'

On the river a flurry of raindrops disturbed the surface. Josie looked up. The offending cloud was directly overhead. She gathered up the cups and the empty bottle. William thought about the mounds of teachests still to be packed before he drove to Nottingham tomorrow to say goodbye to his parents. It would have been nice to sit here all afternoon, trailing hands in the water, talking over old times, remembering last year's sunshine. It would have been nice. He stood up.

He drove her home, as he had done a year before. They negotiated Archway without incident. Outside her front door he parked. The cat was nowhere to be seen. She turned to him, but he spoke first.

'You know, the only thing I regret is that you and Penny never met. She wanted to arrange it, you know. She was very curious about you.'

'About the woman you almost went to bed with, you mean?'

He smiled. 'I don't know really. I told her it never happened. She knew we never had an affair.'

'Aaah yes, but that's what makes it so special. You and I did something worse. We didn't go to bed together. That makes the bond much stronger.'

'I don't know,' he said with deliberate mischief. 'I still say it might have been a nice thing to do.'

'Nice, yes. But not half so potent. We were chivalrous, you and I. Fairy tale stuff. Not all the orgasms in the world can achieve that. For us, mystery remains.'

He laughed out loud. 'Josie, after all this time, I still can't believe that you're a romantic.'

To his surprise she didn't laugh back. 'Everyone needs it, William. Anyway, it's past history now. And we both know that history is romantic.'

She's better, he thought. Funny I didn't notice it before. Or maybe I did. But the tension is gone. She is healed. I wonder if she notices the change in me. He said instead, 'You'd better watch it. You're beginning to sound young for your age.'

'Don't worry about me,' she said, opening the car door. 'You take care of yourself. Have a good time wherever it is you end up. And remember, Confucius he say, Better in principle to be screwed than do the screwing.'

He felt like putting out a hand to hold her back, but he kept his fingers clenched on the wheel. 'And is that the last word from Josie Ridley?'

She leaned over and kissed him quickly on the cheek. 'William, you should know better than that. Take care. And drive carefully.'

This time she made it out of the car, slamming the door behind her as she had on that first night. At the front door she turned and smiled. From nowhere the cat appeared and slid in between her legs. The door closed. He waited, staring up at the first-floor window. After a while he caught sight of her, drawing back the curtain, peering out. He put a hand out of the window in salute. She grinned and waved, as if a little embarrassed at being caught. He pulled out into the road, making sure first that there were no cyclists behind him.